Fishing Secrets from Florida's East Coast

WILD FLORIDA

UNIVERSITY PRESS OF FLORIDA

Florida A&M University, Tallahassee
Florida Atlantic University, Boca Raton
Florida Gulf Coast University, Ft. Myers
Florida International University, Miami
Florida State University, Tallahassee
New College of Florida, Sarasota
University of Central Florida, Orlando
University of Florida, Gainesville
University of North Florida, Jacksonville
University of South Florida, Tampa
University of West Florida, Pensacola

Fishing Secrets from Florida's East Coast

RON PRESLEY

Foreword by M. Timothy O'Keefe

University Press of Florida

Gainesville · Tallahassee · Tampa · Boca Raton

Pensacola · Orlando · Miami · Jacksonville · Ft. Myers · Sarasota

17 16 15 14 13 12   6 5 4 3 2 1

A copy of cataloging-in-publication data is available from
the Library of Congress.
ISBN 978-0-8130-3975-6

University Press of Florida
15 Northwest 15th Street
Gainesville, FL 32611-2079
http://www.upf.com

To my wife, Karen, for unending support,
and my grandson Robert, my best fishing buddy.

CONTENTS

FOREWORD

Those who've read Ron Presley's award-winning *Secrets from Florida's Master Anglers* in UPF's Wild Florida series already know that Ron likes subjects with a sweeping scope. His *Florida's Master Anglers* volume focused on what every saltwater angler needs for routine success out on the water: selecting the right equipment and mastering the appropriate casting techniques with it, landing fish in a variety of situations, and much more. The advice was the accumulated wisdom and experience of twenty of Florida's best fishing guides and charter captains. Purchasing this book truly was like picking the brains of all these top experts.

In *Fishing Secrets from Florida's East Coast*, Ron's newest book in the Wild Florida series, he takes on the seemingly impossible task of describing the best ways to fish the shallow and deep waters along the 350-mile coast between Jacksonville and Miami. Obviously, fishing conditions vary so much along this coast that no single person could possibly claim to know all the secrets of such a broad area. Refining the approach from his last book, Ron has drawn out the knowledge of guides and charter captains fishing Florida's Atlantic coast. This time around, the experts tell you not only how-to, but also where-to.

Despite its impressive geographic reach, it would be a mistake to assume *Fishing Secrets from Florida's East Coast* contains content so localized that it's relevant only to limited sections of the coast. For instance, numerous techniques that work in Jacksonville or Port Canaveral also produce in Miami, though they may not be as equally accepted.

Besides a techniques book, *Fishing Secrets* is also an angler's travel guide. Most anglers I know who trailer a boat and are worth their salt like to visit new waters not only for the scenery change but also to test themselves in a brand new neighborhood.

With *Fishing Secrets from Florida's East Coast*, you won't experience the frustration of traveling to a distant launch ramp and having to guess whether a technique that succeeds back home might work there. All the information you need to make the correct decisions is located right here, in these pages, so an otherwise challenging out-of-town trip can easily turn into a bountiful expedition.

Travel should also be fun, and that means not having to waste time searching for the better places to stay and dine. Ron supplies those specifics, too, all of them recommendations from the local guides who send their clients to these same places. As a bonus, Ron also adds relevant history to each of the different locations so traveling anglers arrive with a capsulized chronicle and a better understanding of their new surroundings.

As you may imagine, it's not easy for anyone to convince professional guides and charter captains willingly to reveal lifelong secrets when their own livelihoods depend on introducing anglers to fishing in their own backyards. Ron Presley, a professional fishing guide and licensed U.S. Coast Guard charter boat captain himself, is part of their brotherhood, giving him access and acceptance most outdoor writers could never earn.

A number of longtime International Game Fish Association (IGFA) records were set at destinations on Florida's Atlantic coast. If landing a new one of your own is appealing, this book is as good a guide as you are ever likely to have.

With *Fishing Secrets from Florida's East Coast*, you won't have to fantasize about it. Just go do it!

M. Timothy O'Keefe
Series editor

Introduction

Florida is known for fishing and for big fish. Bonefish, sailfish, redfish, dolphinfish; the list goes on and on. Florida record fish include white marlin at 161 pounds, Mako shark at 911 pounds 12 ounces, and goliath grouper at 680 pounds. Even light-tackle fish like redfish, trout, and African pompano grow to enormous sizes. The record African pompano weighed in at 50 pounds 8 ounces; the record spotted seatrout topped the scales at 17 pounds 7 ounces, and the popular redfish record is 52 pounds 5 ounces. What do all these record fish have in common? They were all caught on conventional tackle, and they were all caught on Florida's East Coast.

Fernandina Beach, Daytona Beach, Cocoa Beach, Fort Pierce, Palm Beach, and Miami Beach are the locales that claim the records listed above, but plenty more record fish are swimming the east coast Florida waters between the Georgia-Florida border and Biscayne Bay. Fishing those areas is what this book is all about. The fishing information found in these pages is relevant anywhere in Florida, but it was collected from fishing pros who ply their trade on Florida's East Coast.

Every chapter begins with a brief history of the development of each destination, giving the reader an appreciation of what's found there today. You will also find valuable information on lodging, restaurants, marinas, and more fishing-related amenities recommended by one of the local experts. All the destinations have numerous good places to stay, eat, and buy bait and tackle, but only those recommended by one of the experts is included. The list is relatively short, but readers should expect the best in service and convenience from those establishments listed. The sleeping and eating are important, but the emphasis of the book is on each destination's fishing resource.

As you make the journey from north to south along Florida's Atlantic coast, you will read about abundant fishing possibilities, inshore and offshore, available to visiting anglers. The best fishing possibilities for each destination are identified, with specific tips from local professional anglers or local experts on how to catch the big one.

In addition to the popular species of fish for which these Florida locations are known, some offer a "bonus" fishing opportunity. When one of these windfall opportunities exists, the chapter will include the details. Kayak fishing, for example, is growing rapidly in popularity among anglers. If a particular destination offers some outstanding kayak fishing, it will be included in the chapter. Pier fishing and wade fishing are other examples of bonus fishing opportunities covered in the pages of the book. The emphasis is on saltwater fishing, but there are also opportunities to catch freshwater fish at most of the destinations.

A few area hotspots are named by the local experts to give traveling anglers an idea of where to start fishing. These named areas can be easily found by checking with local marinas or bait and tackle shops, or by searching the Internet. Some Internet sites where good local information can be found are also given in the chapters.

You don't have to have a fancy boat or the most expensive rod and reel to enjoy the many benefits of recreational fishing in Florida. The knowledge retrieved and reported from the experts selected for this book will give you a competitive advantage regardless of your fishing platform.

Each chapter ends with a fishing lesson for life segment. These segments are intended to highlight an issue important to the fishing community. The segments can be used to teach your children, other people's children, or maybe your friends you take fishing how to have fun fishing, how to be responsible anglers, and how to care about the resource.

The increasing demands placed on the fishing resource by population growth and all that comes with it are a huge challenge for the future of fishing. We need to start our kids off right—and that has to start with you. These parts of each chapter are intended as a reminder to pass on good stewardship of Florida's fishery resource to our youth.

The book is designed so that its maximum value is derived from the sum of its parts. The book is meant to be read from cover to cover with the expectation of learning something new about fishing from every chapter, even if you never intend to fish the particular location about which you are reading. Some duplication of information is inevitable, but this duplication serves to reinforce the skills and techniques needed to become a better angler. The techniques used by Jacksonville pros to help you catch flounder will also work in Miami. The techniques used to catch snook in Stuart will also help you catch snook at Port Canaveral. Even when duplication occurs, it is only partial, and new information is woven into the local application. If I am successful in my goal, this book will add a vast amount of fishing information to what I call your knowledge base for angling. You will learn where the best opportunity exists to catch a certain species of fish and gain valuable knowledge for catching every major species found on Florida's East Coast. Regardless of where you fish next, this book will arm you with fishing skills and techniques that will make you a better angler for life.

PART 1

Florida's First Coast

1

Jacksonville, Fernandina Beach, Amelia Island, and Mayport

Florida has long been a favorite destination of visitors seeking rest and relaxation. Historians tell us that Fernandina Beach, located on Amelia Island, was Florida's first resort, dating back to around 1870. The shipping trade was booming, and the deepwater rivers gave wealthy travelers easy access to the warm climate and elegant hotels. Many New Yorkers and other wealthy Americans traveled south by steamboat to settle in the Amelia Island area. They built stylish Victorian homes, many of which still stand today. The geography of Amelia Island provided a natural strategic location with its secluded harbor and deepwater passages. From the time of the island's original discovery, the flags of eight different world powers have flown over the isle in recognition of its tactical location.

True progress came to the area when Henry Flagler built the first Florida railroad. Flagler contributed greatly to launching Florida's tourism industry. In addition to the railroad, he built luxury hotels along the way to accommodate the tourists coming to Florida by rail.

Jacksonville, dubbed the river city where Florida begins, has grown from humble colonial roots to a major American city. Jacksonville's development is closely linked to the St. Johns River, which flows through the city to connect with the Atlantic Ocean and major shipping lanes near Mayport.

Mayport began as a true American fishing village. Its proximity to the ocean and the availability of large quantities of fish created a solid economic base for development. The city's growth, like that of most cities along the First Coast, was aided significantly by tourism. Today the city is situated between Mayport Naval Base and the St. Johns River. The Mayport Jetties are a major fishing destination for locals and visitors alike.

Characteristics of the Fishing Area

New visitors to northwest Florida are amazed by the tidal swings that characterize the Jacksonville area. The tides can change from 4 to 6 feet depending on conditions. Captain Tony Bozzella owns and operates a fishing guide service in the area. He says to expect an average tidal swing of about 4.8 feet but be prepared for them to be greater. The tidal flows impact fishing and must be taken into consideration for best fishing results.

Captain Bozzella says, "The tides have a huge effect on the fish bite. They dictate where you can fish, and they can leave you high and dry in the backcountry mudflats if you are not prepared."

The Jacksonville, Fernandina Beach, Amelia Island, and Mayport area is a very diverse watershed. The tannin-stained water of the St. Johns River twists and turns as it makes its way north and east to the Atlantic Ocean. As you move inshore from the inlet at Mayport, the water turns from ocean saltwater to brackish. An outstanding fishery that includes both freshwater and saltwater varieties exists. According to Captain Tony, the freshwater species are more abundant in the feeding creeks and offshoots of the St. Johns. He says his charter trips often catch both saltwater and freshwater fish.

The river provides plenty of docks and manmade structure along the shipping channels where anglers can try their luck.

Underwater rock piles made up of various sorts of debris also provide likely haunts for targeted fish.

As you move deeper into the backcountry, there are vast amounts of spartina grass mixed in with, or adjacent to, mudflats and oyster bars. The spartina grass has adapted to live in the harsh environment of a tidal marsh. The grass easily tolerates changes in water depth and salinity as the tides rise and fall in the marsh. The healthy grass stems provide excellent cover for fish hiding from predators and are a prime target for knowledgeable anglers to fish.

The backcountry creeks have deep holes that can range to 60 feet. Newcomers to the area are often heard talking about being in 20 feet of water one second and on the bottom the next. Learning where these deep holes exist, in proximity to shallow sandbars and oyster beds, is essential to fishing success as well as to angler safety.

Oyster bars abound in the Jacksonville area. Formed where fresh and salt water merge, the oyster bar may be as small as a few clinging shells or as large as a bar stretching over several hundred square feet along a mudflat. Either extreme is likely to have some predator fish nearby. The oyster bars are popular dining places for fish because they provide an abundant source of food. Small crabs, shrimp, pinfish, and mud minnows all hang around the clumps of oysters, waiting to dine on the microorganisms that reside there. It is the perfect example of nature's food chain.

The Mayport Jetties are another prominent part of the area's fishing geography and a favorite of local anglers. Deep water, huge boulders, and plenty of current create a natural feeding ground for predator fish.

The Inshore Bite

A *slam* in fishing terminology refers to catching three different species of fish on the same day. The local inshore slam for

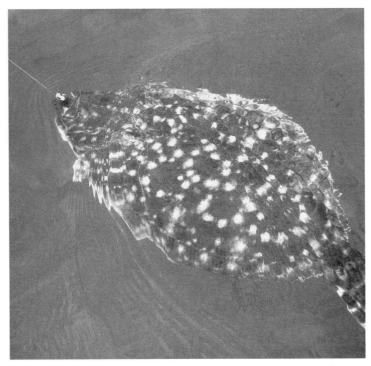

Flounder are one of the three species needed to score a First Coast Slam. This one was fooled by a C.A.L. Avocado/Red Glitter Paddletail Grub rigged on a C.A.L. jig head. Photo by Jerry McBride.

northeast Florida is spotted seatrout, redfish, and flounder. The area is known for its Triple Challenge Tournaments specifically targeting these three species. This local slam differs from the Florida Fish and Wildlife Conservation Commission slam of spotted seatrout, redfish, and tarpon.

Local charter captain and radio show host Captain Vic Tison knows the area well. "I have always thought the FWC/IGFA should recognize these three species as a northeast Florida slam, but they never have. What they call an inshore slam, we don't really have, so it's almost impossible to get one here." The locals adjust the slam criteria so that if an angler catches the triple challenge and adds a tarpon, they call it a grand slam.

Captain Vic reports, "I've caught the grand slam only twice in the past 10 years. I catch the triple challenge of redfish, trout, and flounder every week during certain times of the year." That best time, according to Captain Vic, is April through November. "When targeting the triple challenge, I advise anglers to fish for trout on the high tides. The last hour-and-a-half of the incoming and the first couple of hours of the outgoing tides are best. The flounder and the redfish can be caught in good numbers on lower tides. Both species are best fished during the last couple of hours of the outgoing and the first couple of hours of the incoming tides."

In preparing to catch the triple challenge, Captain Vic checks his inventory of favorite lures. "For trout, my favorite lures include the chrome-bodied Bomber Long A featuring a blue back; the MirrOlure Top Pup with a black back and white belly; or the Heddon Super Spook Jr. in the popular redfish color."

If using live shrimp for trout, he likes to rig a Cajun Thunder float with a 15-inch leader and a 2/0 Eagle Claw Kahle hook. Bait up with a live shrimp and fish over grass flats or oyster bars during the high tides.

When Vic targets flounder, his preferred bait is either Gulp! 3-inch shrimp in the natural color, live mud minnows, or live finger mullet. Pin any of these baits on a slip sinker rig to keep the bait on the bottom, and you are ready for some successful flounder catching.

To finish out the slam with a redfish, Vic rigs live shrimp, live mud minnows, or quartered blue crab on a popping cork. He says, "Use the same Cajun Thunder rigged the same way as for trout and fish up next to the grass on the higher tides." If he decides to use artificial lures to catch the red, he adds Rapala's Skitterwalk in the redfish color to the selection of lures mentioned earlier for trout.

Not only do northeast Florida anglers have a lot of species for which to fish, they also have a lot of choice locations for chasing their favorite targeted fish. Area creeks and flats, the

St. Johns River, and the Mayport Jetty all offer abundant opportunities for angling success.

Fishing the Creeks and Flats

Numerous creeks wind their way through the area, producing prime fishing areas. Captain Tison advises anglers to pick a creek and learn its characteristics inside out. He says every foot of water in the creek should be investigated before you go to a new one. "Every creek here holds fish," he says. "You just have to find out when they congregate at certain spots and be sure that is when and where you fish them." Once educated on how to fish one creek, anglers have taken a huge step toward understanding how to fish the others.

Captain Tison identifies wind direction and tide as the two most important variables to consider when developing patterns for a particular creek. "I tell anglers at my seminars that every time they go out fishing, they should choose a likely creek and work it from front to back while observing wind and tidal conditions." He also advises them to take note of where the natural bait is hanging out and to pay special attention to a spooked fish or group of fish to see where they go. If you have the willpower to investigate a creek without taking your fishing rod, you will learn even more. Be observant and make mental or physical notes of structure, tide level, wind conditions, and any other element of the creek that might influence fish feeding activity. "After learning a creek like the back of your hand, you can go in there and catch fish whenever you want to."

High tides are the time to ease along and fish flooded grass flats or areas where the water is over the oyster bars. At low tide, many mudflats are visible with oyster beds scattered throughout. The edges of those flats and bars should be given due consideration.

New user-friendly reels like the Sharkfin offer longer casts, more time fishing, and less time fooling with tangles.

The creeks provide plenty of oyster beds and mudflats. Captain Vic likes to fish the higher humped-up oyster beds during high tides because they are well covered with water. "I like to use topwater lures across the humps. MirrOlure's Top Pup with a black back and white belly is a good choice. I also like a Rapala Skitterwalk in the redfish color and the spotted trout color. My go-to bait, my old faithful, is the Super Spook Jr. in the redfish color."

Captain Tison also uses live bait over the oyster bar humps. His standby rig over the bars is a Cajun Thunder float with a 14- to 16-inch leader, finished off with a 2/0 Eagle Claw Kahle hook. Bait with live shrimp and cast out over the hump. Lucky anglers can catch redfish, spotted seatrout, flounder, mangrove snapper, sheepshead, and black drum, all using the same technique in the same location.

Captain Bozzella fishes the backcountry mudflats mainly in the winter months using his personally developed line of custom fishing rods. He created TBS rods to cast long and accurately while keeping maximum control and feel of the lure through a fast-action tip. He recommends a 10- to 15-pound braided mainline spooled on a 2500 to 4000 size reel. He chooses reels that hold at least 200 yards of line. "I use spinning style reels that are user friendly in the wind, allowing more time for fishing and less time dealing with wind knots. The braided line adds casting distance, an advantage when fishing the flats." Add a 20-pound fluorocarbon leader, attach the lure with a loop knot to maximize action, and you are ready to fish.

The fall mullet run pulls migrating predator fish south toward warmer waters as they follow the bait. Even with the southerly migration of many saltwater fish, there are plenty of resident fish that stay locally on the warmer mudflats and oyster bars. These year-round inhabitants will be found feeding on crustaceans and mud crabs during the winter months. This is the signal to Captain Tony to head north in the St. Johns River toward the backcountry, where redfish, seatrout, black drum, and flounder will spend the winter. His go-to bait during the winter months is his personally designed TBS Black Bucktail in ⅛ and ¼ sizes. He targets the outgoing tide, fishing depressions in the creeks. "I like to retrieve the jig with low hops along the bottom as if it were a fleeing crab. Weather cooperating, I also look for tailing fish. Sight fishing can be excellent this time of year." The water in northeast Florida gets very clear in the winter, so a stealthy approach is needed to successfully hook up with a sighted fish. Try not to bang hatches or cooler lids, and don't jump down into the bottom of the boat. Don't cause any sudden noise that would spook the fish.

If there is structure in the area choose a lure that does not hang up easily. Captain Tony advises switching to weedless baits like the D.O.A. C.A.L. Series Jerk Bait to avoid the hang-ups. "I like golden bream or a natural pattern if the water is clear, and white or chartreuse if the water is murky or dirty." Rig the jerk bait on a fat gap hook or better yet a Daiichi Copperhead to make it weedless.

Captain Vic suggests fishing the mudflats using a quartered blue crab on a Sure Catch jig. The cut crab emits plenty of smell, and fish will come from long distances to eat it. The jig head features a 2/0 Eagle Claw hook, which is just right for the quartered crab. "I also like using live mud minnows on the same rig. The change to mud minnows normally results in more spotted seatrout and flounder. I also use the Super Spook Jr. and the Top Pups on the mudflats." Captain Vic particularly likes to fish the mudflats during the last two hours of the outgoing tides and the first two hours of the incoming tides. He uses a one-piece 7-foot rod and a relatively small reel spooled with 10-pound super braid for making long casts. "If we are in 8 inches of water, the redfish will naturally spook and stay away from the boat if we're detected. Success depends on avoiding exposure by staying back away from the fish. A long and accurate cast will make all the difference in your success." Since 10-pound-test braided line is the same diameter as 2-pound mono, long casts are easier to achieve.

Fishing the St. Johns River

Captain Bozzella fishes the St. Johns River mainly in the warmer months. He considers March a transitional month characterized by warming water and a new influx of baitfish. "As each day passes following the beginning of March, the water warms a little more and baitfish migrate south in the St. Johns River." Following close behind the bait are the pelagic species such as jack crevalle and Spanish mackerel. "The redfish and big speckled seatrout won't be far behind. As these fish follow the bait up the river, I follow them." Captain Tony says he mostly fishes topwater and subsurface diving plugs this time of year. "Natural colors are my first choice, but clown, white, or chartreuse work well if the water is dirty. Rapalas such as X-Raps, Twitchin' Raps, Flat Raps, and Skitterwalks will also do the job." Tony also adds Bite-A-Bait Fighters and various styles of High Rollers among his choices. "I prefer fishing higher tides, casting over structure for big trout and redfish."

Topwater and subsurface lures will also land you a mix of jack crevalle, Spanish mackerel, ladyfish, mangrove snapper, flounder, and bluefish in the northeast Florida waters. Except for the redfish and trout, all the rest are seasonal and caught mostly in spring and fall.

The St. Johns also provides some great dock fishing. Personal experience or visiting with local anglers can identify the docks that tend to hold redfish. Sometimes a single dock will hold a school of reds just waiting for an easy meal. Once you identify some characteristics of a productive dock, look for other docks with those same characteristics.

Captain Tony uses a shrimp-tipped TBS jig when targeting docks that may harbor a school of redfish. The jig head casts easily and the shrimp adds the sense of smell, which most fish can't resist. Cast the jig/shrimp combo back under the dock and feel for the red to pick it up as you retrieve it slowly toward the boat. A rod with a sensitive tip and a reel spooled with braided line aid the angler in feeling the bite.

The river is characterized by occasional piles of shipping debris like rocks, steel, concrete, and other dilapidated structure. Knowing where these elements are and how to fish them can turn a so-so day into a bonanza. Especially when the tide and current produce a rip along the structure, the debris becomes an ambush point for predator fish. Captain Tony says, "I like to cast up-current and bring the lure back with the current. I generally pick a lure that will not get hung on the debris." Lures that fit the bill here are topwater plugs, floater/divers, and any subsurface lure that does not sink on its own. Once you have hung the lure and worked to free it or break it off, the fish are aware and likely spooked. It's time to move on. More than anything, Captain Tony says, "Find a lure you have confidence in and learn to fish that lure well." Change retrieval speed, twitching sequence, and color until you find the pattern that is working.

The edges of the shipping channel are excellent places to fish for channel bass (redfish). Captain Tony suggests a bottom rig for best results. A 7-foot medium heavy TBS rod fitted with a 3500 sized reel and spooled with 20-pound braid will work well when fishing channel edges. Tony uses a three-way swivel tied to the mainline. Add an 18-inch leader of 30-pound mono and a 5/0 circle hook to one side of the swivel. On the remaining swivel connection, add a 12-inch leader and a weight sufficient for the existing current. Pin one-half a blue crab on the circle hook, cast out, and hold on. Captain Tony says, "Different areas hold fish depending on tide and current. You have to get out there and explore to find the honey holes."

When scouting the channel, look for places that have shallow water next to deep water with some current. The presence of bait and a hard shell bottom make it even better. Another example of a hotspot is a point with water running over it during either an incoming or outgoing tide. A rip is created on one side of the point, and predators stack up waiting to ambush bait as it is swept over the point. Seawalls will also hold fish during certain stages of the tide. The secret is to discover when the fish accumulate along the walls. Once you've discovered this, be sure to mark the hotspots in your logbook or on your GPS so you can return on a future trip, or even later in the day when conditions are more favorable.

Artificial lures can also work well along the channel. Tony says, "I like to get on the edge of the channel and watch my depth recorder for signs of fish. When I spot something with potential I cast up-current and let the jig go to the bottom.

I keep a tight line so I can feel the lure and be in tune with it at all times." Tony says he wants to know exactly what the lure is doing and where it is at all times. He bounces the lure along the bottom waiting for a take. Sometimes a slow roll across the bottom is a good presentation, especially on hard shell bottoms with moving water. When you feel resistance on the line, set the hook.

River fishing may be in water between 20 and 50 feet deep. The savvy angler can use deep jigging techniques to catch fish from these depths. Deep jigging is a technique used when fish are concentrated in one area, as they can be in deep river holes. Using braided line gives anglers a good feel for the action of the lure, and even subtle bites are detected. Super braids are also abrasive resistant, a distinct advantage around steel and concrete debris piles. Use a 30-pound leader and select a jig that will get you down deep quickly. Captain Bozzella uses TBS jigs to take advantage of the large barb that holds the plastic or scented bait in place. The barb keeps the fish from sucking it off the hook on the strike. The large bait-holding barb on the TBS jig also acts as a keel, preventing the lure from rolling over on its side on the retrieve. If the hook rides upright, the angler experiences fewer snags and more hook-sets on fish instead of on the bottom or other structure.

As a general rule of thumb, Captain Tony likes the combination of a D.O.A. C.A.L. tail and a TBS jig for deep jigging. Use a natural color if the water is clean or clear. When the water color is stained or dirty, he switches to a lighter colored body like white or chartreuse for a more prominent silhouette.

Some anglers like to tip the jig with shrimp or cut mullet strips to enhance their angling chances. The key, according to Captain Tony, is to do your homework and understand the conditions you are fishing. Log your successes and be prepared to use the same techniques when similar conditions arise.

The Mayport Jetties

The Mayport Jetties, where the St. Johns River dumps into the Atlantic Ocean, can be a haven for fish. This manmade structure is a half-mile of boulders in 40 feet of water. The jetties hold all the inshore and some of the offshore species available to Jacksonville-area anglers.

When fishing the Mayport Jetty, which some locals call the St. Johns River Jetty, look for drop-offs, holes in the rocks, and hard bottom spots just out in the inlet from the jetty rocks. Anglers catch redfish, black drum, sheepshead, black margates, croakers, and whiting from any of these locations, especially the hard bottom spots.

Targeting sheepshead around the jetties is a favorite pastime of Captain Vic's. "When I fish for sheepshead, from October through April, I usually set the boat parallel to the large boulders on the jetty and position it in about 20 feet of water

Sheepshead are a local favorite around the Mayport jetties.

over the rocks. In this position you can hold the rod out over the side of the boat and fish straight down." Vic uses a 7-foot rod, a Sure Catch sheepshead jig, and a live fiddler crab to entice the convict fish to bite. During these months the sheepshead are in 8 to 15 feet of water, so watch your depth finder to zero in on them. According to Captain Vic, the last week or so of February and right through April the larger female sheepshead are laying eggs and feeding on the hard bottom spots. This is a good time to catch these dinner table favorites, and they can weigh in at up to 14 pounds.

The jetties can also produce good catches of black drum. The best time to target them is October through mid-May. Captain Vic says the drum will be found feeding on hard bottom areas. "I generally fish for the 4- to 15-pound black drum using cut blue crabs." He uses his favorite 2/0 Eagle Claw Kahle hook to present the quartered crab.

When spring rolls around, Captain Vic likes to take his clients on a catch-photo-release (CPR) adventure at the jetties. The targets are huge black drum roaming and feeding near the jetties. This extreme type of fishing requires anglers to beef up their tackle and get ready for a fish fight. "I use a 5/0 Eagle Claw Kahle hook baited with clam and a halved blue crab on the same hook. We call this concoction a 'drum cocktail' and the big boys just can't resist it." A medium heavy rod, a 5000 series reel, 30-pound braid, and 50-pound leader should do the trick.

The jetties also provide great redfish opportunities during certain times of the year. Not surprisingly, these cousins to the black drum can be caught in the same hard bottom areas, using the same techniques and the same baits. Prime time for reds at the jetties is September through December and then again from March through May. Other times of the year, the reds are likely to be found roaming the St. Johns River and its feeder creeks, away from the ocean inlet.

Captain Tison sums up the inshore bite by saying, "We have so many species of fish here that people can target a different one each month. Or, we can target several different ones on the same fishing trip, making the local slam of redfish, trout, and flounder a very good possibility." The different species often hang out in different areas, but they are so close that you can be fishing for redfish one minute and flounder within a 15-minute boat ride.

The Offshore Bite

The Jacksonville area has a great offshore fishery year-round. Depending on the time of year, anglers have the opportunity to catch a variety of offshore species in northeast Florida. Many anglers enjoy high-speed trolling for marlin, wahoo, dolphin-fish, tuna, kingfish, and sailfish. Others like to fish the ocean bottom for one of several varieties of snappers. Red snapper, vermillion snapper, lane snapper, mangrove snapper, and even cubera snapper are available to offshore anglers.

The area also provides fishing opportunities for several different species of groupers. Gag grouper, red grouper, scamp grouper, and warsaw grouper are common catches. Anglers will also find several different varieties of hinds groupers and an occasional black grouper. Bottom fishing anglers can expect to catch triggerfish, black sea bass, cobia, and flounder. Finally, for some real rod-bending action, a few different species of amberjacks are available. Greater amberjack, lesser amber-jack, and almaco jack all roam the offshore waters of northeast Florida.

With all the possibilities the area has to offer, it is a good idea to hire a guide to take you on a few trips before you try it on your own. Guides can teach a lot of tricks that will help in the long run and save time, too. All the techniques needed for off-shore fishing, like tying rigs, bait presentation, and anchoring and trolling, can be learned quickly from a seasoned veteran. A guided trip allows anglers the luxury of asking questions while on the water and seeing the answer demonstrated on the spot.

Amberjack are found around wrecks and rock piles off Florida's First Coast. Photo by Capt. Chad Starling.

Captain Chad Starling, owner/operator of Team Buck Rodgers Fishing Charters, says the geography of the area consists mainly of natural ledges, coral outcroppings, live bottom, and artificial reefs. "I fish all of these at one time or another." The key to fishing different areas is knowing when to fish them.

Captain Chad fishes the artificial reefs year-round, but finds some great amberjack action in the summer. "During the summer months certain wrecks off our coast hold tons of amberjacks. My favorite bait for amberjack is a butterfly jig, but almost any live bait will work well too."

There are numerous brands of jigging spoons on the market and most work well. They are basically a metal body with two single hooks attached to the eye. Most anglers prefer a rod with a long handle to tuck under the armpit for proper jigging action. Captain Chad describes the technique. "Drop it straight to the bottom and give it quick, short jerks all the way to the top. You cover the entire water column from bottom to top. The possibilities include everything from bottom fish to pelagic species. Amberjack in particular crash this rig."

Artificial reefs also hold all the bottom fish available to area anglers, but "water temp plays a pretty big role when it comes to successfully catching fish on the wrecks. I like to fish wrecks when the water temp is in the 60- to 70-degree range."

When Captain Chad fishes for snapper or grouper, he uses a reel in the 4/0 size with a minimal line rating of 50 pounds. The rod varies depending on what species he targets. "When fishing for red snapper or grouper, I use a 7-foot medium heavy action rod. I want the rod to have a lot of backbone for pulling hard against the fish to get them out of their lair. At the same time I like a soft tip for enjoying the fight once you get the fish away from the bottom." The soft tip will also provide the flex needed to prevent the fish from tearing its mouth during hard runs, which can result in a pulled hooked. Captain Chad fishes his baits right on the bottom for snapper and grouper.

There are a variety of good bottom fishing baits normally available at area bait shops, or you can catch your own. The choices include Spanish sardines, live cigar minnows, frozen sardines, frozen cigar minnows, frozen mackerel, and squid.

Natural baits are not the only choice, according to Captain Chad. An artificial product called Fishbites provides a convenient and easy-to-use alternative to natural bait. According to the manufacturer, the Fishbites product gives anglers all the advantages of Mother Nature and then some. It's infused with a concentrated flavor/scent that replicates natural feeding stimulants and creates a powerful scent trail to attract the fish. Captain Chad says, "Triggerfish, sea bass, and vermillion snapper all love Fishbites."

Captain Chad uses braided line with a mono shock leader when bottom fishing. The smaller-diameter braid allows anglers to use a smaller weight, but still keep the bait on the bottom. The sensitivity and feel of the braided mainline allows the bite to be detected easily. When the angler sets the hook, there is more leverage with braid because it does not stretch. The mono shock leader provides enough stretch that the hooks don't rip out on a hard run by the fish or too hard a hook-set by the angler.

The actual terminal rigs used will depend on the targeted fish. For red snapper and grouper, Captain Chad uses a conventional three-way swivel rig. Use 3 feet of 80-pound mono to make a shock leader. Use a Snell knot to attach a 6/0 J-hook. Tie a loop to the three-way for adding weight. "I use bank sinkers mostly, so the loop goes through the weight and then the weight goes back through the loop. It just hangs there. I use lighter line for the loop, say about 40-pound-test line. The reason I do this is if my weight gets snagged I can usually break it loose without having to lose the whole rig." If only the weight is lost, fishing can resume by tying on another loop and adding another weight. The entire terminal rig does not have to be replaced using this technique. Additionally, using the loop method allows the weights to be removed easily for travel back to the dock. Swinging weights in a heavy sea can be a dangerous safety issue.

A different rig is used for triggerfish, black sea bass, and beeliners (vermillion snapper). "I like to use a dropper rig on these species." Prepare a shock leader using 50- to 60-pound leader material and tie two dropper loops before adding a final loop at the end to attach the weight. Use a quality swivel to tie the mainline to the leader. This will prevent line twist. As fish are reeled up from the bottom, they continue to swim in circles until they reach the surface. After being used to catch several fish, the mainline can become twisted and should be changed. "Twisted line will eventually jeopardize the integrity of the line, so when you do get a big fish on, there is a possibility it may break you off."

For the beeliners and black sea bass, bait 4/0 circle hooks with squid, cut bait, or Fishbites. Remember when using circle hooks, no hook-set is required. Just start reeling when the bite is detected.

For the triggerfish, Captain Chad chooses Owner Hooks because the triggerfish mouth is hard to penetrate. A quality hook is needed to pierce the mouth and seal the deal. "Owner makes a top-of-the-line hook with a 'cutting edge' that works great on tough-mouth species like triggerfish." He adds a small piece of Fishbites and drops the baited hook to the bottom. "Triggerfish absolutely love Fishbites! Seriously."

Trolling for kingfish is another popular choice of area anglers. Captain Chad's bait of choice when trolling for kingfish is fresh-caught live bait. Spanish sardines, cigar minnows, pogies (Atlantic menhaden), blue runners, and threadfin herring have produced many king-sized kingfish. The kingfish bite is year-round, according to Captain Chad, but it really fires up during the summer from June to August, when the baitfish such as pogies are prevalent in the nearshore waters.

Slow trolling of live bait is the primary strategy for catching kingfish. Captain Chad describes slow trolling as pulling the bait at less than 2 miles per hour. Other methods include drifting and flatlining live bait, anchored and flatlining live bait, and trolling with artificial baits. "If using artificials to target kingfish, I like to speed up the pace." There's usually no scent to attract the fish to an artificial lure. With no scent trail, anglers are hoping for a reaction strike. Increasing the trolling speed gives the fish less time to think about it and less time to realize the lure is not real. The added trolling speed also creates the illusion that the baitfish is trying to escape. Captain Chad relates, "I think all pelagic fish like a challenge. When they believe the baitfish is trying to escape, they rise to the challenge and try to prevent it."

Rigging for kingfish is an extremely important task. Using copper wire to prevent them from biting through the mono leader is highly desirable. Captain Chad says, "Kingfish will cut through mono like it was a spaghetti noodle, no matter what pound test you use." He suggests using 30- to 40-pound copper wire. The length of the leader varies by personal preference, but Captain Chad likes his short. "I like it short so there's not that much for the fish to see, deterring them from the bait. If it doesn't look right, they won't bite it." He starts with a haywire twist to a #1 live bait hook. Tie on a #6 treble 4x as the stinger hook. The length of the wire between the live bait hook and the treble depends on the size of your bait. Don't make it too short, or you will miss short strikes. Don't make it too long because it will look unnatural. A perfect rig should allow the bait to be hooked through the nose with the stinger inserted close to the tail without too much slack wire. The bait should be able to swim naturally.

Some anglers do choose a longer wire leader. They argue that when a kingfish strikes, it sometimes runs straight away from the boat, and its tail will sever or at least damage the leader. This is referred to as *tail whipping*. The long wire leader serves to prevent this breakoff by a tail whip. Captain Chad does not use the long leader because "a long wire leader detracts from the natural presentation of the bait. Anglers may prevent tail whipping breakoffs, but they greatly reduce the number of hookups because the kings shy away from the longer leader."

To compensate for the short wire leader and to prevent most tail whipping breakoffs, Captain Chad uses fluorocarbon

Tuna are often caught on the way–way back line using a cedar plug. Photo by Capt. Chad Starling.

shock leader between the mainline and wire leader. He says this application serves two purposes.

First, the fluorocarbon disappears in the water, giving the bait a more natural presentation. Since the fluorocarbon material disappears under the water, a heavier fluorocarbon may be used. "If my mainline is 20-pound test, I will use a 25- to 30-pound fluorocarbon shock leader. I tie it to my mainline using a double grapevine knot (double uni knot)."

The second advantage of the fluorocarbon is its abrasion resistant characteristic. It will hold up much better than regular mono when tail whipped by an angry kingfish. "Even though tail whipping breakoffs still occur, I greatly increase the number of hookups because the presentation is more natural."

Other trolling targets on Florida's northeast coast include dolphinfish, sailfish, wahoo, and tuna. The easiest way to fish for all these species is to use skirted ballyhoo. Set your troll at a speed of 6 to 10 miles per hour. All these fish will bite this application.

The most difficult but important part of this fishing is rigging the ballyhoo so it swims straight and upright. Several good videos on YouTube explain proper rigging. Trolling ballyhoo is mainly a spring activity in northeast Florida.

For tuna, a cedar plug is a favorite lure of many anglers. Captain Chad says, "while trolling skirted ballyhoo I will hang a cedar plug way behind the rest of my spread. I call it the way–way–way back pole. I have caught many tuna on the cedar plug and the other species will hit it too. Cedar plugs are outstanding all-around offshore trolling baits."

Wahoo fishing can be done using only artificial lures, but the strategy does require the proper equipment. The pace is fast, at high speeds ranging from 10 to 25 miles per hour. Begin by stocking your tackle box with special lures created specifically to handle this speedy presentation. The average slow-trolling or midline-trolling baits won't stay in the water at those speeds. "The lures must be heavy enough and designed to stay in the water under high-speed conditions." Captain Chad suggests using big bullet-head lures or bonito lures for this presentation. Most quality tackle stores can help match anglers with the proper high-speed trolling lures. If the proper lures are not available, be creative. "Anglers can make do by adding inline trolling weights to available lures. I sometimes add up to 48 ounces of weight to keep the lures down to the intended depth."

Captain Chad adds this advice: "Use a 50- to 80-pound mainline tied to a quality ball-bearing clip swivel. Clip the inline trolling weight to the swivel. Add a 7-foot 400-pound wire leader and attach the lure. Wahoo strike the bait at very high speeds, and the wire leader will prevent loss of the fish due to cutoffs from their sharp teeth or breakoffs from their brute power."

Captain Chad prefers mono over braid when high-speed trolling. "The no-stretch characteristic of the braid sometimes causes the hooks to rip out too easily on the strike. The mono will stretch and give much more flexibility on the strike. This can be the difference between a landed fish and a lost fish."

Once winter rolls around, the trolling is limited mostly to wahoo as other fish have migrated away from the area. The high-speed application allows anglers to cover a lot more water in search of scattered fish.

Kayak Fishing in Jacksonville

Kayak fishing is one of the fastest-growing outdoor activities in the Jacksonville area, according to Mike Kogan, creator of jaxkayakfishing.com. Take a look at any topographic map and you can easily see why. The area is filled with creeks, rivers, bays, islands, and of course the Atlantic Ocean and its beaches. Mike's Web site lists close to 100 areas for kayak anglers to try their luck. Names like Mud River, Deep Creek, and Cemetery Creek all sound like places worth exploring.

The popularity of kayak fishing is strongly linked to economics. Kayaks are inexpensive in relation to powerboats, and maintenance is near zero. With a kayak, anglers do not have the expenses of storage, fuel, or repairs of mechanical and electrical equipment. Additionally, kayaks provide a very personal fishing craft. In a kayak every motion and direction of the vessel is controlled by the operator. Anglers can't get up and run from one point to another as with a powerboat, but that gives more incentive to investigate every square foot of water available during an outing. Kayak fishing is a great discovery process where creeks, deepwater holes, grass flats, and other fish-loving structure are identified and logged in a pursuit to find where the fish hang out. For kayak anglers, fishing is just plain fun and productive.

Choose a kayak based on where you will use it most, inshore or offshore. The possibilities of kayak fishing are endless. Photo by Jerry McBride.

The kayak experience is considerably different from being in a powerboat. Anglers are placed at the same level as the prey, and when the hookup occurs, it's man against the fish. When a big fish is hooked, kayak anglers often go for a ride, at the will of the hooked fish. If you are new to the area, the big decision is where to try fishing first.

The Jacksonville area offers a most outstanding venue for enjoying the sport of kayak fishing. The numerous inlets, estuaries, creeks, and saltwater marshes, along with spartina grass and the ocean, all offer plenty of exciting fishing action. The weather is usually cooperative, and the variety of saltwater fish is a big plus.

Tides are everything in the Jacksonville area, with tidal swings of as much as 6 feet. Tides should be a strategic part of an angling float plan. With correct planning, an outgoing tide can take you from the launch area a mile downriver to a creek you want to fish. That is an easy paddle, going with the tide. Once you reach the destination creek, you work a little harder, paddling against tide toward the back of the creek. The idea is to meet the bait coming out of the creek with the tide. Captain Mike says, "I want to ambush the ambushers." He advises anglers to match the hatch as best they can by using lures that imitate the bait moving with the natural outflow of the current. Captain Mike says, "If you seem to be paddling against the tide all the time, you are probably doing the right thing." As you move out of the creek, you will be paddling against the incoming tide.

Fishing in places like Mosquito Lagoon (chapter 5) and other shallow-water estuaries often requires the utmost in stealth. The fish are spooky and easily flushed. "One thing about the fish around here," says Captain Mike, "they are like teenagers who listen to rock music all day. They don't hear so well." Mike says the rushing, rumbling tides of the Jacksonville area allow you to throw a surface-crashing topwater plug and catch fish instead of spooking them.

The fish to target depends on time of the year. Redfish and spotted seatrout can be caught all year long. Flounder is also fairly abundant and a distinct possibility most of the year. In the warmer months, snook are available, but not a major target for most kayak anglers. As the winter months arrive, sheepshead and black drum become more abundant. Both are targeted for the dinner table as well as just for fun.

As far as when to plan your trip, Mike recommends fishing the outgoing tide, the bottom of the tide, and the first couple hours of the incoming tide. If you plan your trip correctly, you can fish yourself back on the incoming tide and end up where you launched.

Mike has a little advice for newcomers to kayak fishing. Since you need a vessel first, he suggests the first thing to do is determine where you will be doing most of your fishing. Anglers planning to spend most of their time offshore "will need a boat with plenty of interior storage and the stability and size to handle big water. While you can find a kayak that can handle both the surf and inshore estuaries, there will be compromises." Inshore anglers can be more concerned about stealth and speed to cover more water in a day's outing.

Comfort is a huge consideration in kayaks, because long periods of time on the water can take a physical toll on the angler. Mike says, "Going to a local kayak fishing retailer is probably the most important thing you can do. A local dealer will be able to help you understand the options available, rig the kayak to your preference, and perform any service or warrantee work if necessary. And speaking of rigging, remember your seat and paddle are probably the most important items you will select when you initially equip your kayak." Captain Mike also cautions buyers to test-paddle any craft they are interested in before purchasing.

Fishing the Jacksonville Beach Pier

Shorebound anglers in the Jacksonville area have a great fishing platform stretching out into the Atlantic Ocean. Joe Dionne, a local pier fishing expert and webmaster for jacksonvillepier.com, explains that the original pier was taken out by a hurricane. A new and larger fishing pier now serves visiting anglers. The existing pier extends out ¼ mile into the Atlantic. The pier is 303 feet longer than its predecessor, featuring a 20-foot-wide deck that is fully handicapped accessible.

The pier includes several fish cleaning stations, a concession area, a bait shop, and restrooms. At the deep end of the pier the deck braches out into a 48 × 31-foot deck. The result is a T-shaped platform with plenty of room for fishing.

An amazing variety of saltwater fish can be caught from piers. Some of the possibilities include barracuda, trout, flounder, kingfish, and tarpon. Catching pelagics from the pier is covered in this chapter, and general pier fishing techniques and tackle are presented in chapter 3.

Pelagics from the Pier

Big game anglers don't have to own a boat. Joe Dionne says plenty of kingfish, cobia, and other pelagics are caught from the T-end of the Jacksonville Pier. Just to emphasize the big game aspect of fishing from the end of the pier, Joe reports the record kingfish for the pier weighed in at 53 pounds.

Joe goes on to explain that the same techniques used for big game fish off the pier in Jacksonville are not the same all the way along the coast. "The farther south you go, the water gets clearer, and different techniques are used. I think the water clarity has to do with the color of the sand. The farther south you go, the whiter the sand; around Jacksonville the sand is darker and so is the water." The clearer waters of the southern piers allow anglers to actually see the kings and cobia as they swim by. The technique under these clear water conditions is to cast the bait to the sighted kings, a method referred to as free lining.

In the darker water of north Florida, area anglers use a trolley rig (anchor rig) with a breakaway system to target big game fish. Three different rods are used to successfully catch big game fish from a pier. The first rod is referred to as the mud rod, the second is the fighting rod, and a third rod is the bait rod.

The mud rod or anchor rod ranges from a 10-foot one-piece outfit to a 12-foot two-piece rod with the capability of casting 4- to 6-ounce sinkers 300 feet or more from the end of the pier.

Pier fishing is an easy way for shorebound anglers to get a shot at big fish. Proper pier etiquette includes keeping your gear next to the railing.

Reels used are a personal preference of the angler. Some use regular spinning reels, while others use casting reels such as Penn 525, Daiwa Sealines, or the old Penn Squidders. Dionne prefers the Avet MC SX because of its proven performance. "The object is to heave a mud hook as far out into the surf as possible, and the Avet, on a proper rod, will certainly do it." Mud hooks are usually 4 to 6 ounces in weight and constructed from bendable wire. The hook sinks to the bottom and then hooks into the sand and sticks tight until pulled in at the end of the day. A tight line from the rod to the mud hook serves as the trolley line to deploy baits to waiting fish. A 4- to 5-foot-long PVC pipe is attached to the pier railing with bungee cords for the purpose of holding the mud rod securely.

The second rod will hold the bait and be used to fight the fish. The fighting rod can be 6 to 7.5 feet in length, equipped with the angler's reel of choice. "Some anglers use Shimano or Penn reels; I prefer the Avet LX 6:1 spooled with over 300 yards of 20-pound-test line. Plenty of line is important, especially for kingfish that make a long initial run after being hooked."

The third rod is used for catching bait. A small to medium rod and reel combo will work just fine. Set up the bait rod with a Sabiki rig that can be cast to passing baitfish. Be sure to have an aerated bait bucket to keep the bait lively until needed.

Live baits are presented to passing fish on the surface by attaching the bait line to the trolley line using a breakaway release clip. After a strike the mainline breaks away and the release clip slides down the anchor line to the ocean floor, where it will be retrieved at the end of the day when the mud hook is retrieved. The terminal tackle is a traditional stinger rig with treble hooks. The complete rig should be about 8 feet long. A swivel connects the mainline to the stinger, and the release clip is hooked to the top eye of the swivel. The baited line slides down the trolley line to the water. Once a fish hits, the mainline breaks away from the trolley line, and the angler is instantly fighting the fish.

Good fish fighting techniques and a pier gaff are needed to successfully land big fish from a pier. Dionne says, "After the fish screams off a couple hundred yards of line, tighten the drag to tire it out. If you bring the fish close to the pier while it is still green, it could shoot the pilings and you will lose the fish before you get the rope gaff in the water." Dionne adds, "A pier angler without a pier gaff is not complete. Anglers can catch big fish all day, but they have to get them up and over a railing 20 feet above the surface of the water before it counts." He says a good gaff has four sharpened prongs with no barbs that would tear the fish. The gaff is tied to a rope long enough to be lowered at least 5 feet under the water. "A good stick on a fish is usually a head shot, but sometimes it's difficult to target the head, and usually a midsection gets the gaff. If that fish is long and heavy, a pier net is not going to do the job."

Finally, Dionne recommends a good pier cart for carrying equipment to the end of the pier. "Carts are an everyday sighting at the pier. They carry rods and reels, umbrellas, chairs, coolers, food, drink, tackle, bait buckets, and every other thing you can imagine. It is all about convenience, and a pier cart just makes the whole process easier."

Charter Captains and Other Experts

Captain Tony Bozzella

> Hometown: Jacksonville, Florida
> Business: TBS Lures, Jigs & Rods LLC
> Phone number: 904-651-0182
> E-mail address: Bozzella@aol.com
> Web sites: www.tonybozzella.com and www.tbsjigs.com

Captain Tony's advice for visiting anglers: Jacksonville fishing can be tricky to learn, with its big tides, and dangerous, with all the oyster bars covered at high tide and exposed at low tide. New anglers to the area should at least consider hiring a local guide, ask questions, and attend local seminars to learn the area.

Joe Dionne

> Hometown: Jacksonville, Florida
> Business: JacksonvilleBeachPier.com
> E-mail address: jaxpier@gmail.com
> Web site: www.JacksonvilleBeachPier.com

Joe's advice for visiting anglers: Ask questions. Don't feel embarrassed to ask another angler what he or she uses and how to use it. That is how you learn. Walk the pier for a few minutes and observe the anglers in the process of fishing. You can usually tell those who know what they are doing and those who don't. The pier pros are usually geared up with pier carts holding all the necessary tackle. When you find a pro, just sit back and watch. You will learn which rods, reels, and tackle you need to successfully fish the pier.

Captain Mike Kogan

Hometown: Neptune Beach, Florida
Business: Kayak Mike's Charters
Phone number: 904-382-5007
E-mail address: mike@jaxkayakfishing.com
Web site: www.JaxKayakFishing.com; www.321Fish.com;
  www.KayakMike.com

Captain Mike's advice to visiting anglers: New anglers should spend time online researching what kayak fishing is all about, and before purchasing make sure they try before they buy. Kayaks are personal fishing vessels, and anglers need to take the time to find what equipment and layout works best for them and their fishing application.

Captain Chad Starling

Hometown: Jacksonville, Florida
Business: Team Buck Rogers Fishing Charters
Phone number: 904-502-7408
E-mail address: teambuckrogers@comcast.net
Web site: www.teambuckrogers.com

Captain Chad's advice: New anglers to the area should buy a local Hot Spots Chart and bounce around from wreck to wreck. Keep your eyes on the fish finder, looking for wrecks, ledges, and other fish holding structures. The best fishing spots are the ones you find on your own and mark for future use.

Captain Vic Tison

Hometown: Jacksonville, Florida
Business: Vic2Fish & Adventures, Inc.

Phone number: 904-699-2285
E-mail address: Vic2fish@aol.com
Web site: www.Vic2fish.com

Captain Vic's advice for visiting anglers: Select one creek to fish and learn it front to back before moving on to another. Pay particular attention to bait movement, wind direction, structural components, and tidal conditions. Pay attention to details, and it will pay off for you in the future.

Area Hotspots

Inshore anglers in the Jacksonville area will find plenty of spots to start their fishing. All the flats in Hannah Mills, Claboard Creek, and Mill Cove are good starting points. Shorebound anglers can try George Crady Bridge, the Jacksonville Beach Pier, or the Atlantic Blvd. Bridge. Kayak anglers will find good fishing with easy access at Dutton Island Preserve. Surf anglers can try Atlantic Beach or Vilano Beach.

The offshore angler can try Buckman Rubble. Visit www.thiswaytothe.net/reefs/floridanatlanticreefs.shtml for a complete list of north Florida reefs. More great Jacksonville area locations can be found online at jacksonvillebeachpier.com and jaxkayakfishing.com.

Fishing-Friendly Lodging and Glorious Galleys

Singleton's Seafood Shack

> 4728 Ocean Street
> Atlantic Beach, FL 32233-2426
> Phone number: 904-246-4442

Open Sunday through Thursday 10:00 a.m. to 9:00 p.m.; Friday through Saturday 10:00 a.m. to 10:00 p.m. Good enough to be featured on The Food Network's "Diners, Drive-ins, and Dives," hosted by Guy Fieri. This rustic fish camp restaurant features outdoor and waterfront dining. Recommended by Capt. Chad Starling.

The Sandollar Restaurant

9716 Heckscher Drive
Jacksonville, FL 32226
Phone number: 904-251-2449

Delicious food. Relaxing waterfront atmosphere. You can watch the river traffic on the St. Johns River as you eat. Full menu. Recommended by Capt. Vic Tison.

Holiday Inn Express

10148 New Berlin Road
Jacksonville, FL 32226
Phone number: 904-696-3333

Outdoor heated pool and spa, complete hot breakfast, microwaves, and refrigerators in all rooms. Tell them you want Captain Vic's fishing rate and save $20. Ask for Kathy Jones, General Manager. Recommended by Capt. Vic Tison and Capt. Tony Bozzella.

Chowder Ted's

5215 Heckscher Drive
Jacksonville, FL 32226
Phone number: 904-714-6900

Chowder Ted's is a kick-back lunch and dinner spot in a super relaxed "Jimmy Buffet" atmosphere on Browns Creek. Beer and wine and Chowder Ted himself behind the grill, cooking burgers and his famous fish sandwich. Closed Sunday and Monday. Otherwise open until the last person finishes his meal, around 7:30 to 8:00 p.m. No fuel or place to tie up the boat. Recommended by Capt. Tony Bozzella.

Sandollar Restaurant

> 9716 Heckscher Drive
> Fort George Island, FL 32226
> Phone number: 904-251-2449

Sandollar is a full-service family restaurant with a place to tie up the boat on a floating dock. Full menu, dinner and lunch buffets, band on Sundays in the summer months. A great view of historic Mayport from outside dining on the patio waterfront. Full bar. Recommended by Capt. Tony Bozzella.

Bait and Tackle

Rick's Bait & Tackle

> 224 North 20th Street
> Jacksonville Beach, FL 32250
> Phone number: 904-372-4689

Local shop is known for personal service. Owner Rick Hale grew up in the Jacksonville beaches area and is very knowledgeable about all aspects of pier, surf, inshore, and offshore fishing. If you need it, he has it. Recommended by Joe Dionne and Capt. Vic Tison.

Brown's Bait and Tackle

> 5214 Heckscher Drive
> Jacksonville, FL 32226
> Phone number: 904-757-1600

A full-service bait and tackle shop with munchies, drinks, and guide services. No fuel, but does have a dock to tie up on. Also offers a fishing pier for a small fee. Recommended by Capt. Tony Bozzella.

Other Resources

For more information on fishing Florida's east-coast piers, visit www.boatlessfishing.com. This site is loaded with pier fishing information for novices and pros alike.

Fishing Lessons for Life—Fishing With Kids

I will never forget the look on my son's face when he caught his first fish. Many years later, that same smile appeared on my three-year-old grandson's face as he reeled in his first fish, a 6-inch pinfish. Size doesn't matter; catching does. When you plan a fishing trip to include children, forget about what *you* want to catch and concentrate on what *they* will catch. Kids are fast learners and will retain what they learn and apply it later as the need arises.

Since good fishing begins with habitat, it is a good idea to teach kids early on about the importance of protecting the

Catching is more important than size when fishing with kids.

habitat. Educating our kids about our own impact on habitat quality can add up to large returns in the future. Simple things like not littering and picking up litter and trash that others have left are the right lessons to teach. Some trash, like plastic bottles, aluminum cans, and fishing line, can and should be recycled. Always pack a trash bag in with the fishing equipment and fill it up on your next fishing trip. Make conservation an integral part of each outdoor experience. Concentrate on the catching, not on the size of the fish.

2

St. Augustine

St. Augustine, Florida, the nation's oldest city, was founded by Pedro Menendez in 1565. The city's beginning came some 52 years after Ponce de Leon first visited the area in 1513. More than 400 years of history and culture make this seaside city a fascinating place to visit, not just for the fishing, but also for enjoying a step back in history.

The city was the Spanish center of power in North America for almost 200 years before falling to the British in 1763. It came under Spanish control again in 1784 under a provision of the Treaty of Paris. The Spanish control continued for 37 years, until the Spanish sold Florida to America in 1821.

As he had in other cities, oil tycoon Henry Flagler saw the possibilities existing in St. Augustine. His wise investment in the restoration and development of the city as a winter resort resulted in some of the magnificent architecture existing in the city today. Visitors come from around the world to visit Flagler-inspired construction such as the Alcazar Hotel. Now known as the Lightner Museum, the hotel featured a huge indoor swimming pool with a retractable roof. It also featured a casino, spa, and movie theater.

Flagler's first hotel in St. Augustine was the Ponce de Leon Hotel. Its Spanish Renaissance Revival style of architecture was chosen so the hotel would complement its historic surroundings. It operated until 1967, when it was sold to Flagler College. The college retained much of the original integrity of the architecture, making it a popular destination for visitors.

The Cordova, another Flagler hotel, was actually purchased by Flagler from a friend in financial difficulty. The Casa Monica hotel was purchased and renamed the Cordova. Following a series of ownerships and uses, the hotel operates under its original name and is the only hotel in St. Augustine to be given AAA's Four Diamond Award.

Today, the heart of St. Augustine retains its distinctive plan of a 16th-century Spanish Colonial walled settlement, much of which has been preserved or restored. The numerous remaining colonial buildings in the historic district present an impressive array of architecture to visitors.

Famous as the nation's oldest city, St. Augustine offers much more for guests than just fishing. Historic sites and beautiful beaches are attractive to visitors of all persuasions. Nevertheless, the visiting angler will find much angling variety from which to choose.

In addition to the typical seatrout and redfish, cobia roam abundantly in the area. The "brown clown" is often caught off the backs of huge cruising manta rays. Offshore species include plenty of snapper, grouper, and amberjack.

Characteristics of the Fishing Area

Like Jacksonville, the St. Augustine area is characterized by a large swing in tide level. Depending on wind and moon phases, the range can be as much as 6 feet between low and high tides. Local fishing guide Captain Dennis Goldstein says, "First-time visitors should be particularly aware of the tide swing because it can be confusing for finding fish."

The St. Augustine area is characterized by numerous natural and manmade structures. Oyster bars, a deep inlet with rock jetties, tidal flats, sand flats, mudflats, and vast areas of spartina grass all provide structural attraction for fish. Captain Goldstein likes to target flooded flats for redfish. "When flooded, either sand or mudflats often attract numerous redfish feeding on crabs and crustaceans." He adds, "The three bridges in the area provide a haven for all species of fish. Snook, sheepshead, trout, and tarpon can all be found around the bridges." He also identifies the multitude of docks in the St. Augustine area. These docks can be fished in daylight with great success, but he especially recommends fishing them at night, when their lights provide an added fish attractant. The dock lights attract baitfish, which attract predator fish. Captain Goldstein says, "These docks, when fished at night, attract every fish you would want to target."

The offshore waters contain a variety of fishable structure. According to Captain Guy Spear, operator of MisStress Charters, offshore St. Augustine offers many spots of natural (hard) bottom and artificial reefs as you run out to about 180-foot depths. After that, anglers discover true blue water around the continental shelf, a natural ledge that drops from 180 feet to more than 200. Anglers traveling the 52-mile distance to blue water can target a mixed bag of sailfish, mahi-mahi, kingfish, wahoo, and blue marlin outside the ledge. Captain Spear describes the sailfish and blue marlin fishing during the spring and fall as "nothing short of outstanding."

The nearshore artificial reefs offer anglers some of the best king mackerel fishing found in Florida. The kings run in size from snakes (5 to 12 pounds) on the artificial reefs to smoker kings in the 40-pound class along the beach in 25 to 55 feet of water.

Bottom-fishing anglers find opportunities from 60 feet of water out to the continental shelf. Captain Spear says, "The bottom fishing for red snapper is outstanding for nine months a year from 60 feet of water on out to the ledge."

Anglers wanting to catch the *lady in the blue suit*, the name affectionately given to blue marlin weighing more than 300 pounds, will have to fish the 250- to 300-foot depths. Captain Spear says the long boat ride to these waters is time consuming, but worth it if you want to target the big girls.

The Inshore Bite

Every angler enjoys the adrenaline rush of an exploding surface strike. The geographic features of the St. Augustine area make it prime territory for fishing topwater lures. Captain Goldstein identifies water temperatures between 65 and 80 degrees as a necessity for a hot topwater bite. The warmer water temperatures put the fish in the right attitude to strike on top. Oyster bars are found in all the numerous creeks and also along the edges of the Intracoastal Waterway. Especially at high tide when the oyster bars are flooded, topwater lures such as MirrOlure She Dogs, Storm Chug Bugs, and Rapala Skitterwalks work well. Either a walk-the-dog presentation or an aggressive slashing retrieve with a chugger-type bait will produce blow-up strikes and quality fish from these bars. Use braided line for long casts on 10-pound spinning gear for best results. Add a 20-pound fluorocarbon leader and attach the

Braided line, clear leader, and a topwater lure spell success when fished over oyster bars. Photo by Karen Presley.

Shrimp on a popping cork is an excellent way to introduce kids to fishing.

lure with a loop knot for added action. Captain Goldstein says, "You can improve your success while topwater fishing if you get started at first light. After the sun rises, you may want to shift to something subsurface."

If you enjoy live bait action, Captain Goldstein suggests fishing live shrimp on a Cajun Thunder float over the flooded oyster bars. A 3/0 circle hook tied to a 20-pound leader that accommodates the depth of the water provides a simple rig for catching fish from the flooded bars. Pinch the tail off the shrimp, a technique that releases additional scent, and pin it to the circle hook like a worm. Expect to catch a lot of smaller fish when using shrimp or other natural bait, but the action is normally constant. This is a great way to introduce kids to fishing with plenty of action to keep them busy.

At low tide when the oyster bars are exposed, a different tactic is needed. Captain Goldstein suggests fishing the edges of the exposed shells. "When fishing at lower tide levels, I get on the trolling motor and work the exposed shells along the Intracoastal Waterway or the bars in the creeks. Either ⅛- or ¼-ounce jig heads pinned with live shrimp work exceptionally well." If you prefer artificial lures, use the same jig heads, but rig them with Gulp!, D.O.A., or Saltwater Assassin grubs. Keep in mind that the oyster bars are easy to hang up on. Work the jig slowly, but never let it stop completely. If you keep it moving, the hook rides up and is less likely to catch on an oyster. Be warned, an oyster bar is not a good place to bounce lures on the bottom; the bait needs to be kept up in the water column. Captain Goldstein catches redfish, trout, flounder, and black drum using this method over the bars.

Target the mudflats in the winter when the overnight temperatures fall. Pick a low tide and a sunny day to produce great fishing results. "I'm talking about fishing water from 8 to 10 inches deep," says Captain Goldstein. "The sun will heat the water over the flats by 10 degrees and the fish get active." You can sleep in a little on these cold mornings and still have some great fishing. Once the water has warmed, the serious fishing begins. "Redfish stay in there all night, and when the water heats up, the bite heats up too. Anglers can throw Berkeley Gulp, mud minnows, or almost anything under these conditions and they will eat it."

Use a stealthy approach to the flat and make long casts to reach the fish before they know you are around. Small-diameter braided line and a full spool will give you the added casting distance you need. Some anglers like to use a longer rod in this scenario because longer rods give added casting distance, a must in shallow-water fishing.

Wintertime flats fishing around St. Augustine is a good bet for kayak anglers too. The stealthy approach afforded by kayaks allows anglers to get closer to fish in the 8- to 10-inch water. The adventurous kayaker should obtain an area map and explore some of the many creeks in the area for fish-attracting structure. Call ahead and ask some area marinas or bait shops

Beef up the leader when fishing around docks, bridges, and other heavy structure. Photo courtesy of Jerry McBride.

where the prime fishing areas are. They are usually more than willing to help.

Bridges and docks make up another element of the inshore bite in the St. Augustine area. Fish love structure, and the bridges and docks provide it. Free-lining live bait around the bridge fenders or back under the docks is a sure way to hook up with a hungry fish. Upgrade the shock leader to 30- or 40-pound-test mono or fluorocarbon. Fish around structure are going to test your equipment by wrapping pilings or whatever else they can find. The heavier leader is needed to offset the possibility of the accompanying abrasion. The heavy leader may not be enough. Any time you are fishing around bridges or docks, you need to turn the fish as soon as you can to prevent sudden cutoffs on the structure.

The Offshore Bite—Kingfish and Billfish

The artificial reefs located in St. Augustine waters offer anglers good fishing for king mackerel, cobia, and amberjack. Live bait trolling using light tackle is the favored approach by most local experts. Outfits like the Shimano Speedmaster IV rigged with 20-pound line will do the trick on these offshore species. High-speed reels allow anglers to pick up the slack quickly when a hooked and lively king is heading straight for the boat at 100 miles per hour. Live-baiters prefer a fast-action rod like the Star Live Bait rods. The fast-action tip is flexible, allowing the bait to live longer and be more productive.

Experienced kingfish anglers say that up to 80 percent of kingfish are foul hooked—hooked somewhere other than the mouth—because of their characteristically slashing strike and the presence of the stinger hook. This evidence suggests another reason for using a light-tipped rod. The light tip keeps anglers from ripping the hooks out in a prolonged fight with a big fish. Captain Spear says, "I've actually caught kings with only one point of a #4 treble hooked in the dorsal fin. I don't think I would have landed those fish on a stiff rod." According to Captain Spear, the lesson here is to "Always use a light-tipped rod with a lot of backbone (strength) lower in the rod; this keeps you from ripping the small treble hooks out while fighting a fish."

The terminal tackle is made up of 20 inches of 40-pound wire cable for the toothy critters you engage. Some anglers prefer two #4 trebles on a stinger rig, while others replace the front hook with a circle hook. A third option is to use circle or octopus hooks for both hooks in the stinger rig. Space the

A trip to the Gulf Stream may result in hard-fighting, high-jumping action. Photo by Capt. Billy Poertner.

hooks to fit the size of the bait and leave a little wiggle room for the fish to swim when pinning the bait.

In the St. Augustine area, the natural bait is usually Atlantic menhaden (pogies) or scaled sardines. Captain Spear prefers pogies on the beach and sardines on the wrecks. In either case, if live bait is not available, frozen cigar minnows from a local tackle shop are a great substitute and perfect backup should you run out of live bait.

As far as trolling speed is concerned, Captain Spear says, "The trolling speed for kingfish should be set at dead-slow, 1 to 1.5 knots." If you need help in slowing your trolling speed, raise your engine until the preferred speed is reached. This technique also produces a prop wash behind the boat that can attract curious fish to your boat. The best time of the year for this style of fishing is late April through September.

Even with the fishing excitement available on the artificial reefs, Captain Spear likes to travel a little further offshore and chase billfish in the blue water near the ledge. The best times for fishing trips to blue water are spring and fall. April through June and again from late September through November are recognized as prime seasons for billfish in the St. Augustine area. He says, "We fish a little further offshore than most think of fishing in Florida, but the high probability of catching bill-fish is worth it."

Captain Spear normally sets his spread and begins fishing about 40 miles out for sailfish and 50 miles out for marlin. "I've seen days that produce 20 or more shots at sails and as many as 5 shots at blue marlin." These waters will also produce mahi, kingfish, and wahoo.

The trolling setup includes four 30-pound class rigs and two 50 class outfits. The 30-pound rigs are fished on the outriggers and the 50s are split between a downrigger and flatline fished behind the starboard teaser. If using a curved-butt rod, the flatline can be run from the rod tip. When using straight-butt rods, a release clip on the transom will do the job. Teasers are a hookless lure or string of lures that imitate baitfish and act to pull predators into the strike zone. Captain Spear says, "I use rubber squid tied seven in a line to act as my attractant or teaser to pull fish into the spread of baits. I run it from the outrigger." The teaser will be pulled 20 to 50 feet behind the boat, depending on sea conditions. When fishing clam water, pull the teaser close to the 20-foot mark. When fishing rougher water, the teaser should be back further, as much as 50 feet in really bumpy seas. The flatline bait will be pulled even with the last squid in the teaser.

Captain Spear advises anglers who fish outside the ledge to ditch the 30s and fish all 50-pound-class rigs because of the size of the fish they may catch. Another option is to use four 50-pound rigs and two 80-pound rigs. He sums up his reasoning for upsizing in his description of the area: "This is where the beasts live."

Captain Spear recommends using a mix of naked horse ballyhoo, ballyhoo/lure combos, and artificial lures. The term horse ballyhoo is what Captain Spear calls the largest ballyhoo he can get his hands on. It's naked because it is fished with nothing but a 200- to 300-pound-test fluorocarbon leader and a Mustad 9/0 to 12/0 model 7732 or a 10/0 circle hook. If he is using a ballyhoo/lure combination, he prefers small to medium selections like the L & S Ilander and the C & H Flame. Either of these lures in combination with ballyhoo makes excellent bait.

He likes the L & S Ilander so well when rigged with a ballyhoo, he says, "If I were restricted to just one lure for the rest of my life, for big game fishing, I'd choose the L & S Ilander in blue/white." The ballyhoo is pinned with a single hook directly down on the head and the Ilander runs out front.

For pure plastic artificial lures without natural bait additions, Captain Spear recommends the C & H American Express (never leave home without it). He also fishes Bob Schneider's YAP in Halloween (black over orange) in his spread. Finally, the Hawaiian Custom Disco Ball in pink over blue body is among his favorites. "These are three especially effective lures for going after the blue beast."

The Hawaiian Custom Disco lure is made by Pappy's Trains and Custom Lures in Kona, Hawaii. It is the original Disco Ball lure. It is about three-fourths the size of the similar Aloha lure. The Disco has a flat face, whereas the Aloha has a slant nose that gives it a very erratic action. Captain Spear prefers the Disco action, saying, "If I have to use the Alohas, I grind the face flat to straighten out the action and make it perform more like the original Disco."

Among the very large blue marlin, those weighing more than 300 pounds are all female. They are also known to billfish anglers as the "lady in the blue suit." Captain Spear says, "This may sound corny, but you have to fish where they are if you expect to catch one. What I mean by that is you won't be catching a lady in water shallower than 250 to 300 feet." In northeast Florida that means traveling more than 50 miles offshore to begin fishing and then working out to deeper water. He uses a depth finder that will read up to 5,000-foot depths. "I've caught most of my blues between 400 and 1,000 feet of water." The typical fish caught out of St. Augustine range from 150 to 400 pounds and are caught using 50- to 80-pound line.

Captain Spear says his typical spread includes large baits like the Bob Schneider Large Teardrop or large Black Bart on one of the flatlines and a live Spanish mackerel on the other. These flatlines are fished at or just behind the teasers.

For the short riggers, he recommends medium-sized lures like C & H Stubbies running behind an inline bird teaser, Disco Ball, or a lure/bait combo like the C & H Flame rigged with ballyhoo. These medium-sized baits should be pulled about 10 to 20 feet behind the teasers.

The long riggers are outfitted with small lures like the Black Bart Elk Hunt or L & S Ilander/bait combos, preferably rigged with ballyhoo. These baits will be fished 20 to 50 feet behind the medium baits on the short riggers.

Last but not least, the shotgun rigger, the one running in the middle, will be rigged with either an American Express by C & H Lures or another ballyhoo-rigged Ilander lure. Captain Spear says this line should be "WAAAAAYYYY back; if you can see it, it is too close. I'm talking 300 to 350 feet."

Captain Spear reminds anglers that the setup he describes is for fun fishing or club tournaments where there is no restriction on the number of lines anglers can use. These

Marlin weighing more than 300 pounds are known to billfish anglers as the "lady in the blue suit." Photo courtesy of Capt. Tony Bozzella.

no-restriction tournaments are organized by clubs like the North East Florida Marlin Association, headquartered in Captain Spear's hometown of St. Augustine. In tournaments where rules limit the boat to only six lines, Captain Spear recommends eliminating the short rigger on the port side. "I say this only because I really like to run a center rigger (shotgun) line. Anglers could just as well eliminate the shotgun and run a long rigger, but run it WAAAAAYYYY back if you do."

All things are not created equal when it comes to trolling speeds. Slower speeds are used with natural bait and faster speeds with artificial lures. "Troll the naked ballyhoo and the ballyhoo/lure combos at 6.5 to 8.0 knots. Anglers trolling pure lures should bump the trolling speed up to 14 knots for best results." Artificial lures are pretty good, but don't have the perfect natural look. The higher speed does not give the predator too good a look at the offering before it strikes.

St. Augustine Surf Fishing

Surf fishing is one of the least expensive ways to have an opportunity to catch really big fish. Anyone can find a place to surf fish along Florida's East Coast. The St. Augustine area has three prime beach locations available to would-be surf anglers. St. Augustine Beach, South Ponte Vedra Beach, and Vilano Beach offer surf anglers an abundance of fishing spots with easy access.

If you are new to the area, start the fishing day at a local tackle shop that serves the beach you are fishing. The staff in these stores are usually local experts and can give you information on which fish are biting, what they are biting on, and what equipment to use. Depending on the time of year, most east coast beaches offer redfish, pompano, whiting, bluefish, and many other varieties to try your luck at catching.

Since anglers are never sure just what they may catch in the surf, it is a good idea to use at least a 4000 series reel on a medium heavy rod. Twenty-pound braid makes a good mainline. Rod length is a personal preference, but many surf anglers like at least a 9-foot-long rod because of the extra casting distance it adds. Even with the 4000 size reel you may hook some monster of the deep that spools you. Large sharks are one of the species that might do it. There is really nothing you can do but grab the spool and break the line unless you gear up to target the larger species. In that case you don't have the fun of catching the smaller ones.

There are many different terminal rigs to use while surf fishing, but the most popular one is really all you need, especially if you like to keep it simple. Most anglers refer to the rig as a fish finder rig. Begin the rig by adding a ball-bearing snap swivel to a 1- to 4-ounce pyramid sinker, depending on the current. Run the mainline through the eye of the swivel and attach an inline swivel. Add 20 to 24 inches of 30-pound mono or fluorocarbon leader and attach a 3/0 to 5/0 circle hook to complete the rig.

Surf fishing is very popular along Florida's East Coast. Photo by Paul Mac-Innis.

The pyramid sinker on this rig will bury into the ocean floor to hold the bait in place. Once a fish picks up the bait, it feels little resistance because the mainline will slip right through the snap swivel, making the fish less likely to drop the bait. This rig will work on all species of surf fish with minor adjustments. In rough seas it might be necessary to increase the size of the pyramid sinker. The size of the circle hook can be changed to accommodate the size of the fish you are catching. If you want to add a second hook you can. Use a longer leader and tie a dropper loop to accommodate the second hook.

Another simple rig places the pyramid sinker on the end of the fishing rig. Assemble this rig by tying an inline swivel to the mainline and add a fluorocarbon or mono leader to the other end of the swivel. Tie two or even three dropper loops before adding the sinker. Space the drops so they will not reach

each other. Run each loop through the eye of a 3/0 circle or Kahle hook and then back over the hook to secure it to the rig. Hook size and sinker size can be changed to accommodate fishing conditions and size of the fish. If toothy fish like bluefish or Spanish mackerel show up, you may have to change the rig to include a small length of wire before adding the hooks in either of the rigs described above.

The most common Florida surf fishing baits are shrimp, clams, finger mullet, and sand fleas. All are normally available at bait shops. Mullet can sometimes be cast-netted in the surf, and sand fleas can be dug from the beach. If the shrimp are frozen, remove the shell and pin them on the hook like a worm. Remove the head, start the hook point at the exposed flesh, and push it on all the way to the tail. A single clam will usually make two or three baits. Thread the clam on by wrapping and pinning it three or four times. Finger mullet can be used whole or chunked. The chunked bait releases more scent and is preferred by some surf anglers. If big fish are present, use the mullet whole.

Sand fleas can be located and captured using your hands or a sand flea rake. Walk along the beach and watch as the waves come in and go back out. As the waves recede, look for little v-shaped designs in the sand. That shape is caused by the receding water rushing over the sand fleas' antennae. Drop down on your knees and dig in the area with your hands and you will come up with the sand fleas.

Alternatively, purchase a sand flea rake from a local tackle shop. This handy device is a rectangular wire mesh basket on a handle. Insert it behind the v-shaped spots and rake forward. The basket fills with sand and fleas. Wash out the sand and your next bait is left in the basket. The fleas can be easily kept by placing fresh sand in a bucket and letting the fleas burrow down until you need them for bait. Keep the bucket out of the sun if possible for longer sand flea life. Pin the fleas to the hook by inserting the point in the bottom side near the tail and take it all the way through the top shell.

When fishing in the surf, travel light and remain mobile. Don't go to the beach, set up a chair, and stay there all day unless the fish are biting. If you don't get a bite in 45 minutes to an hour, move down the beach a ways. Look for diving birds or flipping baitfish to locate an area to fish. If baitfish appear in the first trough, wade out and fish parallel to the shoreline toward the bait you can see. Anglers often cast as far out as possible and miss these closer fish.

If there are baitfish around, the predators are more likely to be around too. Sometimes a short move down the beach will put you in front of a submerged point or a deep hole that will hold feeding fish. Checking out the beach at low tide will reveal some of the structure that you can fish when the tide is higher.

Most surf anglers use sand spikes to hold their rods. These PVC spikes drive easily into the beach and keep rods and reels out of the sand, which could damage them. Always remain mindful of the tide because as it comes in, it can wash out the spikes and leave your rod and reel in the surf. If that happens, try to apply a freshwater rinse as soon as possible to remove the salt and sand. Change the position of your spikes to keep them above the incoming tide to prevent washouts. Surf anglers don't need a fish landing net because caught fish are simply beached for harvest or release.

If the rod is in a holder, the angler is usually alerted to a bite by a rod that bends over and continues to flex back and forth. Quickly pick up the rod and set the hook. If circle hooks were used, the hook is probably already set, but it does not hurt to set it further with a slow but deliberate lifting motion. Don't use a hard hook-set with circle hooks.

If the angler is holding the rod, it is sometimes difficult to distinguish a strike from the action of the waves because of the force of the moving water. Don't mistake the increased pressure for a bite on the line as a wave rolls in. What you feel with a bite is a tapping action, often in rapid succession. When those taps occur, reel up any slack and continue cranking to hook the fish.

Artificial lures also work well in the surf, and using them makes it easier to cover a lot of water in search of fish. One of the all-time favorite surf fishing lures is the white bucktail jig. The name comes from the fact that original bucktail jigs were made by tying hair from a deer's tail to a lead head jig. The hair was believed to be a natural fish attractant. When in the water, the hair on a bucktail undulates, giving the lure a seductive look of natural bait. Walk up and down the beach making casts up-current as you walk. You can bounce it off the bottom, swim it at mid-depth, or skim it across the top like a fleeing baitfish. Try all these retrieves until a fish is hooked. Once a fish is hooked, make repeated casts to that area before trying other locations. Chances are there is some type of structure under the water, causing the fish to be in that location, and you want to fish it thoroughly before moving on. Remember the action that caught that first fish and repeat the retrieve until it fails to catch additional fish. Silver and gold spoons, jig heads with plastic tails, and other flashy baits work well in the surf, too.

Surf fishing with bait includes a lot of idle time as the angler waits for a passing fish to find the bait cast out on the bottom. Willing anglers can use that wait time productively by bringing two fishing outfits. Rig one with bait and set it in a sand spike; use the other one as a casting rig to fish artificial lures. Don't stray too far from the baited line, because a big fish could pull the spike out of the sand and take your rig. The casting action relieves some of the boredom of waiting while adding more fishing fun.

There are a few cautions to consider when fishing in the surf. One is a warning that comes from savvy beachgoers and experienced surf anglers: don't turn your back on the ocean!

Especially when the ocean is rough, a rogue wave can come in and sweep you off your feet, so stay in tune with your surroundings. Never wade out deeply into the ocean if you are not a good swimmer. Observe and read posted warning signs as you enter the beach area for possible hazards. If there are swimmers on the beach, try to pick an area to fish that will not cause potential injury to the swimmers. Hopefully this courtesy is a two-way street, and the swimmers will also be mindful of the anglers using the beach. If you hook a huge fish, fight it from the beach where you are standing on stable sand, not out in the surf where the bottom is ever changing.

Many of the same baits and techniques used in surf fishing are used in pier fishing, too. See the following chapter for more information on rigging and baits that work in either application.

Charter Captains

Captain Dennis Goldstein

Hometown: St. Augustine, Florida
Business: Hot Fun Sportfishing Charters
Phone number: 904-810-2455
E-mail address: dennisgoldstein@bellsouth.net
Web site: www.hotfunsportfishingcharters.com

Captain Goldstein's advice for visiting anglers: Recognize that you are fishing in a new area and that fishing techniques may be different from those back home. Use local residents to obtain basic fishing knowledge for the area. For best results, hire a guide and take advantage of his local knowledge.

Captain Guy Spear

Hometown: St. Augustine, Florida
Business: MisStress Charters
Phone number: 904-540-4200

E-mail address: guyspear@bellsouth.net
Web site: www.MisStressCharters.com

Captain Spear's advice for visiting anglers: Anglers who bring their own boat should visit with a local charter boat captain or mate; most of them will be helpful. Ask advice and questions about what is going on at that particular time. Don't expect to find secret spots, but you are likely to get good general information about fishing the area. If you are in the area and want to hire a guide on the spot, visit the fish cleaning tables and see what is being caught. If you are scheduling in advance, use the Yellow Pages or Internet and speak to the captain or mate about your expectations for a trip. Don't be afraid to ask for references.

The question of tipping always comes up when thinking about chartering a fishing boat. Tips are never mandatory, but they are always appreciated. Tipping should be based on how much you enjoyed the trip and the crew's efforts, not on the amount of fish caught. An average tip is 15 percent, and more is added for extra effort from the crew and satisfaction with the trip. When you're fishing on a small boat with no crew, the captain gets the tip.

Area Hotspots

Offshore St. Augustine is loaded with structure. Try Nine Mile Reef for cobia, kings, barracuda, and sailfish. Standish Reef is another good spot for the same species. Nearshore anglers can try the Captain's House. It is a St. Augustine landmark located about 3 miles north of St. Augustine Inlet. It is a good area for rolling tarpon in the summer. South of the Inlet about 12 miles is Matanzas Inlet, for tarpon and kings in the summer and cobia in the spring.

The State Road 312 Bridge is good for redfish, trout, and flounder. If you are fishing from a boat, try the abundant oyster bars north and south of the bridge. Downtown St. Augustine offers the Bridge of Lions, a local hotspot for sheepshead, redfish, trout, and flounder. Fish the Bridge of Lions at night and take advantage of the lights while you listen to the music from the numerous downtown bars and clubs.

Surf anglers should try the Guana River Marsh Aquatic Preserve. The area offers four beach access points to the Atlantic, and kayakers will find miles of wetlands to explore.

Fishing-Friendly Lodging and Glorious Galleys

Conch House

57 Comares Avenue
St. Augustine, FL 32080
Phone number: 904-829-8646

Open Monday through Saturday, 9:00 a.m. to 6:00 p.m. Great restaurant, lodging, and marina, all with a Caribbean flare. Recommended by Capt. Chad Starling.

The Inn At Camachee Harbor

3070 Harbor Drive
St. Augustine, FL 32084
Phone number: 800-688-5379

Clean, nice rooms in the heart of Camachee Island Cove. Lots of shops and restaurants nearby. Recommended by Capt. Dennis Goldstein and Capt. Guy Spear.

Kingfish Grill

252 Yacht Club Drive
St. Augustine, FL 32084
Phone number: 904-824-2111

Serving lunch and dinner, full bar, and outside dining. Dockage available. Will cook your catch. Recommended by Capt. Dennis Goldstein and Capt. Guy Spear.

Bait and Tackle

Cast and Cruise at Camachee Cove

3070 Harbor Drive
St. Augustine, FL 32084
Phone number: 904-829-2628

One-stop shopping for your fishing needs. Live and frozen bait, tackle, kayak rentals available. Recommended by Capt. Dennis Goldstein and Capt. Guy Spear.

Avid Angler

2101 North Ponce De Leon Boulevard
St. Augustine, FL 32084-2623
Phone number: 904-824-8322

Complete line of bait and tackle. Reel repair and fly tying classes. Hunting gear too. It they don't have it, you don't need it. Recommended by Capt. Guy Spear.

Fishing Lessons for Life—Catch and Release Fishing

There are no better stewards of the fishing resource than the anglers who spend time enjoying it. A natural appreciation and respect comes from use and enjoyment of the great outdoors. The continued enjoyment of the resource will depend on how we take care of it. I can remember in my youth when the day's fishing often resulted in keeping most of what we caught. A few fish may have been used for dinner, but many were sent to the freezer for later use. Unfortunately, I also remember discarding many of the carefully prepared packets of frozen fish when freezer burn made them unacceptable to eat. All this was done with good intentions, but the final outcome was less than satisfactory.

Today, as I teach my grandson to fish, I also teach him about catch-and-release fishing. Our fishing goals are aimed at fighting and releasing fish for fun, instead of seeing how many pounds we can put in the freezer. There is certainly nothing wrong with keeping a legal limit of fish for the dinner table, but keeping only what you want for a fresh fish dinner makes more sense in the long run than throwing everything you catch in the freezer.

The success of catch and release fishing as a means of conservation depends on fishing techniques, equipment, and fish handling abilities of the angler. The benefits of catch and release fishing, the use of circle hooks and dehooking tools, and proper handling techniques will all be discussed in following chapters.

3

Palm Coast, Flagler Beach, and Ormond Beach

The three quaint beachside communities of Palm Coast, Flagler Beach, and Ormond Beach are characterized by many amenities attractive to outdoor-related development. When the Spanish regained possession of Florida from the British in the late 1700s, a land grant from the king of Spain to Francisco Pellicer created what would become a true national treasure. The Pellicer family never did divide the parcel, as was normally the case with land grants. The property stands today as the only original Spanish land grant contained in its original boundaries. Pellicer farmed the land for many years, growing sugarcane, corn, and cotton. The local creek named after him is the northern boundary of Flagler County.

Visitors can catch a true glimpse of old Florida in this beautiful piece of the state. The Pellicer Plantation, as it was known, later became part of the Princess Place Preserve, a 1,435-acre park containing the oldest homestead in the county. It sits in a unique historical and environmental treasure chest of old Florida. The preserve is located where Pellicer Creek and Moody Creek meet the Matanzas River, a self-evident hub of nature's abundance and a significant draw to those who love the outdoors.

In 1886, Henry Cutting, a New England sportsman, purchased property that included one of the oldest orange groves in Florida. He hired William Wright, a New York architect, to design a hunting lodge for the property. He constructed an Adirondack-style camp setting similar to those he knew in the mountains of New York State. The pristine setting of the lodge was popular among dignitaries and royalty from all over the world, including many socially prominent residents from Chicago and New England. The lodge is thought to be the only example of this type of architecture in Florida.

The preserve is open to the public, and visitors can enjoy nature trails, picnicking, fishing, canoeing, kayaking, camping, bird watching, and horseback-riding trails. Disabled visitors can view wildlife and birds as they enjoy nature along a paved and accessible trail through the park.

Characteristics of the Fishing Area

The physical characteristics important to anglers are considerably different from and simpler than those found further north. Saltwater marshes, freshwater wetlands, and open surface waters offer anglers plenty to choose from. The area is made up mostly of mud bottoms with scattered oysters and oyster bars in the creeks and canals. The Intracoastal Waterway provides deeper water and some basic structure in the form of docks and seawalls.

This stretch of Florida's East Coast is the location of Matanzas Inlet, but offshore fishing will not be considered in this chapter. The inlet is not deemed a navigable inlet by the Coast Guard. Some experienced anglers do traverse the inlet to obtain ocean fishing access. The inlet is considered a local fishing option, but is not recommended for the inexperienced boater.

The area is also home to a fishing pier in Flagler Beach. A small admission charge will gain anglers access to many popular Florida fish. Flounder, pompano, black drum, weakfish, redfish, whiting, and more are all able to be caught off the pier. A tackle shop on site provides plenty of local advice about tackle and bait.

The Inshore Bite

Snook are normally considered a warm-water fish and not readily available to anglers until much farther south along the Florida coast; however, a pleasant fishing surprise awaits visiting anglers to the Flagler Beach area. It's not an area known to outsiders for snook, but for locals, snook are a regular target. Captain Rob Ottlein operates Osprey Fishing Charters out of Flagler Beach. He says, "You can catch snook from the Highbridge area in northern Volusia County, all through Flagler County, and into southern St. Johns County."

Snook on Fly

Captain Rob's favorite way to chase snook is with a fly rod. Snook are a warm-weather fish and more abundant in the spring and summer than they are in the fall. He says if he had only one month to target snook it would be October, when the

Visiting anglers are usually surprised to find snook fishing in Flagler County. Photo courtesy of Capt. Rob Ottlein.

mullet run is in full swing, but he catches them all year long on flies. "It's all good, especially coming out of winter with water temperatures rising to near 70 degrees." He says that once that magic 70-degree temperature is reached, the snook can be seen busting the bait schools. "Anglers can sit in a boat at Highbridge and watch snook bust out of the water on mullet all day long. It is quite a sight."

Captain Rob prefers a #8 or #9 fly rod with a weight forward (WF) floating line when targeting snook. The WF is extremely popular among saltwater anglers because it casts farther than other line types. Since much saltwater fishing is in shallow water, fish can be spooky and long casts are needed.

Leaders are another important consideration when chasing snook with flies. The leader is attached to the fly line with a perfection loop in the leader. Captain Rob chooses Airflo fly line that comes with a factory-welded loop, allowing a loop-to-loop connection for the leader. The primary advantage of loop-to-loop connections is allowing anglers to quickly change leaders from one application to another. "If I'm using a topwater fly, I'll usually use a straight 5-foot piece of 30-pound fluorocarbon leader with a loop knot on one end for ease of connection to the fly line." If he is fishing sinking flies, Rob makes a knotted tapered leader from various segments of mono and fluorocarbon. "For sinking flies I'll construct a leader using a 4-foot butt section of 40-pound mono, a 3-foot section of 20-pound mono, a 2-foot length of 12- or 15-pound tippet, all tied with a double surgeon's knot." Since snook have such rough mouths and the ability to wear through a lighter leader, Captain Rob adds a special bite tippet. "Finally I add a 30-pound fluorocarbon bite tippet coupled with either a surgeon's knot or a loop-to-loop connection."

He advises anglers to keep everything simple. "Personally, I'm not trying to set any IGFA records, just trying to have some fun catching snook." He uses both these leaders as described on 8 or 9 weight fly rods. "I'll switch to a smaller leader when

I use a 6 weight by starting it off with a smaller butt section. Start with 30-pound mono and decrease the size accordingly."

A topwater bite is exciting to most anglers, and Captain Rob is no different. "I like to start the day using a topwater fly. My two favorites are the Todd's Wiggle Minnow and the Rainy's Bubble Head." The Wiggle Minnow is a self-tied fly on a 2/0 hook. It is composed of Crystal Mirror Flash, Polar Fiber, a small foam cylinder, and plastic eyes. The fly's originator, Todd Boyer, says it has a "slow wobble that drives fish nuts."

The Rainy's Bubble Head fly is commercially available at fly shops and online outlets. It casts easily and lands softly on the water for a stealthy presentation. It is hollow in the front of the head to make it pop, and at the back of the hollow area is a small hole that exits the top of the fly. Air exiting the head produces a bubble trail following the fly as it is retrieved. "I think the bubbles help make this an irresistible fly."

The noise made by Rainy's Bubble Head is an important part of the presentation, according to Captain Rob. "I keep the rod tip close to the water and strip the line at different speeds. Depending on the speed, and length of the strip, the fly will make different noises."

Presenting Todd's Wiggle Minnow is similar, but includes a pause. "Keep the rod tip close to the water as you strip line. Move the rod tip parallel to the water's surface, and this will cause the fly to make a small popping noise before diving under the water. After the strip, allow the fly to float to the surface and rest a second or two before stripping again. The strike often comes during this pause."

Captain Rob reports that both these topwater flies have produced big snook for him, but as the day progresses he switches to a sinking fly. "With more light available I will go to more of a sinking fly or switch to a rod with an intermediate line that will make the fly run deeper in the water column." One exception to the rule is in the backcountry in the summer and fall months. "In the backwater where the water color is usually

For Flagler County snook, use topwater and subsurface flies, depending on the time of day and water temperatures. Photo by Capt. Rob Ottlein.

brown in the summer and fall, it doesn't matter that much. I'll use a topwater or a fly with no lead, such as an Enrico Puglisi mullet, that sinks just below the surface when using a floating line. Fish don't seem to be as affected by the sun in the darker water because it doesn't penetrate as much."

When fishing the Intracoastal Waterway, deeper creeks, or canals, Captain Rob reminds anglers of the fact that fish tend to stay deep as the sun gets higher in the sky. In the colder months the fish stay deep in an effort to find warmer water. Fish also get sluggish when water temperatures drop and are not likely to rise to a topwater offering. Either of these situations calls for a sinking fly for best results.

When prospecting with a sinking fly, Captain Rob varies the speed and length of the strip until he finds the one that works. The whole notion of prospect fishing is to find the combination of size, color, and presentation the fish will strike. It is a matter of trial and error. "Sometimes they like a fast strip, sometimes a slow strip, sometimes a long strip, other times a short strip." He also likes to let the fly sink a couple of seconds between strips. "The fish will often eat the fly during the pause while the fly is sinking." Continue to experiment with the strip until a fish is caught and then repeat the pattern.

Tidal conditions make a difference too. Anglers can improve their catch rate by placing flies as deep in the bushes as possible when the tide is high. Snook love to use the cover as an ambush point for unsuspecting prey. At low tide, fish the deepest parts of holes as near the bottom as possible. Fish often hold in those deeper holes waiting for the tide to resume. Anglers definitely should not take the tides for granted. Tides directly and significantly affect fishing activity. The farther you get into the backwater, the less tidal change you have. A 1- to 2-foot change can be expected in the Flagler Beach backcountry and up to 3-foot changes in the ICW. These averages can be higher or lower depending on wind direction, time of year, and moon phase. All these factors have their own effect on the tides. Captain Rob's best advice is to "Fish the tides whether they are incoming or outgoing because the fish are not as likely to bite during slack tides."

Tying Flies

A passion with most fly fishers is the opportunity to fool a fish with a fly they tied themselves. Captain Rob joins others as one who gets pleasure from tying his own flies. He has three favorites that he ties consistently. "I tie an Enrico Puglisi Peanut Butter in chartreuse/white on a 2/0 Gamakatsu SC 15 hook." He also ties Todd's Wiggle Minnow. "Start with a 2/0

Gamakatsu B10 S stinger hook. I like a white body with a light green back and light green Polar Fiber tail." His final favorite is his own design. Using either a Mustad 34007 #1 or #2 hook, he ties on a set of small dumbbell eyes about ¼ inch behind the hook eye. Use flat waxed nylon thread. Wrap the shank down to the hook bend and tie in a 2-inch piece of white neck hackle. Use two or three feathers on each side and include some EP sparkle. Wrap the hook shank between the feathers and dumbbells with white Estaz to form a bulky, fuzzy body. "Finish it off by wrapping the space between the dumbbell and the eye with thread to build up a small head. Apply a coating of head cement and it is ready for some snook action."

Snook on Spinning Equipment

When chasing snook or other species with a spinning outfit, Captain Rob chooses a 7-foot, medium-light action rod. Add a 2500 to 3000 size spinning reel with 10-pound-test braid and anglers are ready for 90 percent of the species available to them. "I add a 20- to 30-pound fluorocarbon leader, depending on what time of year it is. Lighter leaders in the winter when I know the snook bite slacks off and the water is clearer." Snook have very rough mouths and will chafe a light leader, causing it to break, so use the biggest leader you can get by with. Fish the oyster bars with topwater plugs or very shallow running plugs to avoid hang-ups. Even when the fish aren't hungry, they will often strike these lures out of aggression and anger. The fish don't like it when another creature is invading their territory. When the water is warm, the mudflats also yield good results using topwater lures.

Plastic baits are another popular lure for spinning tackle. "I will use plastic jerk baits such as a Bass Assassin rigged weedless on a 5/0 worm hook." Other plastic baits such as grubs and paddle tails can be rigged on ¹⁄₁₆- or ⅛-ounce jig head with good results. The cooler the water temperature, the slower the retrieve should be. One great advantage of plastic baits is the ease of switching colors. When the bite is slow, don't hesitate to try different color combinations. Other things that might help turn the bite around are rattles or some scent. The rattles add the sense of sound to the presentation, and scent adds the attraction of smell to your bait. Either may be just the ticket to the day's fishing success.

For consistent fishing action, Captain Rob suggests using live shrimp. "Hands down, I would have to say that live shrimp are the most consistent and productive bait for snook. I attach a minimum of 30-pound fluorocarbon leader to the braided mainline and add a Daiichi #1 hook. I like to snell my hooks, and these hooks are made for that knot. If I use Owner hooks I use the SSW #1 hook. Either of these hooks is just the right size for a small to medium shrimp."

When weight is needed for longer casts or a swift current, add a BB-size split shot to the fluorocarbon leader. "Add the weight just below the knot that joins the braid to the leader to keep the shrimp down in the water column." If the current is too fast to allow the shrimp to sink, increase the size of the split shot or add another until you get the sink rate required to keep the shrimp down near the bottom.

The Intracoastal Waterway

The Intracoastal Waterway (ICW) offers tons of fishing possibilities in Flagler County. All fish like structure, and the ICW is loaded with it. Anglers will find deep holes, dock pilings, bridge fenders, and drop-offs to fish. Experience will identify which holes are best on which tide, or which dock is best to fish. Anglers should log their successes so they can come back to the productive spots on a different trip.

Captain Rob's methods in the ICW are similar to those he uses in the backwaters. "I like to fish the ICW early and late in the day with topwater plugs. As the day goes on and the sun gets higher, I will switch to deep diving lures." He names the Rapala X-Rap and the Bomber Long A among his favorites. "I like lures that will dive from 4 to 6 feet deep in the ICW, because that just seems to be where the fish are."

The docks in the ICW can hold fish all day long. Use skipping baits like the D.O.A. Jerk Bait to fish the docks from back to front. Skip the lure all the way back under the dock and then retrieve it with slow, deliberate wrist flicks. Let it settle after each flick before flicking it again. The strike will often come as the lure settles in the water column.

The artificials work great, but Captain Rob reminds anglers not to forget live bait, especially shrimp, in the ICW. "When it comes to using live bait, you can't beat live shrimp. Inshore fish from mangrove snapper to large tarpon will eat shrimp." He fishes shrimp in one of three ways. "Shrimp can be rigged under a popping cork, on a jig head, or free lined. My favorite way is free lining." He describes his setup as 15 inches of 20- to 30-pound fluorocarbon leader tied to the mainline, followed by a #1 hook. He adds a split shot near the knot that connects the mainline to the leader. "The size of the split shot depends on the speed of the current. Fish this rig around the docks and structure of the ICW for some hot action. You never know what you will hook on shrimp."

Matanzas Inlet and Vicinity

There are 19 ocean inlets along Florida's East Coast. Six inlets were constructed for navigational and/or water quality purposes. Of the 19, all but two have been modified for navigational purposes. One of those unmodified inlets is Matanzas Inlet. Since the inlet is not stabilized by jetties it is subject to shifting sand and hazardous navigation. The current edition of NOAA Chart 11485 marks the inlet as "Closed to Navigation." The actual pass can change weekly or even the day following a major storm. Most insurance companies and vessel

Even though Matanzas Inlet is considered non-navigable by Coast Guard standards, prime fishing opportunities surround the inlet. Photo by Capt. Ralph Olivett.

tow services will not cover vessels that run aground in Matanzas Inlet because of known hazards. The Intracoastal Waterway is located in close proximity to the inlet, separated only by Rattlesnake Island and a bridge along Highway A1A.

Captain Ralph Olivett operates his charter business in the area of the Matanzas Inlet. His specialty and passion is fishing for redfish on the vast mudflats that characterize the area. "My favorite flats are located just west of the ICW, between the northern areas of Flagler County and the southern extremities of St. Johns County." He describes these flats as extremely shallow with a heavy mud bottom.

In a warning to anglers Captain Ralph says, "You may expect to find high concentrations of oyster bars scattered throughout the flats region. These oyster bars act like land mines to unsuspecting anglers because they are submerged for the hour preceding and following high tide." According to Ralph, a typical tide range in this area is roughly 30 inches. There is an ancient idiom that says "time and tide wait for no man." Captain Ralph subscribes to the saying and warns anglers to be careful. "It's common to see newcomers to the area out of their boats in ankle-deep water because their boat is stuck. They are pushing them toward deeper water after running aground. Fishing the area requires oyster-proof footwear and a willingness to scratch the bottom of the boat."

Local knowledge is often what separates fishers from catchers. Captains like Ralph Olivett have developed their knowledge of an area over a lifetime of fishing and should be the go-to source for local information to improve fishing success. "Out-of-town clients depend exclusively on our local knowledge," says Captain Ralph. "Not only is the most likely species to be caught in your area identifiable, but also the hot bite of the season is available through communications with local captains." He says the typical targeted species in his neck of the woods are redfish, trout, flounder, and drum. "Redfish," he says, "are caught year round, but our favorite bite is during the coldest winter months when the water temperature falls below 62." This typically occurs in January, February, and March. During this time groups of 25, 50, and up to 100 fish or more can be found on area flats. In the warmer months, reds will be available but found in smaller schools. This is critical information for anglers who want to target redfish.

Equipment selection for fishing the area depends on tidal conditions, time of year, and casting ability. Captain Ralph has two favorite rigs for fishing his area. "My first and favorite tournament rod is a 7-foot fast/medium action 8- to 12-pound class rod with a small 2500 size reel. I spool the reel with 8-pound braided line and add 3 feet of 20-pound fluorocarbon leader. To the leader I attach a ⅛- or ¼-ounce jig head." This rig is chosen because it is light and untiring when 500 or more casts a day are likely; it has the flexibility in the tip to *load* and use stored energy to make long casts, and it has enough backbone to set the hook at great distances.

Winter months bring schooling and tailing redfish to area flats. Photo by Capt. Chris Myers.

His second selection is a 7-foot fast-action 10- to 16-pound rod, mounted with a 4000 class reel, spooled with 10-pound braided line. "I would pre-rig the outfit with 3 feet of 20-pound fluorocarbon leader. Depending on conditions, I would tie on a topwater lure or a gold spoon." Calm water and low light conditions call for a topwater offering, while later in the day a spoon may do better. This outfit is chosen for the same qualities given above, with one notable addition. "In many cases a topwater plug or spoon is 10 times heavier than a jig. The rod will flex much more with the added weight. The extra weight and energy of the cast will stress the line-to-leader knot. This is also the reason I would go from an 8-pound test to a 10-pound-test braided line."

Rod guides are an important and sometimes overlooked element of rod selection. Especially with larger line size and leader size, the knots joining the two must pass through the guides easily. If you hear a clicking sound when you cast, it is likely the knot is catching on the eye connected to the rod's tip. Captain Ralph's advice is simple: "When I purchase a rod, I make sure the guides closest to the tip are as large as I can find." The knot and the guide can be damaged if the knot does not stream freely through the guide. The loss in casting distance and the possibility of damaging the guide and weakening the knot dictate proper sizing. Ignoring these possibilities could result in a lost fish.

To explain how to target fish using either rig, Captain Ralph uses an analogy of eating in a restaurant. The restaurant, an oyster bar in this case, is also a condominium for the baitfish where they can hide from predators. The redfish and other species are going to travel to the restaurant to eat.

He begins by saying, "Fish aren't smart; they just eat for a living." Anglers, he says, should put their offerings in the fish's restaurant without the fish knowing the anglers are around. Stealth is highly important in this endeavor. "If the fish are feeding, they are in their restaurant, not out in the parking lot. Make *long* casts to the restaurant and *serve* up dinner as long as you can. Once the bait is out of the restaurant, you must retrieve the offering as fast as you can and make another high-probability cast."

Captain Ralph advises anglers to make as many long and accurate casts as they can to high-probability areas such as oyster bars. He describes the retrieve as "jig, jig, stop, flutter, float, bounce, wiggle, or any other movement you can generate with the bait." Commenting on the proper retrieve, he says, "For God's sake, try to make the bait look alive!" So, fish in the restaurant and not the parking lot to improve your fishing success. "He who spends the greatest amount of time at the restaurant and at the greatest distance from the restaurant wins."

To complete the equipment selection, Ralph loads his Plano tackle bag with four boxes. "The first box contains jig heads of various weights and colors; the second box contains plastic tails in various shapes and colors to pin on the jig heads; the third box is an assortment of gold spoons, topwater and suspending lures; the final box is loaded with hooks, split shots, barrel sinkers, swivels, and popping corks for natural bait fishing." Multiply the two rods times the number of anglers and the fishing party is geared up for anything that may come their way.

He summarizes equipment selection with simplicity when he says, "If I had only one choice of rod, reel, and bait, I would choose the 7-foot fast/medium rig with 8-pound braided line and 20-pound fluorocarbon. My bait would be a ¼-ounce D.O.A. red jig head tipped with a watermelon-colored Berkley Gulp!"

Another example of important local knowledge is the clarity of the water that comes with cold weather. When the water temperature is below 62 degrees, the water becomes gin clear, allowing anglers to actually see the fish they target. Using flounder as an example, Captain Ralph says, "We catch flounder all year-round, but between the months of December and May most all the larger flounder of breeding age move to nearshore reefs for spawning." Local evidence supports the need to fish in late fall and winter for the big doormat flounder.

The Flagler County Sport Fishing Club has kept fishing records for more than 17 years. The last three times the flounder record was broken was during Thanksgiving holiday. The most recent record is 10.6 pounds, set on the Saturday after turkey day. Before that, a huge 9.14-pound flounder set the record on Sunday following Thanksgiving, and before that the mark was recorded at 9.9 pounds on the Monday before Thanksgiving.

Captain Ralph's best-ever flounder charter occurred on a Friday following Thanksgiving. His clients boated 17 flounder, of which 10 weighed more than 5 pounds, and the water temperature was in the 68-degree range. "In our neck of the woods, stuffed turkey means it's time for stuffed flounder."

More evidence of this phenomenon comes from Dr. William Carr, creator of Fishbites, a series of artificial baits that create a potent scent trail by replicating natural feeding stimulants. "During the months of May through November, the Southern flounder spend their time in the vast flats and tributaries leading to them. In the fall when the temp hits near the 68-degree

Doormat flounder are often caught during fall and winter months. Photo by Capt. Ralph Olivett.

range, flounder pour out of the local inlets like race horses out of a gate. They travel to the nearshore reefs to spawn in 40 to 80 feet of water. Then, in May, the flounder filter back in at a more relaxed rate." There is more than coincidence between this recorded data and Dr. Carr's research. Anglers fishing during this time have a great chance to catch a doormat-sized flounder.

Be ready if the water temperature falls below 68 degrees around the end of November, because a period of outstanding fishing occurs. "Mother Nature opens the spawn gates and the flounder pour out of the local inlets in droves," says Captain Olivett. "As those fish move out of the river to spawn, the bite can only be described as hot."

The fishing can be excellent in the near vicinity of the inlet for shorebound anglers too. The inside of the inlet just west of the bridge is accessible on foot, and shorebound anglers are often seen fishing the area. Captain Rob says, "The change of tides is usually the best time to fish the inlet. Normally there is a one- to two-hour window to fish as the tide is changing." If you are in a boat, a good anchor is needed to hold the boat steady in the extremely fast current.

Prepare a bottom rig with appropriate weight to keep the bait on the bottom. A 2/0 or 3/0 hook pinned with live mullet, mud minnow, croaker, or pinfish will work great. Expect to catch flounder, reds, black drum, and sometimes trout using this method. Even snook can be caught in the same way. According to Captain Rob, "This area is where the largest of the species are caught. During the summer you can also find tarpon inside or outside the inlet."

A little further inside the inlet, up around Fort Matanzas and all the way to the end of the point of land north of the fort is a good place for trout and bluefish during the winter months. Best bet for these fish is diving plugs, jigs, or flies.

Outside the inlet are the usual nearshore species. Kingfish, tarpon, cobia, and tripletail are all possible. When the weather allows small boats to navigate the inlet to ocean waters, there are some really good reefs and wrecks to bottom fish. Captain Rob says, "A variety of snapper, grouper, and other bottom dwellers can be found on the wrecks. These spots are real good because they are not hammered like other spots because few anglers navigate the inlet." He reminds anglers that most of the species caught around the inlet are seasonal, except for redfish. He agrees with Captain Ralph, saying flounder is best in the fall between October and November.

The Flagler Beach Pier

The Flagler Beach Pier has stretched into the nearshore Atlantic Ocean since 1927. It was expanded over the years to extend almost 1,000 feet into the ocean. Now, after years of Florida hurricanes and ocean waves pounding on the structure, its total length is 806 feet. The pier provides a fishing platform for anglers seeking many varieties of saltwater fishes. A small fee allows anglers to fish for the day. Seasonal passes are also available, and discounts apply to military and senior citizen users. The pier operates under a no alcohol policy, making it quite suitable for family outings.

Spend at least some of your time on the pier talking with regulars who fish the pier often. They possess the local knowledge necessary to make a day on the pier a fishing success. Make note of their equipment, tackle rigs, and bait. This is one time when copying someone else's techniques may pay off big and shorten your learning curve.

Shorebound anglers can use the pier with a bona fide chance of catching big fish. Tarpon, jacks, kingfish, cobia, and big sharks have been caught off the pier with some regularity. Big fish require big tackle with heavy terminal tackle. The good news is that visiting anglers don't have to bring a thing; rods can be rented by the day, and all necessary bait and tackle can be purchased on site.

Most anglers fishing for big fish use a rod with a lot of backbone and a reel large enough to hold plenty of heavy line. A 7-foot heavy action rod with a 6000 series reel will work in most cases. Many of the locals prefer longer rods, but they can be cumbersome and inefficient for anglers new to the sport. Above all, the outfit must have the backbone to lift heavy fish from the water surface to the pier deck. Braided line will add needed line capacity because of its smaller diameter. Mainline of 70- or 80-pound test is common on pier fishing outfits when targeting big fish. The rig needs to be capable of casting heavy pyramid sinkers far out into the pounding surf. The pyramid sinker is used to hold the bottom and keep the bait in place. If the bottom is soft, the sinker tends to bury into the sand. If the bottom is hard, the flat sides help keep the sinker and bait from rolling in the current.

Everyone fishing on the pier does not target the bigger fish. Plenty of fish can be caught from a pier using a 7-foot rod and a matching spinning reel. Spool the reel with 12- to

20-pound-test line. Because you are fishing in the surf, add terminal tackle to fit the existing current and wind conditions. If wind and current are mild, rig up with a 2-ounce pyramid sinker. For rougher conditions use a 4-ounce sinker. In either case, you use a plastic slider attached to the mainline to protect the knot from damage and to attract fish. Joe Dionne is an expert pier angler, founder of the Florida Pier Anglers Association Incorporated, and originator of jacksonvillebeachpier. com. He says, "You want the sinker to freely slide up and down the line." Add a small bead and then a small swivel to the end of the mainline and tie on a fluorocarbon leader. Joe adds a second small bead to the 12- to 16-inch leader before tying on a 1/0 to 2/0 circle hook. The bead will rest above the eyelet of the hook. Joe says, "The beads supposedly resemble fish eggs. Their purpose is to attract the fish to the bait." He says green and orange beads seem to work best. "It works for me as well as countless other anglers who use the same technique."

When it comes time to bait up Joe recommends *fresh dead shrimp*. He says to visit a local bait shop and specifically request fresh dead shrimp. "The majority of fish off the pier will eat shrimp. This is very important and that is why I emphasize it." He also says that bigger is not always better. "Some anglers think that a whole shrimp is better bait, but all it really does is shorten your fishing day. Why use up all your bait in just a few hours? You can get three or four pieces of bait from one nice shrimp." He advises anglers to carefully remove the head and skin from the shrimp. Use a sharp knife to cut the shrimp meat into three or four pieces or sections depending on the size of the shrimp. He explains, "The purpose of the smaller baits is to allow the fish to get the whole bait in his mouth along with the hook. The catch rate is better, and 1 pound of shrimp kept on ice will last you all day."

Other good baits for the pier are sand fleas, cut mullet, clams, and Gulp! or Fishbites brand artificial bait. These baits can be fished on the same rigs as described above.

Sand fleas are especially good for whiting, reds, and pompano off the pier. Dionne says they can also be effective on the beach when surf fishing. Collecting the sand fleas for bait can be almost as much fun as fishing with them. Some anglers just dig them with their hands, but a sand flea rake, purchased from a local bait shop near the beach, will make the catching easier. Walk along the beach and watch the sand as the waves go out. Look for little V-shapes in the sand to indicate the presence of sand fleas. Dig the rake in and sift out the sand to expose the fleas.

Dionne says the sand fleas, also called mole crabs, are very durable and can last for days if cared for properly. He says to fill a 5-gallon bucket with 5 to 7 inches of wet beach sand. "The moist sand works best, but be sure not to have excess water in the bucket. A few small drain holes in the bottom will drain the excess water out. Once you catch the fleas, place them in the bucket and store in a cool shady spot until you are ready to use them."

Different anglers have different techniques for pinning the sand fleas on a hook. Dionne prefers the bottom-up method. "The method I like to hook sand fleas is from the bottom up. Insert the hook just short of the head and bring it just barely out of the shell." Don't expect to catch anything in particular, because these hard-shelled little rascals are good bait for a variety of fish in the surf.

Another popular pier fishing bait is cut mullet. Dionne says the mullet work great for bluefish and redfish. "I cut the mullet into 2-inch-long sections for pier fishing. If I am surf fishing I use the whole mullet because it stays on the hook better under the forceful casting that is necessary from the beach." Anglers can cast net mullet to obtain bait for free, or buy it from the local bait and tackle shops. Don't forget to have a sharp knife in your tackle box for chunking it up.

The final bait mentioned by Dionne was clams. "Another good bait for the pier is clams. Anglers on the pier refer to clams as pompano candy, because pompano can't refuse them. The pomps love the clams, but because they are tender they can be somewhat tricky to keep on the hook." Dionne uses frozen clams for convenience, but whole clams or shelled clams are sometimes available too. Pin the clam on a hook by folding the flesh and hooking it again and again to increase its durability. Some anglers even tie the clam on with a small piece of thread.

The popular Gulp! and Fishbites brand soft baits are also popular among pier anglers. They are artificial baits with built-in scent to attract fish to the bait. The stimulating scent and the added taste in these new-technology baits cause the fish to bite and hang on while the angler sets the hook. They are gaining much attention and use among anglers in all kinds of fishing applications. They come out of the package ready to use, much the same as natural bait.

Kids and other less ambitious anglers can catch plenty of fish off the pier too. Smaller rigs can be used to target the many other species of fish available in the nearshore ocean waters. Cut bait is all the angler needs to catch pompano, weakfish, whiting, sheepshead, redfish, black drum, and more. These species are caught regularly off the pier. Some pier anglers use chum bags to attract smaller fish around the pilings. This can create great fishing for the kids while at the same time drawing predator fish closer to the pier.

As a matter of courtesy and consideration, park your coolers, carts, umbrellas, and other equipment in the center of the pier, not in blocking position along the rail. This simple act of courtesy will give everyone equal access to the fishing opportunities. Keeping the rail clear of obstacles also increases the safety of all the anglers and the many visitors who are just strolling through.

As a final and important note, Joe says, "Always know what you are catching and know the existing size and creel limit for each species. The FWC patrols the pier frequently and can ruin your day if you have regulated fish in your cooler that don't meet the requirements of fishery laws."

If you catch a few fish for the dinner table, don't fillet them on the pier. It is illegal to cut off the heads or tails. Field-dress your catch on the cleaning tables and throw them on ice until you get home to finish the job.

Charter Captains and Local Experts

Joe Dionne

> Hometown: Jacksonville, Florida
> Business: JacksonvilleBeachPier.com
> E-mail address: jaxpier@gmail.com
> Web site: www.JacksonvilleBeachPier.com

Joe's advice for first-time pier anglers is to use a spinning reel and rod setup and fish the surf break or just above the break for whiting, bluefish, reds, pompano, and other saltwater species. Fishing the surf break assures success and makes anglers want to come back. Joe says plenty of fish can be caught off a pier in only 4 feet of water.

Captain Rob Ottlein

> Hometown: Flagler Beach, Florida
> Business: Osprey Fishing Charters
> Phone number: 386-439-2636
> E-mail address: captrco@cfl.rr.com
> Web site: www.flaglerfishingcharters.com

Captain Rob's advice to visiting anglers: Catching snook in Flagler County is just a matter of putting in time on the water. Use that time to learn the best times to fish for snook, the habitats they prefer, and the best baits for the time of year you are fishing. Don't hesitate to talk to the locals for current and relevant fishing information.

Captain Ralph Olivett

Hometown: Palm Coast, Florida
Business: Palm Coast Charters
Phone number: 386-503-0693 (cell); 386-447-7777 (home)
E-mail address: Captralpholivett@aol.com

Captain Ralph's advice to visiting anglers: Be prepared to fish shallow, wear polarized glasses to locate the hidden oyster bars that attract and hold the redfish, and identify the local tide changes to plan a safe trip in and out of the flats.

Area Hotspots

Offshore anglers will find good fishing at George Hanns, Big George, and the Sail Boat reefs, all east of Mantanzas Inlet. As described above, Mantanzas is considered non-navigable by the Coast Guard, so access is safer from St. Augustine. Inshore anglers will find easy access to miles of grass flats at Bing's Landing on Highway A1A. The area west of Highbridge is a good starting point, and shorebound anglers can fish off the bridge. Two Flagler County beach access ramps are available at Varn Park and Malacompra Park for surf anglers. Pier anglers can visit Flagler Beach Pier. Click the fishing link at www.visit flagler.org for more local information.

Fishing-Friendly Lodging and Glorious Galleys

Devils Elbow Fishing Resort

7507 A1A South
St. Augustine, FL 32080
Phone number: 904-471-0398

Old Florida style cottages along the ICW. Dockage and boat ramp on site. Bait and tackle shop. This is lodging where fishing is the focus. Recommended by Capt. Ralph Olivett.

The Flagler Fish Company

180 S. Daytona Avenue
Flagler Beach, FL 32136
Phone number: 386-439-0000

A fresh fish market and prime beef restaurant. Food is great. Monday through Saturday for lunch and dinner. Recommended by Capt. Rob Ottlein.

The Topaz Motel

1224 S. Oceanshore Boulevard (A1A)
Flagler Beach, FL 32136
Phone number: 386-439-3301

Old Florida style hotel right across A1A from the ocean. Good restaurant on premises. Recommended by Capt. Rob Ottlein.

Beverly Beach Camptown RV Resort

2815 N. Oceanshore Boulevard (A1A)
Flagler Beach, FL 32136
Phone number: 386-439-3111

RV resort with modern facilities. Bait and tackle, gift store, convenience store. Pet friendly. Full hookup with 30/50 amp service, and free wireless Internet access. Recommended by Capt. Rob Ottlein.

Flagler by the Sea Campgrounds

2982 N. Oceanshore Boulevard (A1A)
Flagler Beach, FL 32136-2779
Phone number: 386-439-2124

Small but nice RV campground on the ocean. Pet friendly. Full hookups. 30/50 amp service. Bait and tackle nearby. Recommended by Capt. Rob Ottlein.

Bait and Tackle

Bing's Bait and Tackle

> 5862 N. Oceanshore Boulevard (A1A)
> Palm Coast, FL 32137
> Phone number: 386-447-7310

Full line of bait and tackle. Live and frozen. Kayaking nearby. Recommended by Capt. Rob Ottlein.

Highbridge Bait and Tackle

> 35 High Bridge Road
> Flagler Beach, FL 32136
> Phone number: 386-441-4151

Full service bait and tackle shop. Live and frozen bait. Rod rentals. Boat ramp nearby. Kayaking nearby. Recommended by Capt. Rob Ottlein.

Fishing Lessons for Life—Circle Hooks

There is no easier conservation tool than circle hooks. All the angler has to do is tie one on and let the hook do its job. Circle hooks are designed to hook fish in the mouth instead of the gut. The deeper a fish is hooked, the harder it is to release. Gut hooking is a problem when using live or cut baits because the bait gets inhaled deeply into the fish's throat. Circle hooks tend to hook the fish in the lip, making it much easier to release. Also, the risk of gut hooking is minimized. Where the fish is hooked plays a significant role in its survival after catch and release.

Fishing with circle hooks is a no-brainer when you understand how fish eat. Once a fish inhales the bait, it turns while mashing its jaw to kill its catch. It turns its head and body to avoid competition from other fish for the meal. According to T. J. Stallings, public relations director for TTI Blakemore Fishing Group, "It's this turn that is critical. While the fish is completing this turn, the circle hook will slide back through the mouth and find the angle change, which is usually the corner of the mouth." This is exactly why you don't set the hook when using circle hooks. The fish will do the hooking for you. He says, "That's why some charter captains keep fishing rods in the rod holder when inexperienced circle hook anglers are on the boat." It is a great lesson for the uninitiated.

When choosing a J-hook, anglers select one that will fit the jaw of the targeted fish. With circle hooks, anglers should choose a size that will fit the lip, not the jaw. "Forget the number size on the package on circle hooks as they are confusing and not uniform. Inspect the gap between the point and shank to see if it will fit the lip of the species you are fishing for." Anglers should also check the bottom of the bend to ensure that it is large enough to hold the chosen bait. While many circle hooks feature a near 90-degree bend in the point, choose circle hooks that have a greater bend in the gap for best results. According to Stallings, "Circle hooks with a greater bend in the gap have a slower curve in the point and will result in faster penetration."

T. J. also encourages anglers to choose nonoffset circle hooks. "The term 'offset' means the point is not directly in line with the shank. While this style is easier to bait, offset hooks tend to penetrate deeper into the fish's mouth. *Nonoffset* hooks are much better for the easy release of fish as well as conservation."

Captain Bouncer Smith, Miami charter captain, uses a tiny 3/0 Daiichi Circle Chunk Light for his sailfish charters. Smith has won the World Billfish Foundation award for most tagged and released Atlantic sailfish three years in a row. This patented circle hook features a Stop Gap barb that keeps bait

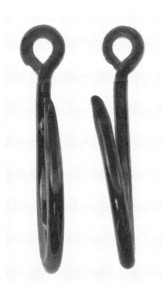

Nonoffset circle hooks result in quicker penetration and a hook-set in the corner of the mouth. Photo courtesy of TTI Blakemore Companies.

from getting double-hooked or fouled. Smith says, "Quality pays when it comes to choosing hooks."

To show young anglers how this hook works, simply hold a circle hook on its topside and run it back and forth across your palm. The action demonstrates that the hook will not penetrate the flesh until it changes angles. Next, explain that if the hook is allowed to change angles by being pulled slowly out of the fish's mouth, it will dig in and hook the fish in the corner of the mouth. This demonstration also makes it clear to the young angler that it is not necessary to set the hook when using circle hooks. All that's needed for the hookup to occur is to start winding when a bite is detected. Teaching kids early about the use of circle hooks will persuade them to use them correctly, enhance their fishing experience, and instill a sense of conservation in their fishing activities.

4

Daytona Beach and New Smyrna Beach

Known as the location of the world's most famous beach, the city of Daytona Beach experienced a history similar to that of the rest of Florida's northeast coast. The area was under Spanish influence until about 1821, when America defeated the Spanish and brought new possibilities of development and recreation for America's rich and famous. Newcomers to the area were not coming for personal rest and relaxation alone. The profit motive was alive and well, causing the Daytona Beach area to appeal to many well-off Americans as an investment opportunity. Early coastal development depended highly on railroads, and two local rail lines were developed. The St. John and Halifax River Railway served the early settlers; it was later purchased by Henry Flagler and added to his Florida East Coast Railroad system.

The first hotel in the area, the Palmetto House, was built by Matthias Day, a business tycoon. He is credited with the founding and improvement of the area. In addition to the first hotel, he developed many more commercial enterprises in the Daytona area. As the original area developed it was named after Mr. Day. In 1926 the three major settlements of Daytona, Daytona Beach, and Seabreeze were joined as one city. This union created a centralized government for the area and improved the flow of private and governmental funds to the area.

Daytona Beach is known by many for a beach that allows motorized vehicles to travel on the hard-packed sandy surface. This vehicle access provides visitors ease of entry and the convenience of carrying ice chests and umbrellas to the beach. In addition to the beach, the city is known as a mecca for motorsports. It is the headquarters city for NASCAR and the Grand American Road Racing Association. Almost all Americans recognize Daytona Beach as home of the Daytona International Speedway and a premier destination for Spring Break.

Some say fishing is secondary in Daytona Beach, but there are plenty of fishing opportunities available. Non-anglers will find plenty to do at this destination while the anglers in the group have their fun fishing.

Numerous marinas, bait shops, and charter fishing guides provide all the interested angler will need for a successful day of fishing in the area. Since the backcountry fishing around Daytona Beach is virtually the same as that already described to the north of the city, this chapter will concentrate on offshore fishing. Mosquito Lagoon is close by and offers some specialized backcountry fishing, but it will be considered in the following chapter since the two regions overlap. Although most are listed as operating out of Daytona Beach, the offshore boats gain access to the Atlantic Ocean through Ponce Inlet near New Smyrna Beach. By most designations New Smyrna Beach falls in the Space Coast area of Florida, but because of the inlet it is best included in this chapter with Daytona Beach.

Characteristics of the Fishing Area

Ponce Inlet is the only inlet in Volusia County with ocean access and egress. Learning the topography of the ocean floor is a must for area anglers searching for the best fishing spots. Everything from old tires, lawn mowers, and sunken boats to old bridge debris is now on the ocean floor, creating habitat and feeding areas for Daytona Beach's fishing.

Anglers gain access to the Atlantic Ocean fishing grounds through Ponce Inlet. Shorebound anglers can fish from the pier over the jetty.

The nearshore water, out to about 30-foot depths, is characterized by meadows of turtle grass that support baitfish and attract predators. As you travel out the inlet and pass the red bell buoy, the ocean floor drops to about 65 feet before gently sloping downward. After about 18 to 20 miles, anglers reach 90-foot depths and an area known to locals as the party grounds. This name has stuck over the years, because the area has long been a favorite destination of local head boats (party boats), where anglers were charged by the head for a day's fishing.

Some anglers, looking for true big game fishing, make the long trek to the Gulf Stream east of Ponce Inlet. The blue water of the Gulf Stream offers anglers a great opportunity for big fish, including wahoo, sailfish, marlin, and dolphinfish.

In that vast area between the party grounds and the inlet are several sunken vessels and wrecks. The GPS coordinates for most of these structures can be found on commercial fishing charts. Captain Budd Neviaser operates Huntsman Charters in the Daytona Beach area and has a long history of fishing these abundant waters. He says, "Learning the location of wrecks, reefs, and other structure is the key to successfully fishing area waters. I personally find the Waterproof brand charts to be the most accurate in providing the needed information for a successful offshore fishing trip." He says there is also a local fishing club chart developed by local anglers available to visiting anglers. Ponce Inlet has a variety of fish offshore, inshore, and along the jetties. "I can think of at least 30 different species of fish," says Captain Budd, "that I have personally caught in these waters."

Anglers fishing out of Ponce Inlet should keep an eye on the fathometer. "The fish-finding screen of your electronics will interpret and display a picture of the actual bottom as it rises and falls. It will also indicate the presence of fish above the bottom." Captain Budd advises anglers to keep an eye on the screen as they run their trolling pattern, record the location of potentially fishy spots on the GPS, and return later to fish them.

Bottom-Fishing Daytona: Triggerfish

Trolling with ballyhoo, mullet, Spanish mackerel, bonito strips, and/or artificial rigs for kingfish (king mackerel), dolphin (mahi-mahi), and wahoo is a favorite sport of many novice and experienced anglers. Captain Budd, however, is a bottom fisherman at heart. "I personally enjoy bottom fishing better than trolling. In my opinion, it requires more skill and finesse than pulling bait behind the boat." His favorite pastime of bottom fishing can be accomplished with live bait, dead bait, or artificial bait, depending on angler preference or fish appetites. He says bottom fishing challenges the angler to give action to the bait as opposed to action created by the boat when trolling. The normal bottom targets are triggerfish, genuine red snapper, a variety of other snappers, porgy, or any of a number of grouper species.

Choice of baits may dictate what is caught. Captain Budd says, "Using live bait limits your chances of catching anything but cobia, red snapper, mangrove snapper, and grouper; however, dead bait or cut bait will not only catch cobia, red and mangrove snapper, and grouper, but other species like porgy, vermillion snapper, and triggerfish. Triggerfish, in my opinion, are the best eating of all of these fish." Although triggerfish are difficult to target specifically, there are a few things an angler can do to catch them.

The correct rod, reel, and line selection for targeting triggerfish can make the angler's job easier. Start with a strong rod with lots of backbone for retrieving fish from deep water. Captain Budd uses Star Delux rods because of a built-in shock-absorbing action that keeps pressure on the fish instead of the angler. He believes in long rods with a lively tip for bottom fishing. "I prefer 7- to 8-foot rods with very active tips, either a fast or extra fast action. The flexibility of the rod allows the angler to feel every tap on the bait. When a fish grabs the bait, the lively tip will alert the angler to the bite."

Add a 6/0 high-speed reel and you are ready for all comers. Captain Budd's choice is Penn brand reels. "Penn produces sturdy dependable reels that take the abuse of rugged bottom fishing. They are easy to take apart for cleaning and lubrication, and parts are readily available if needed." He spools his reels with super braid line over monofilament filler. "I use synthetic line exclusively. My personal preference is Fins 50- to 80-pound-test line when bottom fishing, because it eliminates the stretch of monofilament line and the weight of wire line." Triggerfish are caught in deep water, and the hook-set ratio is better if the line does not stretch. Additionally, the synthetic line eliminates the weight associated with using wire or Monel type lines. Fishing straight down with wire line will fatigue most anglers during an eight-hour day of fishing.

When filling the line spool, start with a thin base of Dacron line. Dacron is made from interwoven strands of nylon material that prevent the monofilament backing, which goes on the spool next, from slipping on the metal spool. Connect the Dacron and mono with a uni knot and fill the spool to approximately 75 percent capacity. Captain Budd says, "Color makes no difference. Use 30- to 50-pound monofilament backing before attaching the synthetic line. Finish filling the spool with 50- to 80-pound braid and you are ready for the terminal tackle." He uses this combination of lines because it results in a thin line in the water, virtually eliminating the resistance of the current. Depending on moon phases, the current can be very fast and make holding the bottom difficult to accomplish. Triggerfish are bottom feeders, and the bait must be kept near the ocean floor, not swept upward and away by the current. The thinner line creates better performance by cutting through the water, allowing the bait to hold well to the bottom.

The terminal tackle used for catching gray triggerfish consists of 10 to 15 feet of clear monofilament or preferably fluorocarbon leader. Captain Budd explains that the fluorocarbon leader is more expensive than monofilament, but leader-shy fish that won't come near the mono may take the bait when presented on fluorocarbon. The rig has a simple double loop knot placed on each end of the leader and two dropper loops spaced between the ends. "A dropper knot is formed by making a small loop in the leader line and twisting the line three to five times and then bringing the loop equidistant between the twists in the line and tightening the twists." Captain Budd says the loops should not be greater than 4 to 7 inches long because longer loops will not hang straight out from the main leader line. If the initial loop is too long, anglers can make one or two simple overhand knots in the loop to stiffen it. Additionally, the dropper loops should be far enough apart to eliminate tangling in each other.

Triggerfish are known as bait stealers. Sharp teeth and small mouths quickly remove bait from the hook. Photo by Capt. Budd Neviaser.

A hook is placed on each dropper loop by sticking the loop through the eye of the hook, swinging it around the bottom of the hook and tightening the loop around the eye of the hook. Size 4/0 hooks work well for bottom fishing in general, but Captain Budd goes smaller for triggerfish. "I personally prefer a hook size of 1/0 when targeting triggerfish exclusively. They have a small mouth, requiring a small hook to be successful. I use Owner hooks for bottom fishing because they are extremely sharp and penetrate easily." Combined with no-stretch braided line, sharp piercing hooks are a must for deepwater hook-sets on triggerfish. Connect the dropper rig to the braid using a quality barrel swivel.

A bank sinker completes the bottom rig. The bottom loop of the leader is placed through the sinker, which is dropped back through the loop to finish the rig. The loop allows sinkers to be changed easily if the current dictates it.

Most reefs off Daytona Beach will have some triggerfish hanging around. Triggerfish are extremely aggressive feeders and have a reputation of being bait stealers. Their small mouths are lined with very sharp teeth that quickly shred the bait and remove it from the hook. "When they are present in large numbers, the competitive spirit takes over and no other fish has a chance to reach the bait before a triggerfish grabs it. This competitiveness is why I love fishing for triggerfish." He says he would rather fish for them using very light tackle, but since there is such a variation in size and species of fish on most spots, heavier tackle is needed for the larger fish like grouper that will be caught from the same spots while targeting triggerfish.

The actual fishing becomes a game of finesse. Captain Budd explains, "I prefer to barely touch the bottom of the ocean with the weight. This allows me to feel the slightest nudge of fish activity. With practice, anglers will be able to sense when the fish takes the bait." He goes on to warn that if anglers lay the weight on the bottom, detection is not as likely and the hookup ratio will be narrowed noticeably. Alternatively, if the weight is held too high off the ocean floor, the number of bites will be less than when barely touching the ocean floor. Triggerfish use undulating motions of their dorsal and anal fins to ascend and descend vertically and to hover over the bottom searching for food. Their feeding zone is narrow and near the bottom. Captain Budd's technique is aimed at early bite detection and keeping bait in the strike zone longer.

Captain Budd recognizes that bottom fishing requires patience, skill, and a sense of timing to set the hook on bottom fish. "Unlike many other types of fishing, it is imperative to set the hook with the reel—*not the rod*! A couple cranks of the reel and the fish is hooked, and the angler should keep on cranking.

If you accidentally throw your rod tip straight up or close to vertically, crank the line rapidly to keep pressure on the line as you drop the rod tip toward the fish." A tight line is necessary, because the slightest slack in the line will likely result in losing both the fish and the bait. If you missed the hookup, drop the rig right back down for another chance. If there is no more action, the boat has moved off the fish or your hook is empty. Bait up, move if necessary, and try again.

Understanding the behavior of triggerfish helps anglers catch more of them. The gray triggerfish, the species found off Daytona Beach's coast, uses its powerful teeth to dislodge and crush small mussels, sea urchins, and barnacles. Its natural tendency to eat small critters means anglers should use small baits to catch it. Captain Budd's choice of bait is squid. "I feel the best bait is frozen or fresh squid for triggerfish. Prepare small baits that are easy for them to get into their relatively small mouths."

Once a triggerfish is in the boat, anglers should handle it carefully. Their anterior dorsal fin is made up of three spines. The first spine is quite sturdy and long. It is not uncommon for the fish to have that first spine extended and locked in place. Unsuspecting anglers can be stabbed by the spine. Amazingly, the first spine will not retract without depressing the second spine. When relaxed, all spines fit back naturally into a groove on the fish's back. This unique characteristic is Mother Nature's way of protecting the triggerfish from larger predators by making it harder to eat and swallow. Captain Budd says, "Most anglers, if they have not seen a triggerfish before, are amazed by the fact that they cannot push the first spine down into the groove without releasing the trigger—the second spine." The locking characteristic of the first spine belongs to the triggerfish alone and explains its common name. The self-preservation intent of the locking spine on triggerfish can become a hazard to anglers, so beware.

Fishing Daytona Beach: Nearshore Tarpon

For Captain Fred Robert, Daytona Beach fishing is everything he ever dreamed of. As in most other areas, from Central Florida north, the most sought-after inshore fish is the redfish, but Captain Fred, known to friends as Frenchy, identifies the best part of Daytona Beach fishing as the variety of fish available. "The most significant fish here is redfish, but I consistently catch many more varieties." Fred traveled the world, in his words, "just for fishing." Fishing adventures in Madagascar, Thailand, Mauritius, Cuba, Jamaica, Hawaii, and Africa, to name a few, gave Fred a vast amount of experience to apply to his fishing pursuits in America. "I would stay in one place for two to six months before deciding to travel to another destination to fight another kind of fish. It was a dream I had since I was three years old." Now he says, "I live here for 10 years now, it is like heaven. I feel good about America and fishing is good." He names ladyfish, snook, sharks, and cobia among his favorite targets, but tarpon fishing is his true love.

Fred chooses a Shimano Trevala rod for tarpon. Tarpon are mighty fighters, and rods must be able to withstand the punishment of fighting big fish. He adds a Shimano Stella reel that provides plenty of line capacity and a smooth working drag. The size of the reel will depend on the size of the targeted tarpon. Juvenile tarpon can be caught on small reels, but when Fred targets the big boys (his personal best is 250 pounds), he steps up to a Stella 8000 spooled with 50-pound braided line.

The terminal tackle begins with a small swivel and 80-pound fluorocarbon leader for maximum invisibility. A smaller leader can be used when smaller fish are targeted. "I like extra sharp hooks, like Gamakatsu or Owner, to penetrate the hard bony mouth of tarpon. The size of the hook will depend on the size of the bait and the size of the targeted fish." Sizes range from a number 3/0 to a number 9/0 circle hook. Captain Fred uses a Palomar knot to connect the swivel and hook to the leader.

Tarpon are mighty fighters and require quality equipment to land. Photo by Capt. Carl Ball.

Captain Fred is well known for his tarpon-catching ability in Daytona's nearshore ocean waters. His favorite techniques include searching for pods of bait along the beach, finding patches of turtle grass, and searching for and locating objects floating on the ocean's surface.

Captain Fred says there is one important factor that no angler should forget: "The best way to find tarpon is to find bait. The best way to find bait is to find birds feeding on the bait schools. I look for schooling pogies or herring with an expectation of finding tarpon." Once bait is found, a cast net is used to capture it from the same bait school that he will later fish. You can't get any closer to matching the hatch than that.

Tarpon are normally on the move, and chances of finding and catching them are better if the angler is on the move too. Tarpon can be caught by trolling or drifting. Captain Fred says he catches more fish by drifting. "I like to drift-fish for tarpon.

Drift-fishing live or dead bait makes a very natural presentation to hungry tarpon. The idea is to be moving the same as the current. The tarpon feed up-current and pounce on the bait moving toward them." Fred instructs his anglers to cast perpendicular to the boat, allowing the bait and the boat to drift in the same direction. Fred says this works especially well when the tarpon are feeding on the surface.

Trolling for tarpon is best at very slow speeds. Captain Fred recommends live mullet or ladyfish for really big tarpon. "Run the engine very slow and troll live bait. A very lively mullet, not less than 15 inches long, is excellent big tarpon bait; however, the best of the best is ladyfish. Big tarpon strike ladyfish as if they had an uncontrollable addiction." Trolling can also be used in conjunction with artificial lures on days when natural bait is hard to come by. "When I troll artificial lures I use large Bomber or Sebile lures. The big lip makes them dive and have lots of action." Just as with natural bait, Fred says slow trolling is a necessity for tarpon. Set your path to troll directly through a school of herring or other bait to improve results. "If you troll too fast it is very rare to have a strike. Truthfully, I prefer using natural bait on a circle hook. It works better, and I don't have to remove a treble hook from a thrashing fish."

Once a tarpon is hooked, both the angler and the boat operator have unique responsibilities for landing the fish successfully. Captain Fred says, "The angler must keep the rod at 10 o'clock to place constant pressure on the fish. Not much higher, not much lower. When the fish jumps, give him the rod to keep him from throwing the hook." This technique, known to tarpon anglers as "bowing to the king," creates slack in the line between the rod tip and the fish to prevent the tarpon from throwing the hook with its characteristic violent head shakes.

When the fish is not jumping, the line must be tight. "While the tarpon is swimming, anglers should position the rod to pull in the opposite direction. This puts more pressure on the fish to wear it out quicker." After setting the drag at 30 percent of line-breaking strength, Fred advises anglers to feather the spool with a finger to add or subtract drag when needed. "Lay your finger on the top of the reel. If the tarpon decides to run, release some pressure and let it go. The angler should fight with authority, but also with patience." Keeping heavy pressure on the fish at all times will shorten the fight and improve chances for survival on release.

The boat operator has fighting duties too. "Many times tarpon take almost all the line from the spool and the captain must follow the fish. When this is necessary, it is best to go slow and not straight to the fish." This helps keep tension on the fish. The worst thing to do is to follow the fish without applying pressure just to gain line on the spool. The tarpon will gain a second wind, and the fight will be extended. The fight with big tarpon is an inch at a time. Take line when you can and always keep pressure on the fish.

In addition to bait pods, Captain Fred looks for patches of turtle grass. This species of seagrass survives out to a depth of about 30 feet. Named after the green sea turtles that graze on seagrass beds, this thick-bladed, flat, and ribbonlike grass can grow in length to 14 inches. It provides excellent cover for baitfish that in turn attract larger predator fish. Fred runs the beach in search of bird activity indicating the presence of bait. The turtle grass meadows attract baitfish, and the birds find and dive on the bait. He prefers this kind of proactive fishing because it engages the angler more with the environment. "I like this kind of fishing, because it is like hunting. Looking for birds or trying to read the water to find a small wake made by a cruising manta ray or spotting the flash of baitfish on the surface adds great excitement to the adventure." For experienced anglers, proactive fishing certainly adds more photo opportunities to the day's adventure.

Other nearshore structure to look for is any floating debris such as wood, plastic sacks, buckets, or buoys. Captain Fred

Cobia are often a bonus catch when cruising rays are found on a tarpon outing. Photo by Capt. Bouncer Smith.

advises anglers to look for anything floating on the surface. Small debris can be excellent for attracting bait and predators, even the smallest of it. One major type of structure isn't floating at all—it is swimming. "When I am fishing for tarpon, I also look for large manta rays. I might add a bonus to the day's fishing. The rays are often accompanied by cruising fish."

As the rays swim near the bottom, they stir up all kinds of delectable goodies for the nearby fish. Many cobia have been caught by tossing a bait or lure off the back of a cruising manta ray. If you see a ray, especially the larger ones, look closely for signs of a cobia. Captain Fred says, "It is so cool to see this enormous manta ray and then a big magic brown monster appear next to it. My excitement rises as a cast is made to what you know is a very big fish and an excellent dinner." Cobia can be overlooked if they swim close to the ray. Even if you don't see them, make a cast and check it out. Sometimes the cobia(s) will fire out from under the ray and take your offering even when you didn't spot them. Captain Fred adds, "One big cobia is enough to feed you and your friends. At least think about not eating even this one; maybe you will catch him bigger next time. Personally, I like the philosophy of catch, kiss, and release."

Dolphin Fishing in Deep Water, Including the Gulf Stream

There are many fish species available to anglers venturing out to the Gulf Stream departing from Ponce Inlet. Wahoo, sailfish, blue and white marlin, shark, little tunny, and sometimes mackerel are all targeted by anglers in the Gulf Stream waters; however, there is one remaining target that has a special attraction to deepwater and Gulf Stream anglers; that fish is dolphin. Dolphin are a highly sought-after fish. They offer thrilling jumps and hard-charging runs that challenge any angler in a fight. Additionally, they make excellent dinner fare. In restaurants they may be on the menu as mahi-mahi or dorado, but regardless of name, they make great eating.

Before the Trip Begins

Preparation for a Gulf Stream trip starts the day before. Once the decision is made to go dolphin fishing, captains and their mates and most recreational dolphin anglers spend the day or evening before rigging baits for the next day's fishing. Captain Budd Neviaser says, "The first thing to do in preparation for a dolphin trip is to sharpen hooks. Even if they are fresh out of the box, all hooks must be sharp to increase the hookup ratio." He says more fish are lost as a result of improperly sharpened hooks than most people would think.

The edges must be razor sharp so the hook can penetrate the jaw. The point of the hook will be triangular in shape when it has been sharpened correctly. The outside of the point will be flat, and the remaining two edges will be filed at a 45-degree angle to the flat side, creating the triangular profile. A finished hook should be sharpened so each of the three sides of the point cuts like a razor.

Once the hooks are sharpened, they become part of the trolling rig. There are many bait options available to anglers, but the basic rig preferred by Captain Budd is either rigged ballyhoo or silver mullet. Novice anglers should either fish with an experienced captain or study the many books and Web sites available for learning to rig the trolling baits.

For targeting dolphinfish in Florida, the best dead bait, according to Captain Budd, is small to medium-sized ballyhoo and/or rigged silver mullet. These baits are about 8 inches long and will be eaten by any size dolphin. "Most knowledgeable anglers do not use large (horse) ballyhoo because they limit the catch to large dolphin only. The 20- to 25-pound fish are fun to catch, but because dolphins are sought for the dinner table, most anglers want to catch smaller ones too." The smaller baits allow anglers to take on all comers, large and small alike, because the big fish will chow down on the 8-inch baits too.

Black mullet are not recommended by Captain Budd. "Black mullet do not make good trolling baits because they are too oily and they fall apart when trolled. I want solid bait that will last on the trolling rig, that's why I prefer the ballyhoo and silver mullet."

After the baits are rigged, the wire leader is coiled and the ballyhoo held up by the coil to ensure that the inner part of the bend of the hook does not touch the front of the exit hole on the belly of the ballyhoo. "If the bait is not rigged correctly, it will spin like a top. The dolphin will not strike bait that does not swim naturally." Captain Budd advises anglers to remedy the situation by taking a sharp knife and cutting the belly forward of the curve of the hook until the hook rides freely. This will cure the spinning problem, and the bait should perform by swimming naturally.

No trip to the Gulf Stream should begin with fewer than 12 to 18 baits rigged and ready to fish. Once the baits are rigged, fill an ice chest about two-thirds full of ice and place a layer of newspaper over the ice to keep the baits fresh and dry. Place the rigged baits on top of the newspapers and remove the drain plug from the cooler to avoid a buildup of water. Captain Budd suggests shaking kosher salt over the baits to toughen them up overnight. "The salting process will make the baits tougher and last longer. It's not a necessity, but well worth the effort."

The next step in preparation for the trip is to check the equipment. Anglers should inspect line guides and rod tips for damage. To check the line guides, run an old pair of panty hose though the guides. If there are nicks and abrasions present, the panty hose will catch and identify the problem. Damaged guides or tips should be replaced or repaired if possible.

Next, the reels should be checked to ensure they crank smoothly and the drag operates correctly. Captain Budd follows recommended guidelines for setting drags. "I set my drags at one-third the breaking strength of the line on any particular reel." If a reel contains 30-pound line, the drag should be set at 10 pounds. Experienced anglers learn to set the drag by feel, but developing the skill should begin by using scales available for the task. "Once set, the mate would ensure no one fooled with the setting. We check them periodically to be sure they had not been changed." This double-checking speaks to the importance of drag in landing fish, especially big fish.

Check the fishing line carefully too. If any nicks and abrasions are found in the line guides, the main line may be damaged too. It would be a shame to lose a trophy dolphin because of damaged line. Any damaged line should be replaced immediately.

In the interest of efficiency, drinks should be iced down the night before so it does not have to be done the next day. One person should be assigned the task of obtaining food for the trip. Select the clothing needed based on the weather forecast and include any medications that might be needed. The captain will have a first aid kit on board, but each individual's personal medications must not be forgotten. These things may seem minor, but if left until morning, they can delay departure.

The Ride Out

The ride out to the fishing grounds is an adventure in itself. The conversation includes questions about exactly where the fishing begins; who is going to be first in the chair; how the weather will affect the trip; and of course, what happened on trips in the past. Passing the time sometimes results in story telling as each angler endeavors to chronicle a fishing event better than the other anglers can.

The ride time is also an opportunity for the captain to instruct the anglers on what to look for. Anglers are usually instructed to start watching for birds, weed lines, or rips in the ocean that might indicate the presence of fish. According to Captain Budd, "Nothing is more informative about active feeding occurring on the surface of the ocean than bird activity." His advice is to slow down when you see birds and watch their behavior. "There are distinguishing actions made by birds that will give clues to the angler as to what type of fish is causing the bird activity." He explains that if the birds come down to the ocean surface and dart this way and that and then rise up into the air again, most probably they are with a school of tuna that is surface feeding. "The reason for this is that tuna that come up to the surface to feed, eat for a short time and then dive again. When the tuna dive, the birds rise up into the air, giving them better visibility to follow the school."

Dolphin create a different behavior in the birds. Surface-feeding dolphin will swim into the current and feed on the bait for an extended period of time. Therefore the birds have no need to fly back up into the air to follow the school. They will stay just above the school before diving into the feeding frenzy and grabbing the scraps.

At this point where the birds and bait are detected, the captain will deploy the baits, if not already in the water, and troll a deliberate path around the outside of the school. Captain Budd instructs, "Stay at least 10 to 20 yards away from the school; closer in rough conditions but further away when seas are calm. The dolphin will spot your trolled baits on the perimeter and hammer them."

Live weed lines are one of Captain Budd's favorite trolling opportunities. He makes the point that the operative word is *live*. "When the crew finds a weed line, I position the boat to troll down the line. I am always looking for life under the weed line. A good weed line will have plenty of small fish, sea horses, and other marine life just beneath it. This is a live weed line and you should troll it." If there are no visible signs of life under the weeds, it is what Captain Budd calls "a dead weed line" and trolling it is a waste of time. "I have watched inexperienced anglers troll dead weed lines for hours, wondering why they are not getting a bite."

Rips are another important characteristic of good fishing locations. Rips are usually caused by two currents of water being adjacent but moving at different speeds. There is normally a temperature difference between the two currents also. Rips are created by shoals, ledges, reefs, rock piles, and even wrecks where the current lifts after hitting the structure. When the uplifted current reaches the surface, it creates the rip line with the adjacent current. According to Captain Budd, "You can see the difference in color in the two bodies of water and frequently, but not necessarily, a disturbance in the water where the two currents meet. Often the line where they meet will be irregular, depending on what created it." Fish hang out along the rips waiting to eat without expending energy. The bait is moved by the rip and the fish simply lay in ambush.

Captain Budd also keeps an eye on water temperature during the ride out. "Dolphin are a temperature-sensitive fish and prefer water temperatures greater than 78 degrees Fahrenheit. In my mind, 78 to 85 degrees is the preferred range. In fact, I will not start trolling until the water is 78 degrees. All the experts say that dolphin will only be found in 100 feet of water or more, but that is just malarkey. I have caught dolphin just beyond the surf if conditions are right."

Setting the Spread for Dolphin

The trolling begins by setting out the spread. The spread varies with the size of the boat and the captain, with every captain having individual preferences. Regardless of boat size, every captain wants his baits and spread to appear as natural and enticing as possible. Very small boats without outriggers usually fish with just three lines. They can troll two flatlines at different distances and one far back behind the boat, often referred to as the wayback line. Small boats with outrigger capability usually troll with five lines. They can troll one line from each of two outriggers, two flatlines, and one deep line called the shotgun. Larger boats can have as many as three outriggers and run up to nine lines depending on equipment. "There are no set rules to setting a spread. It is something of personal preference based on experience and sea conditions. I would say it is usually asymmetrical and designed to position baits over the largest possible area of water, including various depths in the water column."

Most boats making the trip to the Gulf Stream are equipped with downriggers and fish a maximum number of lines. Regardless of the number of trolling lines being fished, there are some fundamental principles to follow in placing the spread. The basic idea when trolling with outriggers is to have the baits spread out away from the boat. The outriggers are covering different water than the flatlines. Captain Budd likes to place the baits on the face of the waves that developed from the boat's wake. "I might position line number 1 on wave number 3, line number 2 on wave number 4 and so on, depending on how many lines I am fishing. My objectives are to cover as much water as possible and make the presentation look natural."

The flatlines and the shotgun line are pulling swimming mullet or swimming ballyhoo inside the area covered by the outriggers. For trolling with dead bait, he recommends a speed between 4 and 6 knots depending on ocean conditions. "With rare exceptions, I never troll faster or slower than 4 to 6 knots. The actual speed is determined by the action of the baits and the water conditions. At speeds less than 4 knots the baits usually do not swim naturally and above 6 knots, on my boat, the baits jump out of the water." Captain Budd goes on to explain the exceptions in terms of bait performance. "Depending on sea conditions, wind direction and strength, current, direction of travel in relation to those factors, and the hydrodynamics of the object being trolled, occasionally I bump it up a notch or two to make the bait present properly. Speed is not the important factor. It is the presentation of the bait that is the important thing." Sometimes teasers are used in spreads to create commotion and attract predators to the spreads. Teasers are hookless lures trolled along with the baits. They are intended to give the fish the idea that an easy meal is at hand. Once the fish are attracted by the teaser, they are also likely to see the baits in the spread and strike one.

Hooking and Fighting Dolphin

Most dolphin hook themselves as they take the bait, especially if the hook is sharp. It is not necessary for the angler to set the hook. Captain Budd says, "It is not uncommon to see the actual strike and an unknowing angler grab the rod and sling it over the shoulder in a hook-setting move. They point the rod at the fish and start cranking. Frequently there is a brief fight and the fish is gone." According to Captain Budd, that fish did not just spit the bait, he was lost because the angler did not use proper dolphin fighting techniques.

In analyzing the series of events, Captain Budd gives a detailed explanation of what happened. Assuming that the point of the hook was sharpened as it should have been, the fish grabbed the bait and was hooked. The point of the hook cut through the membranes in the fish's mouth and out through the skin. The dolphin panicked and started to pull and jump away from the pressure that had been placed on it. As the angler yanked the rod tip up and over his shoulder, the cutting edge of the hook enlarged the point of entry as a result of the excessive pressure and created a hole. Then as the angler swung the rod tip back down, slack was formed in the line and the baited hook escaped from the enlarged hole and the fish was gone. He further explains that if the hook had not been properly sharpened and the bait was sitting in the fish's mouth, the over-the-shoulder maneuver described above would serve to yank the bait out of the fish's mouth. So what is the proper way to hook and fight dolphin?

Captain Budd answers that question with these instructions: "Raise the rod tip slightly and begin cranking the reel handle. The fish will pull, jump, and do aerial acrobatics, but as long as the angler keeps steady and firm pressure on the fish he is in control of the fight." To bring the fish to the boat, the pump and reel technique is used. Gradually raise the rod slightly, never over your head, and then crank the reel to add line to the spool as the rod tip is lowered. The angler should remember to keep constant pressure on the fish at all times. A bent rod is a tight line.

It is the angler's responsibility to bring the fish close to the boat and ready for the gaff. As the fish gets within gaff range, the angler should back up and raise the rod tip enough to allow the gaffer to get between him and the fish. Captain Budd says, "A good gaffer will stick the point of the gaff above and

Dolphin are great fighters as well as good table fare. Photo by Capt. Budd Neviaser.

beyond the fish and, in a smooth motion, drive the hook of the gaff into the shoulder of the dolphin. The fish is then lifted into the boat and straight into the fish box." All the while the angler should concentrate on giving the gaffer all the slack line needed to lift the fish into the boat and into the fish box.

During the fight the other anglers should bring in any lines that can potentially tangle with the one the fish is on. After the fight is over and the fish is in the box, everyone helps set the spread again and the fishing continues.

Charter Captains

Captain Budd Neviaser

Hometown: Edgewater, Florida
Business: Huntsman Charters

Phone number: 386-566-3137
E-mail address: captbudd@cfl.rr.com
Web site: www.huntsmancharters.com

Captain Budd's advice for visiting anglers: Make certain the boat is oceanworthy before departing. Equipment should include outriggers, VHF radio, GPS, and a fathometer with fish finding capability. Ensure that the boat carries sufficient fuel to make the trip. Purchase a Waterproof chart of the Ponce Inlet area and head toward the party grounds and start trolling.

Captain Fred "Frenchy" Robert

Hometown: New Smyrna Beach, Florida
Business: fishing-guy.com
Phone number: 407-948-5035
E-mail address: myfishingguide@gmail.com
Web site: www.fishing-guy.com

Fred's advice for visiting anglers: Enjoy every day that you can fish even if the fish don't bite. It is still better than staying home in front of the TV watching a fishing movie. Respect the fish and the resource. The more we anglers respect the fish, the better the resource will be. The fewer fish you kill, the more there will be for the future. The best part of the fishing is the catching, especially on light tackle, but don't go so light that you kill a fish intended for release. Match tackle to fishing conditions and targeted fish. Catch, kiss, and release.

Area Hotspots

South Bridge in New Smyrna is a good place to start fishing. Just about every desirable inshore species can be caught around the bridge, including tarpon in the summer. A short drive will get you to Haulover Canal, where fishing can be from a boat or shore. Big reds and big black drum are often caught there. Easy access for shorebound anglers can be found at

Ponce Inlet. South of the inlet, along the beach, is where the locals fish for kings, cobia, and tarpon.

Plenty of wrecks and reefs dot the offshore landscape. Check an offshore map for locations.

Fishing-Friendly Lodging and Glorious Galleys

Captain Fred's

> 105 Peninsula Avenue
> New Smyrna Beach, FL 32169
> Phone number: 407-948-5035

Two-story private house, sleeps up to eight. Three hundred feet from the river, one mile from the boat ramp. Kayak rentals available. Owned and operated by Capt. Fred "Frenchy" Robert.

JB's Fish Camp and Restaurant

> 859 Pompano Avenue
> New Smyrna Beach, FL 32169-4906
> Phone number: 386-427-5747

JB's features fresh Florida seafood from local professional anglers. Casual relaxed atmosphere on the shore of Mosquito Lagoon. Open daily. Kayak rentals available. Recommended by the author.

Norwood's

> 400 Second Avenue
> New Smyrna Beach, FL 32169
> Phone number: 386-428-4621

Fine seafood, wines, and aged Angus beef. Lunch and dinner since 1946. A New Smyrna tradition. Recommended by Capt. Budd Neviaser.

Flip Flops Grill and Chill

103 South Pine Street
New Smyrna Beach, FL 32169
Phone number: 386-424-0161

The name tells you how casual this place is. Stop in after a day on the water and enjoy. Old town location, locals love it. Recommended by Capt. Budd Neviaser.

That's Amore

103 South Pine Street
New Smyrna Beach, FL 32169
Phone number: 386-957-4956

Located between the ocean and the Indian River. Great Italian food including pizza and panini sandwiches. Recommended by Capt. Fred "Frenchy" Robert.

Bait and Tackle

Fishin' Cove Bait and Tackle

129 N Riverside Drive
New Smyrna Beach, FL 32168
Phone number: 386-428-6781

Live and frozen bait. Tackle and supplies. Convenient New Smyrna location. Recommended by Capt. Budd Neviaser.

Cecil's Bait and Tackle

197 N Causeway
New Smyrna Beach, FL 32169
Phone number: 386-428-2841

Full line bait and tackle shop. Live and frozen bait. Artificial lures. Open daily. Recommended by Capt. Fred "Frenchy" Robert.

Fishing Lessons for Life—Dehooking Tools

Increased fishing pressure caused by population growth in coastal and inland regions of Florida have systematically led to more stringent size and bag limits on fish. The immediate result is that more and more hooked fish have to be returned to the water. The regulations will be effective as a conservation tool only if the fish live after being caught and released. Anglers must make every effort to return a lively fish to the water.

Using a dehooker increases the chances that a released fish will live to fight another day. Photo by Karen Presley.

Part of the equation of success is how long the fish is removed from the water, and dehooking tools can shorten that time.

There are many dehooking tools available to anglers. My personal favorite is the ARC Dehooker. I can remove either circle or J-hooks from fish without ever having to touch them using this simple device. Dehookers come in all sizes to fit the fish you target. Practice with your child using this simple tool, even on the smallest of fish. Teach him or her the pleasure of allowing a released fish to fight again another day.

Kids and adults alike will have more trouble using a dehooker on a fish that is hooked deep in the mouth or gut. If the fish is hooked internally, it is often better to simply cut the line as close to the hook as possible and let it go. The key in all releases is to cause as little stress as possible, giving the fish a fighting chance at survival. This means handling it only briefly and returning it to the water as soon as possible.

If you don't own a dehooking tool, get one and teach your kids to use it too. Not only will this tool allow more fish to swim off and grow up, you will spend more time fishing with your kids and less time taking fish off the hook.

PART 2

Florida's Space Coast

5

~~~~~~~~~~~~~~~~

Edgewater, Oak Hill, Mims, and Titusville

This destination on Florida's East Coast does not have an inlet connecting the Indian River Lagoon with the Atlantic Ocean. Accordingly, chapter 5 will emphasize backcountry fishing with a tad of freshwater angling thrown in, too. Freshwater and saltwater fishing can be easily accomplished in a given day from any of the local towns. Offshore anglers can use any of the local venues as a base camp and travel north to Ponce de Leon Inlet or south to Port Canaveral if they want to engage in big game fishing in the Atlantic. Those two inlets are described in other chapters, and both are characterized by great boat launch facilities and outstanding fishing opportunities. Driving time to either Ponce or the Port is less than an hour.

The area includes more than 30 miles of coast line and adjacent backcountry waters. The locale has long been part of the fishing industry in Florida. Today it is more recreational fishing than commercial fishing and is well known for its abundant fishing opportunities, including the world-famous Mosquito Lagoon and the Banana River No-Motor Zone.

Around the turn of the century, new and improved infrastructure was a priority with the local leaders. Schools and roads were on the top of the development lists, but a bridge across the Indian River ranked closely behind. The completion of that bridge gives witness to the foresight of those early leaders. Once the bridge connecting Titusville to the beaches

In the days of the shuttle launches, anglers could enjoy fishing and rocket launches on the same day along the Space Coast. Photo by Paul MacInnis.

known as Desoto and Playalinda was completed, the groundwork for tourism was laid. Recreational visits to the area have grown ever since.

It was not until the late '50s and early '60s that suitable accommodations for traveling anglers and their families became a reality. The real boom in economic activity came not from the tourist industry, however, but from the space program and the influx of workers it generated.

As people took up the quest to visit space, the Kennedy Space Center was funded and constructed on what is now the Merritt Island National Wildlife Refuge. The growth of the Space Center fueled economic development, including motels, hospitals, shopping centers, golf courses, churches, subdivisions, and a public hospital. Swarms of tourists would not be far behind.

Titusville is still one of the best locations along the Space Coast to view rocket launches from numerous public locations.

The tremendous fishing possibilities existing in the area were long known and enjoyed by local residents before it became a destination for traveling anglers. Early accounts suggest that either inshore or offshore anglers could easily catch their dinner, and much more, in a few hours of fishing. Now, anglers come from around the world to fish in the Indian River Lagoon.

Characteristics of the Fishing Area

With no tidal influence, this destination's fishing possibilities are limited mostly to sandbars, grass edges, and sandy areas in grass flats. The only exceptions are manmade structures. Several bridges span local rivers with docks and seawalls found in some locations. Mosquito Lagoon and the Indian River are both excellent destinations for redfish and spotted seatrout.

The backwaters are not pure saltwater, but what scientists call brackish. Brackish water has more salinity than fresh water but not as much as seawater. Salinity is expressed by the amount of salt found in 1,000 grams of water. For example, if there is 1 gram of salt in 1,000 grams of water, the salinity is 1 part per thousand, or 1 ppt. According to the Office of Naval Research, brackish water has 0.5 to 17 ppt salt. Less than 0.5 ppt is labeled freshwater; more than 17 is considered seawater, with the average seawater measuring about 35 ppt.

Most visitors are amazed to learn that the average depth in these backwater areas is only about 3 feet. Most of the waters are what anglers refer to as grass flats, and they characterize much of the region. Most sightfishing is conducted in water that is 18 inches or less. These vast grass flats are home to many saltwater predators and also serve as a nursery for juvenile fish.

Giant redfish and seatrout can be found on the deeper side of the shallow sandbars. The deeper water, if it includes a food source, can be an excellent location for both. Anglers should look for bars holding plenty of mullet or other baitfish and pole or troll slowly alongside the drop-off looking for fish. These deep sides can also be an excellent location for targeting trout on topwater in the morning or with jigs all day long. Poling along the shallow side of the sandbar can reveal tailing redfish as well as trophy-sized seatrout.

The deep edge of the flat where the grass ends and transitions to a sand bottom is an excellent location to target seatrout during the summer and fall. Plastic lures like D.O.A. C.A.L.s on a ¼-ounce jig head or the D.O.A. Deadly Combo, which includes a rattling cork and an artificial shrimp, can be used for some nonstop fishing action. Trout, ladyfish, and jack crevalle are often willing to take the bait.

The Intracoastal Waterway traverses the area and makes north to south travel fairly easy. Newcomers should be warned, however, that getting out of the channel can get you in trouble fast. More than one unknowing boater has been left high and dry after discovering how quickly the water depth can change after leaving the channel. Since there is no tidal influence, the situation will not get better. You just have to get out and push or call for help from a tow service if you can't dislodge the boat yourself. A good map that shows water depths is a must for new anglers to the area, and a GPS is useful for navigating the area.

Sightfishing in the Indian River Lagoon

Sightfishing is an art in and of itself. It definitely requires a few more skills than soaking shrimp or pinfish under a bobber. As the name implies, the fish is actually spotted before casting a lure or bait in its direction. There are a few things anglers should know before attempting this artful type of fishing. According to Captain Chris Myers of Central Florida Sightfishing Charters, high on the list of important skills for successful sightfishing is casting ability. He recommends taking time to practice casting skills before you hit the water to improve your success when you are on the water. He says, "Sightfishing the flats of central Florida requires the ability to cast to the fish quickly and accurately. In general, the better you cast, the more you will catch." The casting skill cannot be overemphasized—if you miss with the first cast, you don't often get a second chance. Captain Myers says this is especially true in his home waters of Mosquito Lagoon and the Indian River. "The fish in this area are heavily fished and have become increasingly spooky over the years. It is important to make your first cast count."

Captain Myers outlines four additional skills that are important to sightfishing anglers. In order of importance, his essentials are stealth, polarized sunglasses, casting, proper bait or lure selection, and a proper presentation.

With respect to stealth he says, "If you can't get close to them, you can't catch them." In clear, shallow water it is essential to approach fish as quietly as possible. In places like Mosquito Lagoon and the north end of the Indian River where fish are heavily pressured, they become spooky and will bolt at the least bit of noise. He says poling or wading is the best approach, but if you can't do that, at least use a trolling motor.

It is called sightfishing for a reason. You have to spot the fish first before casting. "If you can't see them, you can't cast to them." Visually spotting the fish requires anglers to have a good pair of sunglasses. Using good sunglasses, spending time on the water, and learning to read the water helps sightfishing anglers develop the skills to sight the fish and make the cast.

Polarized sunglasses aid anglers in spotting tailing or pushing redfish on a flat. Photo by Capt. Chris Myers.

Captain Myers' third essential is casting, but as noted above it is extremely important and worth repeating his advice. "Practice your casting skills before you get on the water." It doesn't matter if you use a baitcaster, spinning gear, or fly rod, the more you practice the more successful you will be in your fishing pursuits. When asked about the biggest mistake fly fishers make, he responded, "Not having practiced a way to get the fly out at least 50 feet with one or two false casts is the biggest mistake I see." It is a lot easier to make the quick cast with a spinning outfit or baitcaster, but the flyrodder needs to practice until he or she can achieve the long casts needed on the flats. The old maxim of practice makes perfect applies nowhere more than in fly-fishing in shallow water.

Next in order of importance is choosing and using the proper natural bait or lure. Appropriate lure selection relates to what anglers call matching the hatch. One example would be winter on the flats. In the winter the flats are void of mullet and the reds are eating small crustaceans like shrimp and crabs. The best baits are going to be real shrimp or crabs or artificial lures that imitate them.

Finally, Captain Chris calls for "proper presentation of a bait or lure to result in more hookups." The presentation is when the whole deal comes together. The angler has approached the fish quietly, wearing polarized sunglasses to see them; practice at home has made the angler proficient in casting; the bait has been selected based on the natural menu of the targeted fish; the cast is made to place the bait or lure in front of the feeding fish where it will either be seen or smelled; the strike occurs, and the fight is on.

Redfish on Fly

With no tidal influence or hard structure available, Indian River Lagoon fish relate to sandbars, grass edges, and sandy areas in grass flats. Captain Myers says, "While these various structures will attract gamefish and baitfish, the majority of the redfish do not relate to any specific structure. Instead, they will choose a certain depth of water in areas that hold the best source of food." The successful fly angler, or any angler for that matter, will do well to remember the fishing conditions where the first fish is caught and target similar conditions to catch another.

Anglers should begin the fly-fishing adventure by choosing a fly that mimics the food source of the redfish at the time of the year the fishing occurs. Captain Myers advises anglers to "Use small crabs and shrimp patterns in the winter and bait-fish patterns in the warmer months to improve your success."

Sometimes fish on the flats show up quickly, and there is little time to react. Captain Myers suggests having a system in place that will allow you to cast quickly when a fish is sighted. He feels so strongly about this technique, he made a video to instruct fly-fishing anglers how he does it. The video can be viewed at www.youtube.com/watch?v=aQtjJ8LjNk0.

Always remember the importance of stealth when fishing the flats. Anglers should approach fish slowly and quietly,

Choose the right fly and make the right presentation to be rewarded with a nice redfish. Photo by Capt. Tom Van Horn.

paying close attention to the shadow made by the fly rod and line while casting. "Any shadow can spook the fish," according to Captain Myers. "Do not allow the fly line to land on or near the fish or you will see it only for a second."

Most fly fishers are extremely dedicated to their sport, but a little flexibility can help them catch more fish on fly. When conditions are not good for sightfishing, because of clouds or dirty water, Captain Myers advises anglers to pick up a spinning outfit to make blind casts to fishy areas. "Spinning gear allows anglers to cover a lot of water quickly and locate fish that they may not find with only fly rod in hand. Blind casting a fly for redfish is usually not effective unless you are fishing tidal areas where you can pinpoint locations where fish will be congregating." Once fish are located using the spinning gear, return to using the fly rod.

Most fly-fishing on the flats is accomplished using a 7 or 8 weight rod spooled with a floating line. Captain Chris likes a 9- to 10-foot leader tapered to 15-pound test before adding his favorite fly.

Captain Chris often fishes with no-name flies that he has created at his fly tying bench. He says, "I just make them up as I go." Size, profile, and color are important components of any lure, and flies are no exception. Selecting or tying flies should reflect the old adage of matching the hatch. "I usually tell anglers to use bendback-style flies, crab patterns, and shrimp patterns for year-round sightfishing on the flats."

Bendback-style flies are tied on a hook where the shank is "bent back" to cause the fly to ride with the hook point-up when fished. The point of the hook is often hidden in the body of the fly, adding to its weedless characteristic. For this reason bendbacks are often used in shallow water where hanging up on the bottom or shallow grasses would happen too often with

The point of the hook is often hidden in the body of a bendback fly, adding to its weedless characteristics. Photo by Capt. Chris Myers.

Redfish and drum feed heavily on crab patterns, especially in the winter. Photo by Capt. Chris Myers.

a fly that rides with the hook point-down. Many baitfish can be mimicked with a bendback fly.

Crab and shrimp patterns are go-to flies for many saltwater fly fishers. "The crab pattern," says Captain Chris, "can be made with many different materials and should be a staple of any inshore saltwater fly angler. Redfish and drum feed heavily on crabs, and seatrout will eat them as well."

There are many variations of shrimp-style flies, and they are readily available in the market place; they are, however, easy and economical to tie with just a little practice. The figure on top of the facing page shows several of Captain Chris's hand-tied shrimp patterns that he uses on the flats. Everything on the flats eats shrimp, making this an extremely popular pattern.

Other flies recommended by Captain Chris are baitfish styles like the Enrico Puglisi mullet or pinfish. He ties these on

Shrimp patterns are popular because everything on the flats likes to eat shrimp. Photo by Capt. Chris Myers.

number 2 to number 4 hooks for use in the summer and fall months when baitfish are abundant on the shallow-water flats.

Fighting big fish on fly requires careful consideration by anglers. In addition to rod selection, Captain Chris warns anglers to be familiar with the limits of their tackle. When a big red is caught, the angler should know how much pressure can be

Baitfish patterns are used in the summer and fall months, when baitfish are abundant. Photo by Capt. Chris Myers.

applied with the selected equipment. Take leader material for example. "Have a friend hold a scale attached to the end of the leader while you pull as hard as you can. You will be surprised at how hard you can pull without coming close to breaking the leader."

Be familiar with all your equipment and know its limits. As far as fighting a big red on fly, "Always pull opposite the direction the fish is traveling while holding the rod low to the water. Do not raise the rod straight up when the fish is near the boat or the rod may break." In the interest of conservation, use your skills and equipment to make the fight as short as possible before releasing the fish. Be sure to keep constant pressure on the fish to tire it quickly and keep it on the hook.

The Banana River No-Motor Zone—As Natural As It Gets

The No-Motor Zone (NMZ) on the Banana River can only be described as a special outdoor place. It is not for every angler, but those willing to pay the necessary price will discover a fishing opportunity beyond their wildest dreams. As the name implies, access is by nonmotorized vessels only. This restriction includes any vessel having an attached or non-attached combustion engine or electric trolling motor capable of being deployed. The cost of admittance is the willingness to be confined to a canoe or kayak, except when wading, as the fishing platform—and the ability to paddle your way to some great fishing action.

Established as a manatee refuge in 1994, the Banana River Lagoon's No-Motor Zone consists of 35 square miles of the most pristine estuary to be found on Florida's east central coast. Since it is bordered by the Kennedy Space Center (KSC) on the west and north and the Cape Canaveral Air Force Station (CCAFS) on its east shores, the NMZ is accessible only from the south. Its 10,500 acres is under the control of NASA and the Merritt Island National Wildlife Refuge. Anglers are not allowed to set foot on any KSC or CCAFS property while fishing. Since the NMZ is located within the boundaries of the Merritt Island National Wildlife Refuge, all anglers are required to obtain a federal fishing permit for the park. Permits are self-administered and available online at no charge.

Because of security requirements at the Space Center launch facilities, no fishing has been allowed in a 20-square-mile area of the Banana River Lagoon north of the NMZ for more than 50 years. This is one of the first marine protected areas (MPAs) in the country, and it is connected to the NMZ. Captain Tom Van Horn, editor of *Coastal Angler Magazine*-Orlando and professional fishing guide, is a frequent visitor to the NMZ. He says, "Due to the existence of the connecting MPA and the long paddle required to access prime fishing areas, the NMZ is famous for big, stupid, and happy fish. That said, be sure to step up your tackle size to meet the challenge." Captain Van Horn always carries at least one 20-pound-class rod to handle both redfish and black drum in the 30-pound size and larger. He adds, "Fresh blue crab and cut ladyfish will win over most of these bruisers and bring them to your hook."

The NMZ is primarily an open saltwater flat with sandbars and spoil islands the only noticeable structure. Its three vast flats consist of some of the most luscious seagrass beds to be found anywhere in Florida. Captain Tom says, "It's as natural as it gets." Extensive grass flats run parallel to both the east and west shorelines, with the third flat running right down the middle of the zone.

Captain Van Horn takes wind velocity and direction into account when planning a trip to the NMZ. "When fishing in the NMZ, anglers typically focus on paddle fishing with the location being dictated by the direction of the wind." With three main flats to choose from, wind direction and velocity are the first things he wants to know about. "When there are westerly winds or light breezes I like to launch at KARS Park. This location gives access to a flat that ranges from 1,000 yards to a mile

Canoes or kayaks are the only way to access the NMZ. The paddle is usually worth the effort. Photo by Paul MacInnis.

wide, and it stretches the entire 7-mile length of the zone." The KARS Park launch is made available to the public for a reasonable five-dollar fee, and anglers are fishing within minutes of launch.

When the winds are from the east, Captain Van Horn prefers fishing the east flat. Access is easiest from an unimproved launch area near the Port Canaveral cruise terminals. Anglers can travel north on Phillips Parkway, cross the drawbridge, and locate an appropriate launch area on the shoreline before reaching the Cape Canaveral Air Force Station. Vehicle entry is not allowed beyond the gates at the station. "I simply launch off the causeway, being sure to park my vehicle clear of the highway right-of-way because illegally parked vehicles will be towed."

The third or middle flat is also accessed alongside Phillips Parkway. This luscious grass flat runs north through the center of the NMZ. Since it is the most exposed of the three flats, mild winds are the most enjoyable time to fish the middle flat.

A specially rigged canoe is the fishing platform of choice for Captain Van Horn on the NMZ flats. He has modified a canoe to fit his personal requirements. "The vessel I guide and fish from on the No-Motor Zone is a specially modified Indian River Canoe. It is custom rigged with a set of stabilizers from Kay-noe (www.kay-noe.com). These creative floats can be deployed once the fishing area is reached. The stabilizers give the boat steadiness which allows both anglers to comfortably stand and fish."

All sightfishing anglers know that the higher the line of sight, the easier it is to see fish. Captain Tom covers this requirement with both casting and poling platforms on his canoe. "My canoe features an aluminum poling platform attached to the stern and a casting platform on the front deck. Compared to a flats skiff, the canoe poles very easily and makes super shallow water accessible to fishing." The canoe also has advantages over kayaks, the other popular vessel for NMZ fishing. Compared to most kayaks, a standard canoe can easily carry extra gear like a full-size cooler, additional rods, tackle, and standard safety gear. "The down side to using a canoe is weight when launching and the fact that I can only carry one angler at a time."

The NMZ features its own slam. Captain Tom names the Banana River Lagoon slam as redfish, seatrout, and black drum. Catching all three species in the same day is a crowning accomplishment for NMZ anglers. To catch the slam, Captain Tom starts the day with topwater lures. "My day typically starts fishing topwater plugs like the Rapala Skitterwalk or Subwalker for larger fish in the slam category. If I am finding smaller fish like ladyfish and seatrout, I like the Storm Chug Bug or Rapala Skitter Pop." The strong hooks on the larger plugs will prevent anglers from losing a big redfish or black drum from straightened hooks. Fish weighing more than 20 pounds are not uncommon.

Sometimes the topwater lures are all that are necessary to catch the slam, but if you haven't accomplished it by midmorning, it is a good strategy to switch over to plastic baits or flies.

"I particularly like to sightfish with light plastic lures like a D.O.A. Shrimp. Casting to a sighted fish requires a soft landing, and the D.O.A. shrimp will deliver with hardly a splash." Other successful baits in the NMZ include plastic jerkbaits when baitfish are on the flats and imitation crabs in the winter months, when crustaceans are a stable food source.

Stealth must be a constant consideration of anglers in the NMZ. The water is shallow and clear, and the fish can be spooked easily. Captain Tom describes them as "happy and stupid," but anglers should not step loudly in the canoe or cause it to rock and send out waves that might alert nearby fish. Anglers do not want to broadcast their presence if they expect to sight the fish and catch them too.

Getting out of the canoe and wade-fishing can be an excellent fishing strategy. Wading provides better visibility and also plenty of stealth. Although the Banana River No-Motor Zone is within the boundaries of the Kennedy Space Center, it's not rocket science in terms of wade-fishing. Captain Tom admits that casting from a drifting kayak or canoe can be challenging and uncomfortable fishing, and wading is a good alternative. He says that once fish are located, it is easier to present the lure or bait if the angler gets out of the boat and slowly walks toward the fish. "This method has the advantages of the canoe or kayak and is more comfortable and efficient for the angler."

There are plenty of shallow sandbars and spoil islands with bottom firm enough to support wading in the NMZ. According to Captain Tom, "These solid bottoms are often the same areas where redfish and seatrout will hunt down baitfish." He does have a couple of tips for getting out of the vessel. "When exiting the boat, the most important thing to remember is to stake out the boat. If you don't, the wind will steal it when you're not looking, and it's a long walk back to the launch site. After securing your vessel and equipment, simply step out and begin to wade." While wading, always use the stingray shuffle to avoid an unwanted injury from a pesky ray. By sliding their

Get out of the canoe and wade for a more comfortable and efficient experience. Photo by Paul MacInnis.

feet on the bottom while wade-fishing, anglers will push the stingrays safely out in front of the angler's path.

The NMZ is famous for very large inshore redfish and black drum that can be taken on lure or fly, but natural bait may be the ticket for the larger fish. "I hardly ever enter the Zone without an assortment of fresh bait," says Captain Tom. "Remember, these fish are big, 20 to 40 pounds, and they love cut bait. I have great success catching the brutes by letting them quietly find a big fat chunk of fresh ladyfish or halved or whole blue crab."

Anglers need to plan an appropriate time frame for making the trek into the NMZ. According to Captain Tom, the deeper you go into the Zone, the happier the fish are. "I tell all anglers to keep moving until you find fish, so a full day is suggested when considering an NMZ trip. On many occasions I have covered more than 15 miles round trip, but that is exactly why the fishing is excellent." This is good advice for any fishing destination and worth repeating. As a friend once told me, "If the fish ain't biting, move the boat."

Fishing the Bridges for Monster Black Drum

Black drum come in all sizes. They are identified as the largest member of the drum family, ranging from small ones called puppies to the Florida record of more than 90 pounds and the world record exceeding 110 pounds. Scientific evidence reveals that black drum can live for as long as 35 years, so growing big is natural. Large black drum are known to congregate around the bridge pilings in the Indian River Lagoon and are often targeted by local anglers during the late fall.

Black drum are cousins to the popular redfish, but their shape is distinctively different. They have a high arched back and an inferior mouth for feeding on the bottom. They use whiskerlike barbels on their chin to locate food as they feed along the bottom. The barbels help the drum smell and taste their prey. Their bodies are gray or black, and the young ones have four to six distinctive vertical stripes, almost looking like a sheepshead when in the water. Their teeth are described as cobblestone-like with the capability of crushing oysters and other shellfish.

Black drum's favorite food consists of clams, barnacles, oysters, mussels, crabs, and shrimp. They are known to have a relatively light bite because once they find food, they inhale it and crush it with crusher plates in their throats. They are just sitting there during the process, and sometimes the angler is not aware of the bite until the drum moves on looking for its next victim. This feeding behavior makes it a good idea to check the bait often. It is not unusual for them to steal the bait without the angler knowing.

To begin the quest, idle up to the bridge pilings and scrape barnacles from the pilings using an appropriate tool. Several common garden tools will do the trick. Experience or local knowledge will tell you if some pilings are better than others to fish. The released barnacles act as chum to draw and hold the black drum to the area where you will be casting your bait. Next, anchor the boat upwind from the bridge so the bow points into the wind. The stern should be at least 25 feet away from the pilings to provide room to fight a big fish. Cast baits to the fishing area and place the rod in a holder to wait for the bite. This setup is necessary and effective when a hookup occurs. These fish have a natural instinct to go back around the pilings when hooked, and it is almost impossible to get the big ones into open water without a little help from the captain. Once a big drum is hooked, the captain fires up the engine and drives the boat right up the anchor line, pulling the fish away from the pilings. Once in open water, the angler has a much better chance of landing the fish.

When targeting the big ones, it is essential to beef up the tackle to improve landing success. Use a rig with at least 30- to 40-pound braided line and 40- to 50-pound fluorocarbon leader. I recommend a 5000 series reel or larger. Start the terminal rig by tying a Bimini twist or spider hitch in the braided mainline to double its thickness. Slip the tag end of the double line through a ½- to ¾-ounce barrel sinker and attach a strong swivel to the braid using a uni knot. Use another uni knot to add about 18 to 20 inches of leader material with a 5/0 Daiichi circle hook tied on the end. Using this slip-sinker rig allows the drum to pick up the bait and move it to the crushers without feeling any resistance.

Choose an appropriate bait and cast it out near the pilings where the barnacles were scraped. If this spot does not produce a bite in 30 to 45 minutes, repeat the process on another set of pilings until the fish are found. It is not unusual that a school of drum will be concentrated in a specific area of the bridge, and it is up to the angler to find them.

My personal favorite bait is jumbo shrimp or blue crabs. When using crabs I pull off the claws and use them as additional chum. I cut the crabs in half and pin them on the circle hook by penetrating the shell from the bottom side just inside the horn. With the jumbo shrimp I like to cut off the tail and insert the circle hook through the exposed meat and up through the top of the shell. The exposed flesh of de-tailed shrimp or halved crab increases the sense of smell in the presentation.

Once the drum finds food, it inhales it, then crushes with its throat-located crushing plates. The shells are separated from the flesh and ejected as the fish moves on looking for more food. As the fish begins to move off and the bite is detected, the angler should start reeling, remembering there is no hook-set when fishing with circle hooks. As the hook comes out slowly and changes angle, the fish will be hooked in the corner of the mouth and the fight is on. These fish are very strong when first hooked, and a tight drag is necessary to turn their head toward the boat and away from the bridge. This is the point in the action when the captain helps by driving the boat away from the pilings to pull the fish to open water.

Once the fish is clear of the pilings, it is up to the angler to practice good fish fighting techniques to land the fish. The angler should keep a tight line on the fish and always pull in the opposite direction the fish is moving. Keep constant pressure on the fish at all times to shorten the fight and improve the fish's recovery time on release.

Fresh Water Cobia in the St. Johns River

The local waters of the St. Johns River are a short drive from the central Florida coastline. Saltwater anglers can add a little variety to their fishing trip by testing the freshwater destination for some jumbo catfish. Jokingly referred to by Captain Van Horn as freshwater cobia, the channel catfish of the St. Johns River are welcome additions to his angling adventures.

One of the great things about fishing in central Florida, other than the year-round fishing opportunities, is the diversity of angling options. Regardless of how nasty the weather in the saltwater arena, anglers can always find good protected fishing locations in the freshwater rivers and lakes. The local waters of the St. Johns River are a short drive from the central Florida coastline and a prime fishing destination. The St. Johns River basin presents many seasonal light tackle and fly-fishing options to visiting anglers. Among those opportunities are bass, crappie, bluegill, shad, and catfish.

Captain Tom Van Horn grew up in the area and is a true local expert and historian when it comes to the St. Johns River basin. He says, "The area of the St. Johns River I fish was actually one of the first saltwater lagoons before the last ice age. As the ice caps froze, the waters receded and the lagoon developed into one of the few rivers in the world that flows north." He explains further that the upper reaches of the river from Melbourne to Lake Harney have an elevated salt content capable of supporting a variety of saltwater fish species, crustaceans, and flora. He says that even though this stretch of the river is more than 150 miles from an ocean inlet, it is not uncommon to catch ladyfish, mullet, blue crabs, and flounder.

Another angling option is the first American shad spawning run in the contiguous United States. The shad run normally begins in January and continues through March. Bedding bluegill and shell crackers are abundant in May and June, and fall crappie fishing is about as good as it gets. The largemouth bass fishery is a year-round affair for local anglers. One of Captain Van Horn's favorite targets is the St. Johns River catfish. He targets the whiskered critter in January through March when they are spawning.

It just so happens that those first three months of the year correspond with some of the nastiest weather on the Space Coast, so the catfish give Captain Van Horn an alternative fishing location. "I love to fish, and when Mother Nature makes inshore saltwater fishing a challenge with rough conditions, I can always catch plenty of fish on the St. Johns."

Freshwater cobia offer a welcome addition to Central Florida's angling adventures. Photo by Capt. Tom Van Horn.

Visiting saltwater anglers can join Captain Tom and add a little variety to their saltwater fishing trip by testing the freshwater destination of the St. Johns River for some jumbo blue and channel catfish, or as Captain Van Horn calls them, freshwater cobia. The catfish of the St. Johns River are welcome additions to central Florida's angling adventures, and Captain Tom has some advice for catching them.

Catfish prefer to spawn in moving water. The greater the current, the better they like it. When the spring rains come and the water levels rise, the current picks up as well, making it the right time to go catfishing. Captain Tom explains that as the river level rises, the current runs faster on the outside edges of the bends. These outside edges develop naturally deeper channels. "These deeper areas are where you want to fish for the spawning catfish."

The St. Johns River catfish can range from 6 to 30 pounds. Captain Tom recommends using 20-pound-test tackle. "I use a 7-foot medium heavy Evolution rod with a 4000 series Daiwa reel." His line is 20-pound Spiderwire with a 30-pound-test leader. "These are respectable fish with bad attitudes, and there is a lot of submerged structure to deal with. The heavier tackle will increase your success in actually landing one." Terminal tackle is a ½-ounce barrel sinker slid up the first piece of leader. Next a small barrel swivel is added to keep the weight from sliding down to the hook. Attach an 8-inch leader on the other side of the swivel; add a number 2 circle hook, and you're ready to fish.

Tom's secret bait is a big chunk of freshly peeled shrimp. "Yes, I said shrimp. It's an easy bait to find, and the catfish love it." Fresh or frozen *eating* shrimp from the fish market at the grocery store is excellent if you can bring yourself to use them as bait instead of eating them. Just imagine that you are going to convert the 4-inch shrimp into a 30-pound catfish and bait up. Cast your baited circle hook on the bottom in the deeper bends of the river and wait for the bite. "Be sure to hold your rod or secure it in a rod holder. These brutes will relieve you of an unsecured rod before you know what happened."

Fishing the St. Johns, or any other area for the first time, can be aided by the services of a local guide. Captain Tom says, "My best advice is to fish with an experienced guide who knows the area and the techniques the angler needs to be successful. It's easy fishing, but to shorten the learning curve, fish a few times with an experienced guide who is willing to show you the ropes. Think of it as an investment that will save you time and money in the long run."

Charter Captains

Captain Chris Myers

Hometown: Orlando, Florida
Business: Central Florida Sight Fishing Charters
Phone number: 321-229-2848
E-mail address: info@floridafishinglessons.com
Web site: www.floridafishinglessons.com

Captain Chris's advice to visiting anglers: To target redfish, look for water less than 18 inches deep. Poling or wading will get anglers closest to the fish. Stealthy approaches are highly important since the fish are extremely spooky in the clear shallow water. Do not use the main motor to drive to your fishing spot. Doing so will spook all the fish off the flat. Instead, pole in or use a trolling motor to reach the fishing area. Using polarized glasses and keeping the sun behind you, watch for tailing fish or cruising fish below the surface and only cast to fish you can see.

Captain Tom Van Horn

Hometown: Chuluota, Florida
Business: Mosquito Coast Fishing Charters
Phone number: 407-416-1187
E-mail address: mosquitocoast@cfl.rr.com
Web site: www.irl-fishing.com

Captain Tom's advice to visiting anglers: Never fish the NMZ on a south wind. There is only one way in and one way out with nowhere to hide from dangerous weather. It is best to paddle into the wind at the beginning of the fishing trip and use the wind to your advantage on the ride back home. The NMZ is the property of NASA and controlled by it. Anglers need to know that the NMZ is closed for the four days prior to rocket launches and is patrolled by NASA security in airboats and helicopters, so heed all warnings and obey all rules when fishing the NMZ.

Area Hotspots

Mosquito Lagoon anglers will find Hong Kong Flats and George's Bar excellent for trout and redfish year-round, especially in winter. Try the flats behind Clinkers Islands for redfish and big trout; on the deeper side, trout, ladyfish, and jacks are prevalent spring and fall. For a small fee, kayak and canoe anglers can enter the Banana River No-Motor Zone at KARS Park and paddle north for some great redfish, trout, and black drum fishing. Peacocks Pocket is a favorite redfish flat on the Indian River. It is easily reached from Kennedy Point Park on U.S. Highway 1 just ¼ mile south of SR-50 on the Indian River. Visit www.brevardparks.com for more Brevard County boat ramps.

Fishing-Friendly Lodging and Glorious Galleys

Dixie Cross Roads

1475 Garden Street
Titusville, FL 32796-3389
Phone number: 321-268-5000

A Titusville tradition. Full seafood menu, known for fresh shrimp that come from a fleet of more than 25 full-time commercial shrimpers. Open seven days. Recommended by Capt. Tom Van Horn.

Mosquito Lagoon Fish Camp

311 River Road
Oak Hill, FL 32759
Phone number: 386-566-6303

Clean, comfortable waterfront lodging on the Mosquito Lagoon. Free dockage outside your door. Be fishing in minutes. Recommended by Capt. Tom Van Horn.

Bagel World Cafe

1427 Garden Street
Titusville, FL 32796
Phone number: 321-267-8841

Great place for the early starter. Opens at 5:00 a.m. Great sandwiches to take on the boat or breakfast on the way to the water. Choose from 23 flavors of New York style bagels. Recommended by Capt. Chris Myers.

Super 8, Titusville

3480 Garden Street
Titusville, FL 32796
Phone number: 321-269-9310

Nothing fancy, just right for serious anglers. Convenient to Mosquito Lagoon. Recommended by Capt. Chris Myers.

Bait and Tackle

Daniel's Bait & Tackle

2301 U.S. 1
Mims, FL 32754
Phone number: 321-268-1896

Near Mosquito Lagoon. Everything you need from live bait to artificial. Plenty of local knowledge here, just ask. Recommended by the author.

Fishing Lessons for Life—Fish Handling

Proper fish handling is an important lesson to be learned by young and old anglers alike. There is an old saying among catch and release anglers that any fish is too good to be caught only once. Proper fish handling techniques are necessary to make this adage reality. Dehooking tools and circle hooks discussed in the previous chapters are a great start, but there is much more a savvy angler can do to ensure a live release. Poorly handled fish can result in dead fish that no one else will have the joy of catching.

A principal rule and effective technique is to wet your hands before handling a fish you intend to release. This practice reduces the amount of slime removed from the captured fish. The slime coating is a natural mucoprotein coating covering the skin and scales. This protective slime coating contains enzymes and antibodies that fight infection and help keep fish healthy. When wounds or abrasions are incurred in the landing process, they allow disease organisms to attack the fish and result in further stress and disease.

Along these same lines, never use a rag to hold a fish unless you are keeping it for dinner. Gripping a fish with a rag removes a huge amount of its protective coating and leaves it vulnerable to disease. When the slime is removed, the fish has lost its first line of defense against infection.

It has already been suggested that larger fish should not be held vertically because of potential damage to internal organs. To avoid this condition, some anglers use body slings to hold fish near the boat while removing the hook and for resuscitation before release. These cradles consist of two poles with a net draped between them. A large fish can be pulled into the net to remove the hook without ever being taken from the water. The fish can then rest in the support of the net until ready for release or in wait of a quick photo.

If a fish is hooked deeply in the gullet or in the gills, scientists advise leaving the hook in. Removing a deeply set hook often results in more damage than the hook alone would cause. Simply cut the line as near the hook as possible to give the fish a better chance of survival. The hook will eventually rust out. Remember, too, any hook will come out more easily if the barb is pinched down.

Culling is another activity that results in dead fish. Holding a fish in the livewell until a larger one is caught reduces survival rates after release. Oxygen levels are usually low and water temperature is usually higher than normal, resulting in a stressed fish. It is better to simply decide if you are going to keep a fish or not. If you decide to keep it, put it in the cooler on ice for a tastier dinner and forget about culling.

Since fishing regulations require anglers to release many of the fish they catch because of closed seasons or size limits, fish handling is an important conservation issue. It is an issue that should be addressed by fishery management officials, charter fishing guides, and individual anglers. All should be setting a good example for others to follow, especially with young anglers.

6

~~~~~~~~~~~~~

Cape Canaveral, Cocoa Beach, and Merritt Island

This central Florida destination's history and development is tied closely to America's space program. The area was once populated by several small towns, but they vanished as the development associated with the space program grew. Those small towns live on, but only in the names of streets and historic churches.

Before the quest for space made its impact on the area, growth and development centered on the citrus industry. The area's sandy soil was ideal for citrus production. The area once stressed the cultivation and production of pineapples, but later production concentrated on citrus. The world-famous Indian River oranges and grapefruit come from the sandy soil that characterizes the area.

The majority of the population and of commercial development of Merritt Island lies in the central part. The populated area, once known as Merritt City, now includes the local high school, library, government offices, and a busy shopping district.

The area is the home of Canaveral Lock, the largest navigation lock in Florida. The lock was constructed by the U.S. Army Corps of Engineers in 1965. It provides secure safe passage of vessels from the Banana River through Port Canaveral and into the Atlantic Ocean. The current dampening lock creates a port that is very safe for entry and exit of all kinds of vessels, from small powerboats to large container ships and cruise ships.

Tidal-current velocities are greatly reduced by the lock, and hurricane-induced tides are prevented from entering the Banana River. The lock also prevents saltwater intrusion from the Atlantic into the Banana River Lagoon. This lock was built large enough to allow NASA to retrieve the original Apollo rocket's first stage. The booster was retrieved at sea and transported back to NASA through the lock. More recently the lock was used to return shuttle boosters to NASA for reconditioning and reuse.

Characteristics of the Fishing Area

The Cape Canaveral, Merritt Island, and Cocoa Beach area have all the same fishing attributes described in chapter 5, with the addition of a busy inlet port and substantially more residential docks and seawalls. A barge canal connects the Indian River with the Banana River, offering good refuge from northerly or southerly winds. A third named body of water, Sykes Creek, extends south from the barge canal until it intersects with the Banana River. Sandbars, grass edges, and potholes in grassy flats provide excellent fishing opportunities in all the area waters. The region becomes more populated in close proximity to the water, and more docks, seawalls, and residential canals are available for fishing than in the area to the north. The canals are especially appreciated when high winds cause anglers to look for calmer waters to enjoy.

Captain Mike Badarack operates Space Coast Sportfishing Charters out of Satellite Beach, Florida. He likes to remind anglers of the lack of tide in the area. "Our area differs from many others in Florida because it is not a huge tidal-driven fishery. The Cocoa Beach/Merritt Island area along the Indian and Banana rivers really has no tidal influence." The reason for the lack of tide is the Canaveral Lock. Unless you look at a tide chart you would have no idea whether it's high or low tide in the ocean, because it does not transfer through the locks to influence the water level or current in the backwaters. "The fish in these areas are generally *residents* and don't seem to need a tide change to encourage them to feed. The most productive spots are the areas with good habitat, including seagrass beds, mangrove trees, and a limited amount of oyster bars in the lagoon. Of course the presence of small baitfish and shrimp is the other ingredient of area hotspots."

Inside Port Canaveral the geography is different. The port has very little seagrass because it is constantly dredged to allow safe passage for cruise ships, large commercial vessels, and military ships that commonly use the port facilities. The only seagrass will be found along the edges in shallow areas. There is some current in the port, and anglers will notice the change of tides. In contrast to Sebastian Inlet, the tides in Port Canaveral are quite mild, but noticeable, whereas Sebastian Inlet is considered hazardous to inexperienced captains. As far as fishing in the port, Captain Mike says, "You do see more fish feeding activity at the beginning of each tidal phase as the fish appear to be more aggressive and ready to eat." He says there are oysters attached to most every seawall, dock, and rock pile scattered throughout the port. "There are also numerous oysters attached to both the north and south jetties. Both jetties are great for snook, but trying to land them along the sharp oyster beds is the challenge faced by anglers." All these oyster-encrusted areas are productive because of the baitfish that linger around them for protection. Just west of the jetties are large mudflats that hold baitfish up in the shallow water. "When bait is present in the shallows, large predators come crashing through looking for easy meals. When these conditions exist, it is a great fishing occasion."

The fishing opportunities emphasized in this chapter include the fabulous nearshore fishing offered just outside the port; a night fishing opportunity inside the port; and fishing of a different sort, shrimping the inshore waters near the port.

Nearshore Fishing Outside Port Canaveral

Space Coast area visitors are often surprised that many of Florida's biggest fish can be caught within a mile or two of the beach just outside Port Canaveral. This abundant fishery is very accessible by smaller boats throughout the warmer months of the year, when Atlantic waters tend to be calm. The best fishing fires up as early as May and continues as long as the water is warm and the seas relatively calm. Anglers armed with a few basic techniques and gear find it possible to catch some monster fish, including tarpon, king mackerel, cobia, barracuda, and jack crevalle, all using the same fundamental techniques.

Once anglers leave the confines of Port Canaveral, the nearshore fishing areas are not based on structure, but on food. The best fishing occurs when migrating baitfish are making their way along the beach. These bait schools will be found from the first breaker near the beach to within a few miles off the beach. Large predator fish like tarpon, king mackerel, cobia, sharks, barracuda, and jack crevalle are drawn to these bait pods and feed on them aggressively.

This bait migration provides a superb fishery available to small and large boats alike. A great deal of fishing is conducted from 100 yards to 5 miles out from the beach. Skilled anglers can catch the fish of a lifetime—all within sight of the beach.

East Central Florida Captain Keith Kalbfleisch is an expert in the nearshore Atlantic waters outside Port Canaveral. Captain Keith is owner/operator of Saltwater Adventures of Central Florida. He concedes that there are a number of ways to catch big fish outside Port Canaveral, from sightcasting to chumming, but his favorite technique is slow trolling. He says, "One of the most effective ways to catch a variety of fish in the nearshore waters is to slow troll." He describes slow trolling as

Barracuda are one of the species available nearshore out of Port Canaveral.

a fishing technique designed to present live bait in a natural manner while covering a large span of ocean. "Slow trolling is easy to do for any angler. It can be accomplished in a small boat with no special gear required." While this technique is Captain Keith's specialty on the Space Coast, it will work anywhere in Florida for a variety of species.

Slow Trolling Live Bait

Slow trolling is done primarily with live bait, and obtaining that bait is sometimes the biggest challenge of nearshore fishing. Captain Kalbfleisch identifies three basic types of natural bait he uses on the Space Coast. They are pogies, greenies, and mullet. His favorites are not the only baits that will work in these productive waters. "There are times when the bite is on that nearly any bait will work. These three bait types, however, are normally available and effective in bringing fish to the boat."

Locals call them "pogies," while on the northeast coast they are called "bunker," but whatever the local name, these are great fishing baits. Pogies are also known as Atlantic menhaden, and they populate the Central Florida beaches for four to five months during spring and summer. According to Captain Keith, "They are nicely sized live baits and, when they are schooling in the nearshore waters, can be an easy bait to procure." Menhaden are an oily fish that leave a scent trail in the water for predators to follow.

Pogies are algae eaters and cannot be caught on hook and line. Procuring a livewell full of pogies requires catching them in a cast net, so practice your net-throwing technique before you go. "You will find our local pogies along the beaches in 10 to 20 feet of water, and they can be spotted by the small splashes they make as they feed. Once sighted, aim the boat in their direction, coast up to them, throw your net over the school, and fill your livewell." Well, let's face it, Captain Keith's description is ideally what will happen, but sometimes it takes more than one cast to obtain enough bait for a day of fishing.

The second type of live bait Captain Kalbfleisch seeks is called greenies. Greenies is a generic designation given to a variety of baits common to the Space Coast. Threadfin herring, Spanish sardines, scaled sardines, and cigar minnows are all generally referred to as greenies. These baits are characterized by white bellies, silver sides, and green backs—thus the name greenies.

The main difference between these baits and pogies is their feeding habits. Greenies are plankton eaters, so they eat smaller fish in the food chain like shrimp and other smaller ocean creatures. Since they are actually predators, they can be caught on hook and line. Captain Keith explains that Sabiki rigs are the normal technique used to catch them. "Sabiki rigs are a chain of small lures that resemble miniature fish. Once a school of greenies is located, simply cast or lower the rig and retrieve it through the school. When you get one hooked, slowly retrieve the rig and others may strike the other hooks." While there are a variety of good brands of Sabiki rigs on the market, Captain Keith advises anglers to purchase the rigs made with actual fish skin wings (not plastic). He recommends a size 4 or 6 for greenies.

Captain Keith's final choice is mullet, another algae eater and not normally catchable on hook and line. Unlike the pogies and greenies, mullet are found mostly in backwater lagoons except in spring and fall, when they make an annual migration along the beach. They are normally plentiful enough to be netted on the way to the port from roadside or dockside locations. They are also more likely to be available from bait stores than the other varieties.

The best livewell for any of the three bait species is one with round corners and a good source of oxygenated seawater. The round corners prevent the bait from developing red noses caused by bumping into the sides of the well. The red-nosed baits do not look healthy or natural. The water source provides oxygen, which keeps the bait lively. Captain Keith says, "Lively baits catch more fish, and a good livewell is an essential part of the nearshore angler's equipment."

Anglers planning to venture out in nearshore waters should have a contingency plan if the live baits do not cooperate. Captain Keith obviously prefers live bait for his trolling expeditions, but he has some frozen bait on board just in case it is needed.

"My favorite frozen bait is cigar minnows. I find they troll better and last longer than most alternative baits." He pins the cigar minnows on a Gamefish rig sold by Hookup Lures. These premade rigs consist of a swivel, a short length of wire cable tied to a ½-ounce jig with a number 4/0 hook and another length of wire from the jig to a treble stinger hook. The rig comes completely assembled, so all the angler has to do is tie the mainline to the swivel and bait it up.

Hold the jig head and hook the cigar minnow through the

nose from the bottom side and place the treble hook in the back of the bait. Fish the bait as you would a live one, with one exception. "When using dead bait, I don't want the fish to get too good a look at it, so I increase my trolling speed to create a little more diversion."

Sometimes artificial lures will do the trick and fool a fish into biting. They also cut out the time needed to cast net or catch baitfish by hook and line. Captain Keith's choice of artificial lures is narrow, but he does keep a few of his favorites on the boat. "As for lures, my favorites are Bill Lewis Rat-L-Traps in silver or blue/silver, or a green-lipped plug like a Rapala."

Slow-Trolling Equipment

The choice of fishing gear is an individual preference. Most types will work in nearshore applications. Captain Keith prefers conventional revolving-spool reels, but says that spinning gear works great too. "Try to use a rod with some flex in the tip so it won't yank your bait as you troll it, but has enough backbone to land a hefty fish. I use 30-pound braided line, but if you want to be sporty you can use 20-pound line. I would not recommend going lower than 20 pound since some of these fish can be very large." He reports catches of tarpon that often top the 150-pound mark. When a really large fish is hooked, anglers should apply lots of pressure on the fish. The intent of using pressure is to land it as quickly as possible, so when released it is likely to live. This conservation element of fishing requires the use of beefy tackle when hooked up to trophy fish.

Two basic rigs are all that are necessary for slow-trolling applications, according to Captain Keith. He starts his rig by doubling the braided mainline using a Bimini twist. A Bimini knot doubles the strength and size of the mainline in preparation for the next connection. "I add 6 to 8 feet of 50-pound fluorocarbon leader to the mainline using a double uni knot. Finish the rig with one of two systems, depending on the targeted

Toothy critters like kingfish require wire rigs.

fish. Use a double-hook rig that is snelled on wire leader when targeting toothy critters like wahoo or kingfish. The double hook rig is connected to the 50-pound leader with an Albright knot. If the target is tarpon, the wire is not needed. For tarpon I use a 4-foot length of 80-pound fluorocarbon leader with an 11/0 circle hook as the terminal tackle."

Once the terminal tackle is in place, it's time to go fishing. Captain Keith's target is the area beaches in 20 to 50 feet of water. Anglers are in constant sight of the beach in this nearshore fishing adventure, but the possibilities of big fish are great. The pursuit begins by running the beach in various water depths with an eye out for signs that fish are present. These signs, according to Captain Keith, are bait schools, rolling or surface busting fish, baits skipping on the surface, or birds working the surface where a bait pod may have been pushed up to the surface by predator fish. Even one skipping baitfish can lead anglers to hook up with a predator fish. "Other things I look for are temperature changes and color changes in the water. These variations in water condition often attract bait and, in turn, trophy-sized nearshore fish." Temperature changes can be very important, as cold-blooded fish seek their own comfort range. "I also like slow trolling around structure on the bottom. Use your sonar to locate natural reefs, hard bottom, or artificial reefs. Once found, mark these locations on your bottom machine for future trolling opportunities."

After finding a suitable fishing location, bait up and start fishing using the slow-troll method. Captain Keith prefers live bait when available. "Take a live baitfish and place the lead hook just in front of the bait's eye. Place the trailing hook through the bait's back, leaving enough slack in the attaching line to allow the bait to swim naturally." Careful placement of hooks is necessary for keeping the bait alive and achieving a natural presentation, so time spent rigging it right will pay off. If there is no slack in the line connecting the two hooks, the bait will troll like a stick in the water instead of lively looking bait.

Once in fishing mode, Captain Keith's spread will feature three lines deployed at varying distances behind the boat. "I like the first bait way back, at least 150 to 200 feet behind the boat. My second bait will be positioned about 70 feet behind the boat, and the final bait will trail only 30 feet behind the boat." Proper placements of the fishing lines in the spread will allow anglers to cover more water without getting the lines tangled while trolling and make it easier to retrieve them without tangles when fighting a fish.

With properly placed rod holders, a small boat can fish three or four lines without fear of tangling. "I will typically set my *shotgun* or *wayback* line on the starboard side in the forward rod holder; my short line is also placed on the starboard side in the aft rod holder; my midlength line is fished from the port side." This thoughtful placement allows the shorter lines to slide under the longer line as the boat turns. If the fishing is

Bonito, known as little tunny, are frequently caught while slow trolling in the Atlantic.

slow, anglers can run a fourth line on a downrigger to increase the odds of a hookup. The fourth line would be fished under the midlength line on the port side. Captain Keith says the port and starboard sides can be switched, but the combination of long and short lines on one side of the boat and midlength and downrigger lines on the other side is a productive and efficient spread that will keep tangles to a minimum and fishing time at a maximum.

There is no reason to expect one species over another on any of the lines. Kingfish, tarpon, sailfish, bonito, and many more species will be caught using this setup. "I find that all species hit all lines," says Captain Keith. "I have even had tarpon hit the short line in an explosion of water right behind the boat. It is a thrill you will never forget!" He does comment, however, that when fish are pressured by heavy fishing activity, anglers are likely to get the majority of strikes on the long line.

The actual trolling method is described emphatically by Captain Keith as S-L-O-W-T-R-O-L-L. "I set my trolling speed at no more than 2 knots. Specifically, I want the bait to live, and I want a natural presentation. Both results require trolling at slow speeds." Once the speed is set, the next part of the slow-troll method includes driving the boat in *lazy S-curves* until the reel starts screaming. "I have used this technique for years; it is a tried and proven technique for catching monster nearshore fish."

The Inshore Bite—Night Snooking at Port Canaveral

The snook fishery in Port Canaveral has long been known as a snook hotspot by local anglers. Accessibility has changed somewhat over the years because of security issues, but the port remains a haven for some monster snook under the lights.

It is a well-known fact among snook anglers that snook feed better at night, so it's no surprise that dedicated snookers often wait until the sun goes down to go in search of their targeted prey. Plenty of snook are caught during the daylight hours, but a lot more really big ones are caught after nightfall. Some seasoned captains even say the later the better, and many trips are started after the midnight hour. The best reason to go night snooking is because they bite better, but there are other reasons that make night fishing in the port attractive.

Captain Badarack says, "One of the great things about fishing the port at night is less crowded fishing conditions. There is nearly a complete absence of boat traffic from tankers, charter boats, and submarines; anglers do not have to deal with huge swells created from passing vessels; and, finally, the heat is much easier to deal with since much of this fishing is done in the summer months. These conditions allow anglers to work shorelines and bridges and around cruise docks much more easily than in daytime hours."

Night fishing for snook at Port Canaveral includes fishing a drawbridge, lighted docks, numerous seawalls, rockpiles, and jetties. Captain Badarack fishes them all but prefers the jetties and the oyster-lined seawalls around the docks. "I will fish the jetties and seawalls on either tide in the inlet. As long as the water is moving it helps the bite. My favorite months are May through November."

Given the possibility of catching a really big snook, anglers need to beef up the tackle, beginning with a rod that has plenty of backbone. "My rod choice is a 7-foot St. Croix medium/heavy action rod rated for 17- to 25-pound-test line. Any good quality reel such as a Penn or Shimano that can hold 200 yards of 20-pound-test mainline will work fine." Big snook can take a lot of line out before coming to the boat, so it is extremely important to plan for it. Captain Mike adds about 3 feet of 40-pound mono leader before adding a hook or lure.

Snook adventures can start just before sundown in the port. "Fishing during the dusk part of the evening can be really good, but more important, when live bait fishing, I like to catch my bait while I can see what I'm doing." Snook will hit almost any live bait. Live shrimp and mullet are often available at area bait shops. Pinfish and croakers can be caught by hook and line using shrimp bits or cut squid as bait. Pogies can be caught in cast nets and greenies on Sabiki rigs.

Captain Mike's alternative to starting at dusk and fishing until midnight is to get started around 4:00 a.m. and fish until about 8:00 a.m. "Starting in the early morning means a lot of the night anglers have cleared out, and the charter boats and tankers don't usually start running out before 8:00. You will have the place mostly to yourself."

When it comes to bait selection, Captain Mike does not have a clear favorite, unless there is a lot of live bait present in the port. "I really don't have a preference for live bait over artificials; however, if there is a lot of live bait in the area, I will definitely use live bait first. Artificial lures tend to be less effective when so much live bait is present in the area." Artificial lures become the backup bait under these conditions.

Almost any swimming plug on the market will work on Port Canaveral snook, but Captain Mike has his favorites. "I like swimming or popping plugs that make a lot of commotion when fishing at night for snook. Many plugs work well; I usually throw Bomber or Rapala brand lures." Captain Badarack prefers swimming plugs that he has altered by personal preference. "When I use swim plugs, I remove the treble hooks and replace them with 2/0 offset J-hooks. I land a ton more fish on the single hooks; they are very effective." Especially with the larger snook, the multiple treble hooks often hook the fish at odd angles and cause hooks to bend and pull loose during the fight. "It seems when both sets of treble hooks are pinned in the fish, they fight against each other and you end up losing the fish. I get a more solid hookup and land more fish using single hooks." The other advantage is the ability to release a fish without having to do major surgery to remove multiple treble hooks. Those treble hooks are hard on the fish, too, reducing their survival rate when released.

When he changes to jigs, Captain Mike's favorite colors are chartreuse and white or red and white. When he goes larger, he likes a Hogey lure in pink or white. Choose a jig head appropriate to the depth of the water you are fishing. If you want it to go deeper, quicker, increase the size of the jig head. The size of the lure is pretty much a match the hatch decision, but sometimes a lure larger than the bait that's present will garner more strikes. It is always worth a try.

The bigger Port Canaveral snook reportedly come from the old abandoned cruise terminals located between Jetty Park and the main boat ramp. These cruise terminals once housed The Big Red Boat cruise fleet and the Sterling gambling ships,

Oyster-lined seawall pilings and docks harbor monster snook at Port Canaveral.

but presently the docks are vacant. Security regulations require anglers to stay 25 feet back from the dock. Encroachment inside that 25-foot boundary is likely to result in a citation from the Coast Guard or Port Police. Security agents patrol the area on foot and will let you know if you get too close.

The docks feature shade, seawalls, and pilings, all attributes that attract big snook. Sometimes the snook can be seen crashing bait trapped up against the seawalls. Other times the snook are sighted holding lazily in the shadow lines created by the terminal landings.

Captain Mike has his own strategy for enticing those big port snook to bite. "I like to free-line live shrimp, mullet, pogies, or greenies around the docks." He prefers hooking the baits in the lip as opposed to a meaty part of the body. "I prefer to hook my finfish baits through the lips. They seem to stay lively much longer; baits are more aerodynamic and cast a little further; and when you reel them in they are not dragging backward. Nothing takes the life out of the bait quicker than forcing water through their gills backward." In general, Captain Mike wants his bait to look as natural as possible, and he prefers the lip hooking technique to achieve a natural presentation and lively bait.

He also prefers larger live baits over small ones. "I like larger live baits, something that will stand out from the norm and not blend in with the live bait in the area. I want my bait to be perceived as something different and more appealing to a passing fish." He also warns anglers to always be ready for the strike. Most of the snook will be very close to the structure and will strike within the first five seconds the bait or lure hits the water.

Under certain conditions, where a cast cannot be made under a dock because of low clearance, a different method of hooking can be used. The bait does not stay alive as long, but when hooked in the back, behind the dorsal fin, live bait will normally swim away from the boat and under the structure, where the snook lay in wait. Circle hooks work well in this application. Just remember when using circle hooks, don't set the hook, just start reeling when the bite occurs.

Artificial lures should be cast back under the docks for best results. "If I am fishing with lures, I throw them as far back under the dock as I can. I work the lure back toward the boat, expecting a strike just as the lure hits the shadow line created by the dock lights shining over the landing. Be ready for the strike, and turn the fish's head toward you right away using the backbone in the rod. You have to horse them out under these conditions or they will break you off on the pilings every time." The drag setting should be cranked down pretty good for this type of fishing. Captain Mike says it is important to get them going in the right direction immediately. After you clear them from the structure and get them to open water, you can worry about drag setting and fighting them to the boat. The

Nighttime is prime time for Port Canaveral snooking. Photo courtesy of Capt. Mike Badarack.

longer the fight goes on, the more likely a hook pull will occur, so lighten up once you have them in the clear.

The water in the port is dredged regularly to keep the shipping and cruise lanes open. Water as deep as 40 feet offers a safe haven to weary fish in many areas of the port. If the freelining or topwater lure action is not panning out around the docks, go deeper. "If the fish are not active on top, I like to put on an ounce or two of lead with about a 3- to 4-foot leader and fish the drop-offs, deep bottom, or along the rocks." This deepwater strategy is especially productive during warmer months when the snook are seeking a certain comfort level that they find deeper in the water column.

Fishing the jetties on the north and south sides of the inlet is also productive for Canaveral snook, especially during the fall and spring mullet runs. The water is relatively shallow around the jetties but deeper in the channel. The 8- to 10-foot water drops off to 40 feet just inside the inlet. Captain Badarack says,

"The big snook often cruise the drop-off and then ambush bait-fish up in the shallower part along the jetty rocks." The jetties are well known and popular. They are easy to fish and attract lots of anglers, so get there early to reserve your spot.

There are some hazards to look out for when fishing in the port. The first is the tsunami zones created when cruise boats, tankers, or large headboats pass by. The large waves created by these vessels are very dangerous. "I have seen numerous boats get swamped and sink because they were not watching out for this hazard." The zones are located just west of the north jetty in the sandy cove area. There are signs posted alerting boaters to the dangers, but too many ignore the warning. "If you're in the zone when a cruise boat, tanker, or headboat goes by, you are going to experience some huge waves. They will swamp you if you are not prepared."

The entire port is a minimum wake zone so be sure to obey this rule. "It is not good to have angry charter boat captains chasing you down after you cause their boats to bounce off a piling or seawall. The police will ticket boaters every time for this offense." Minimum wake means the vessel is fully off plane and the bow is settled in the water. Law enforcement officers are watching to see if there is white water behind your boat, or if your bow is lifted. These are signals to law enforcement officers that you are traveling too fast.

All the security zones are posted on a signboard near the boat ramp in the port. Boaters should familiarize themselves with all security zones and understand the regulations. "If you enter a security zone, you will be confronted by Homeland Security agents pointing .50-caliber guns at you, and you could be arrested. Law enforcement is very serious about the security rules, so make sure you know where you are and where you are going." Don't forget, vessels must stay 25 feet off any seawall, or the enforcement agents will board your boat and ticket you. You are also likely to get a good verbal scolding for breaching security.

Fishing in the port at night does require dealing with a few extra regulations, but when that big snook starts taking drag, the effort is worth it. Don't forget the camera when night-fishing snook at Canaveral; you might just catch a fish of a lifetime.

Roadside Shrimping

In the spring and early summer, the causeways, bridges, and canals around Port Canaveral are populated by a unique bunch of individuals seeking a tasty treasure of a different sort. Shrimp-loving folks can trap, cast net, or dip shrimp from the local waters. Although this activity takes place all year long, June is a favorite month in Central Florida. Locals know and visitors should realize, it is wise to show up as early as noon to stake out prime real estate for the night's shrimping endeavor. First come, first served is the law of the land, but the real fun begins when sunlight fades to darkness and the lighted waters become alive with a delectable bounty.

Shrimp belong to a group of animals known as decapod crustaceans because they have 10 walking legs. Nutrient-rich estuaries such as those in the Banana River and Indian River lagoons provide an ideal habitat for juvenile shrimp to develop. Once they reach maturity, they swim out to the open ocean to spawn. Scientists report that a single female shrimp can produce 1 million eggs; unfortunately, only a tiny percentage survive. The eggs depend on tides and currents to carry them to the estuaries where they mature. The time span from egg to adult is about one year. Many of those surviving for a year will not survive to spawn because of predators.

Scientific studies show that the size of the shrimp harvest in any given year is more dependent on environmental factors than on the number of eggs laid. Freshwater introduced into the estuaries by spring rains reduces salinity and the ability of the juvenile shrimp to survive. If winter lingers, keeping water temperatures below normal, it negatively affects survival rates. With all these things seemingly working against them, there is one more extremely import factor in the long-term health of the species. That factor is habitat. The preservation of a vibrant and healthy natural habitat that provides food and protection for juvenile shrimp will be required if the shrimp population is to thrive well into the future.

The general consensus among shrimpers is that shrimp stay in deeper water throughout the day and move into the shallows around the causeways and other structures at night. That behavior is the main reason recreational shrimpers should wait until dusk to place the traps and start shrimping. The whole process could be described as somewhat of a ritual that includes staking out a claim, waiting for dusk, setting the traps, and collecting the bounty.

Staking the Claim

Staking the claim is the first step in preparation for a night's shrimping. Area seawalls are favorite locations for knowledgeable shrimpers. Arrive early at your selected location and set your equipment out along the area you want to shrimp. Place the traps about every 8 feet along the water's edge as soon as you arrive to keep other prospectors from moving in on your location. Equipment will include shrimp traps, underwater lights, long-handled dip nets, a generator, and plenty of snacks and beverages to hold you through the night.

What you should be looking for is a location with flowing water where shrimp begin to congregate before heading to deeper water to lay eggs. There is a common misconception that shrimp move into estuaries to lay their eggs. The fact is, shrimp move out to sea to lay their eggs, and it is that part of their life cycle, when they are gathering together for the pilgrimage to deeper water, when trapping shrimp is at its best.

Finding the right location is like an angler finding a *honey hole* for a day's fishing. Much of the decision is based on past

The action doesn't start until dark, but shrimpers in the know show up early to claim the prime shrimping locations.

experience, but newbies can gather information on location by browsing shrimping Web sites and blogs.

Some factors that can translate to a good catch are depressions along a seawall that let a trap sit a little lower in the water, a sudden rainstorm that cools the water and provides additional runoff and increased water flow, and, finally, faster than normal winds that serve to move water around the seawalls. You should pick a location that takes advantage of any of these possibilities. Checking the weather forecast and planning accordingly may actually improve your success. Many shrimpers also cite the four days before a full moon as prime shrimping time, so if your time is flexible, include this fact in your planning.

Waiting for Dusk

Since the shrimp don't run until the sun goes down, you need to develop a strategy for the wait if you arrived early to stake your claim. Checking your equipment to be sure it is in working order is important, but don't miss the opportunity to visit with other shrimpers set up in your area. In the same way that Facebook creates a social network of friends and acquaintances on the Internet, shrimping communities also evolve into a social network of sorts where new friends are made and information is exchanged. This is the time to ask questions about current shrimping conditions and what to expect.

Setting the Traps

Just before dark, walk along the seawall and move the traps from the holding position on top of the seawall to the water alongside the seawall. Maintain the 8-foot distance between each trap. The 8-foot placement is not a legal requirement, but rather a common courtesy practiced among shrimpers. Occasionally an unknowledgeable shrimper will encroach on another's territory, with harsh words usually the result. Proper etiquette is a serious matter among shrimpers, so keep your distance.

There are a few legal requirements that apply to the traps. Legal traps cannot exceed 36 inches long by 24 inches wide by 12 inches high. The traps cannot be equipped with devices that serve to funnel shrimp into the traps. You can legally tend four traps, but be sure each is labeled with a nameplate including your name and address. FWC officers have the authority to inspect traps in use, and any trap not attended by the person whose name is on the tag is subject to confiscation. This means you must be in sight of your trap if a marine officer stops by for a check.

Collecting the Bounty

With the traps placed against the seawall where shrimp are expected to run, electric lights are placed beyond the traps

Underwater lights make it easier for anglers to dip singles while waiting for the shrimp traps to fill.

to illuminate the water between the lights and the seawall. The subtle glow from electric lights placed below the water's surface creates an almost eerie appearance of the area being fished. The lights are not intended to attract shrimp, but they make it much easier to dip singles while you wait for the traps to do their job. The submerged lights shine upward, making the silhouette of a swimming shrimp easily spotted. The same thing can be accomplished with lanterns hanging over the water, but they produce unwanted glare, and the visibility is not as good. Most serious shrimpers use submersible lights that operate from portable generators.

The net used to collect singles is connected to a pole that may be as long as 20 feet. Legally the net cannot have an opening larger than 96 inches around the perimeter. The mesh will narrow down to a small, confining circumference at the opposite end of the opening. Shrimp can be dipped and trapped in the end of the net without having to empty it each time. If the shrimp keep coming then you just keep dippin'.

Veteran shrimpers recommend pulling the traps in two-hour cycles for best results. If you pull them too early, you may spook other shrimp away from your location, and if you don't pull them often enough, some may escape. You should not leave your traps in the water after the sun comes up. If you do, you run the risk of pinfish and other shrimp-loving fishes moving in and eating the night's catch. Just don't oversleep.

You do need a recreational saltwater fishing license to engage in shrimping. There is no size limit on shrimp, and you are allowed to collect five gallons of heads-on shrimp per person, per day. It is always advisable to contact the nearest FWC office for local restrictions or new legal requirements.

Tripletail on the Canaveral Buoy Line

Tripletail are a prehistoric-looking creature with a body that appears to have three tails. In reality the profile is simply the anal and dorsal fins, but their proximity to the actual tail gives the appearance of a fish with three tails. Tripletail are tropical fish found in warm-water locations all over the globe. This curious fish is often found near structure like seawalls and docks inside the port and around floating objects outside the port. Even floating plastic sacks may have a tripletail harboring below. The buoys marking the ship channel outside Port Canaveral are prime locations to try your luck at catching a tripletail. The fish are attracted to the buoys because they provide a source of food.

To maximize your tripletail adventure, load the livewell with small to medium-sized shrimp from one of the local bait shops in the port. Rig up a couple of medium heavy or heavy action rods with a 400 series reel spooled with 20-pound braided line. A rod with some backbone is needed when you hook up to pull the fish away from the chain that connects the buoy to a large concrete block on the ocean floor. The heavy rods may be a bit of overkill for smaller fish, but you will be glad you have them if you hook a big one. The Florida record is more than 40 pounds, and numerous 30-pound-class tripletail have been caught off the Canaveral buoy line.

Sometimes tripletail will congregate around the cement block on the bottom, but other times you will actually spot them holding shallow in the shade of the buoy itself. They can be at any depth but are normally close to the chain. Prepare a rig for each situation so you can grab the one you need at any given buoy. Rig one rod with 30- to 40-pound fluorocarbon leader and a 5/0 circle hook. This rig will be used for shallow fish. Normally no weight is needed on this outfit. Prepare another rod by adding a jig head in place of the circle hook. The jig needs to be heavy enough to get you to the bottom when the fish are holding deep. Currents and winds may influence this decision, so rig accordingly. Now you are ready for fishing the Canaveral buoy line.

Approach each buoy slowly and take a good look. If you can see fish holding under the buoy, grab the rig with no weight and free-line a shrimp to the fish. Cast slightly beyond the buoy so the shrimp will fall slowly into the strike zone. When the tripletail are holding shallow like this, the angler usually sees the strike. Turn the fish away from the buoy as quickly as you can so it does not wrap the chain and cut the line. The boat operator can help by placing the engine in reverse and pulling away from the buoy.

If no tripletail are spotted on the approach to the buoy, pick up the rod with a jig head so you can fish deep. Break off the tail fin of the shrimp, place the point of the hook in the exposed flesh, and push the shrimp up to the jig head. Removing the tail fin allows an extra dose of scent to emanate from the shrimp and might help trigger the bite. The angler should position him or herself on the bow of the boat and be prepared to drop the baited jig head straight down to the bottom. The boat operator slowly approaches the buoy and attempts to hold the boat in position as the angler makes the vertical drop.

The first drop should go all the way to the bottom unless it is intercepted on the way down. Slowly retrieve the jig with slow cranks on the reel and frequent pauses. It is not necessary to apply action to the jig; just hold it at various depths as you prospect for the fish. Every inch of the water column should be covered until fish are found holding at a certain depth. As you move on to fish other buoys, chances are the fish will be holding at the same depth as previous buoys. A good strategy to find the same depth again is to count reel rotations as you work the bait up from the bottom. Remember where you get a strike and go back to that depth on the next drop.

Deep fish can be harder to land from around the buoys because more fishing line is exposed to the possibility of wrapping the chain. The first few seconds after the hookup are most important to keep the fish free of the barnacle-encrusted cable. The angler has to do his part by applying plenty of pressure, but the boat operator needs to help. The boat engine should be shifted into reverse and the boat backed quickly away from the buoy, especially on the larger fish. Vertical dropping the buoys is a team sport, and communication between anglers is necessary to make it come off successfully and safely. The angler must be prepared for the sudden motion of a boat in reverse as the driver responds to a bent rod on the bow.

Tripletail are mighty fighters and don't give up easily. Unlike a kingfish that might make one long hard run and be finished, tripletail will make one run after another trying to get back to the structure. Anglers have to be on their toes and react to each of the powerful runs, or they will end up losing the battle. The braided line is a plus in this application because it does not stretch. All the power applied with the rod is transferred directly through the braid, giving the fish little hope of turning back.

Tripletail will also strike artificial offerings. Imitation shrimp, paddletail jigs, and small crankbaits will work at times. Anglers should look for any floating objects and approach them

Teamwork between captain and angler pays off when fishing for tripletail on the Canaveral buoy line.

quietly when found. The closer the boat comes to the fish, the more likely they are to sound, so stealth is an important strategy. Tripletail will lie on their side under floating debris waiting for an easy meal. They come to life and ambush their prey when it gets too close. Once you spot them, make a cast beyond the sighted fish and retrieve the bait back near the tripletail and let it fall. It they see the bait, they are likely to strike, and the fight is on. It is an exciting sightfishing experience in the open ocean.

Tripletail are not limited to ocean fishing. Many kayakers, canoers, and powerboat anglers find them inside, along the channel markers of the Indian River. Artificial baits like the D.O.A. Shrimp work well in the river. The same fishing principles hold: fish the entire water column around the markers for best results and be prepared to pull them quickly from the structure.

Once the battle has been won and a tripletail is ready to be landed, certain precautions are in order. Like many saltwater fish they have teeth that can injure an unsuspecting angler, so use caution when removing hooks. The dorsal fin has very sharp spines that can easily puncture human flesh. Since gill plates are as sharp as a razor, holding them by the gills is not recommended without protection. A pair of gloves on board to handle the tripletails is a pretty good idea. Some pros advise landing them with a net and transferring them straight to the cooler if dinner is your goal.

Continue to use caution at the fillet table because that armorlike exterior makes cleaning trips a little bit of a challenge. Those spines will still stick you if you're not concentrating. Keep knives sharp to eliminate the need to apply too much pressure to the blade and cause an unexpected slip into a spine. After the cleaning is complete, the reward will be worth the effort. Once the armor is pierced and removed, a white delectable meat awaits the lucky chef. In a forum at the hulltruth. com about eating tripletail, one user posted, "They're terrible to eat. Please fillet them out (no bones for easy disposal), pack on ice, and send to me."

Area Hotspots

Anglers in the Port Canaveral area will find fish very close to the inlet. Check your map for Canaveral Bight to the north, fish the buoy line outside the port, or travel south along the beach until you see the steeple of the Cocoa Beach First Baptist Church. Once you reach the steeple, deploy your trolling rigs and fish from 20 to 40 feet of water until you locate fish. An Internet search for artificial reefs in Brevard County will produce more wrecks and reefs to try.

A few hotspots in the Banana River include the area adjacent to Canaveral Lock, the residential docks south of State

Road 520, and the flats north of Pineda Causeway on the west side of the river.

Some outstanding beach fishing can be found in the Satellite Beach area because of the rocky outcropping found there.

Charter Captains

Captain Mike Badarack

Hometown: Satellite Beach, Florida
Business: Space Coast Fishing Charters
Phone number: 321-863-0561
E-mail address: captmikebadarack@gmail.com
Web site: www.spacecoastflyfishing.com

Captain Mike's advice to visiting anglers: The best advice I can give when fishing the port is to cover as much water as possible and change your presentations if what you're fishing with is not working. If you're fishing the jetty with live bait up top and nothing is going on after a half hour or so, tie up a sliding sinker rig and work the bottom for a while. If one fishing spot doesn't produce, change locations. With all the structure in the port you may only have to move 100 feet to find some fish. Remember, you are not the only thing moving; the fish are too. The objective is to be in the same place they are, so move until you find them. Try all the different structure—the oysters, docks, pilings, sand bottoms, etc. Keep moving until you find where the snook are holding, and you will get some solid action.

Captain Keith Kalbfleisch

Hometown: Winter Park, Florida
Business: Saltwater Adventures of Central Florida
Phone number: 321-279-1344
E-mail address: Capt-Keith@saocf.com
Web site: www.Capt-Keith.com

Captain Keith's advice to visiting anglers: Always check with local anglers and area bait shops for current fishing conditions and techniques. If you pay close attention to the details of their techniques, a short conversation at the dock or in the shop may result in an improved day on the water. Sometimes the difference between a huge success and a fishless day has to do with the smallest details, and those details are known and often shared by locals. Use them to your advantage.

Area Hotspots

Inside Port Canaveral is good for nighttime snook. The north and south jetties are both good for Spanish mackerel in the winter months and mangrove snappers all year long. The summer tarpon fishing is nothing short of outstanding along the beach when baitfish are present. The Banana River between the Canaveral Lock and the 520 bridge is a good place to sight-fish reds. On the south side of Highway 520 along the west shoreline are numerous docks that hold reds, snook, and trout. Those same docks are great for sheepshead in the winter. For the adventurous angler, the Thousand Islands area of Cocoa Beach has some great fishing. Much of it is best fished in a canoe or a kayak.

Fishing-Friendly Lodging and Glorious Galleys

Grills Seafood Deck and Tiki Bar

> 505 Glen Cheek Drive
> Cape Canaveral, FL 32920-4501
> Phone number: 321-868-2226

Casual waterfront dining. Located in Port Canaveral beside the boat ramp. Full menu includes some great sandwiches. The locals love this place. Recommended by the author.

Bait and Tackle

Fisherman's World

750 Mullet Road #A
Cape Canaveral, FL 32920-4526
Phone number: 321-784-5285

Located in Port Canaveral. Everything for the inshore or offshore angler. Drinks and sandwiches. Opens early, seven days a week. Recommended by the author.

Handler Fishing Supply

677 Dave Nisbet Boulevard, Suite 119
Port Canaveral, FL 32920
Phone number: 321-799-9708

Friendly, reliable staff. Specializing in offshore and inshore saltwater fishing. Rod and reel repair. Open every day. Recommended by the author.

Fishing Lessons for Life—Taking Good Photos

If you are going to take a photo, try to leave the fish in the water until just before you're ready to click the picture. This procedure is not only good for the fish, but it also increases the possibility of an outstanding and memorable photo.

Everyone on board should share operating procedures of his or her camera with other anglers so it does not have to be explained at picture-taking time. Once the photographer is ready, the fish should be removed from the water while carefully supporting it horizontally. Teach the kids not to squeeze the fish when they hold it. Let it lie gently on their outstretched hands. Squeezing can damage internal organs and should be avoided. If conditions permit, a really great photo can be achieved by having the angler get out of the boat for the picture. In this scenario the fish can be held with a gripper tool in one hand and supported horizontally with the other without ever coming out of the water for the photo. Kids should be wearing their life jackets for obvious safety reasons.

A little preplanning will have the child dressed in photogenic clothing to provide contrast and enhance the effect of the picture. Having fishing equipment in the photo is also a good idea if possible.

If the fish is large, have an adult behind the child to help support the fish for the photo. Caps or hats can be removed or repositioned to avoid shadowing of faces. Another tip is to leave the flash on constantly. Even in daylight photos, an active flash will help remove the shadows cast by various objects.

A photo is a historical record of a fun time with your kids or other fishing partners, so take the time to snap a good one. When your kids see the trouble you go to in order to get a good picture and release the fish unharmed, they have learned another important conservation lesson.

7

Melbourne and Sebastian Inlet

This area of Florida developed rapidly with the coming of the space program to Brevard County. Its early development, however, was associated with two settlements near the location where Crane Creek flows into the Indian River. Those two settlements became known as Eau Galle and Melbourne. A visitor driving though the area today would not distinguish the difference between the two as they have merged into one continuous commercial and residential area.

Melbourne developed into the larger of the two cities and became the center of government and commerce. As with all Florida East Coast settlements, the Indian River and its potential for trade and recreation played a major role in developing this area of the Space Coast from Melbourne to Sebastian Inlet. The area's connection to the water began to fade in 1893 when the railroad arrived to serve the area. The river was not needed for transportation, and more inland development began around the railroad tracks.

South of Melbourne, where Turkey Creek joins the Indian River, the town of Tillman developed, complete with a local post office. The area experienced a surge of growth in 1919 when the Indian River Land Company marketed the area to Midwest settlers. Records show that 105 families of German and Slavic descent moved to the area as a result. The present-day name of the town is Palm Bay, changed in 1925 to more accurately describe the tropical setting of the growing town.

Following the Indian River farther south leads visitors to the town of Sebastian and Sebastian Inlet. The settlement was first named St. Sebastian after the nearby river with the same name. Today both the river and the town are known only as Sebastian. The inlet was the result of a local desire for an inlet connecting the Atlantic Ocean to the Indian River. After many failed private attempts to open an inlet, the Sebastian Inlet Association was formed, and lobbying the legislature for an inlet began. A permit was obtained, and the Army Corps of Engineers began the seventh effort to open the inlet. The inlet was completed and officially opened in 1924. It has since become a popular spot for outdoor enthusiasts, and is now the location of the Sebastian Inlet State Park, a favorite location for angling, camping, surfing, and other outdoor recreational pursuits.

Characteristics of the Fishing Area

The Melbourne/Sebastian Inlet region is characterized by miles of mangrove shorelines, residential docks, grass flats, oyster bars, spoil islands, and several freshwater rivers that empty into the Indian River Lagoon system. The Banana River joins the Indian River at Indian Harbor Beach and continues south as the Intracoastal Waterway. The junction of the two rivers is marked by a local landmark known as Dragon Point. The Indian River continues southward past Sebastian Inlet toward its end near St. Lucie Inlet. Turkey Creek flows into the Indian River near Palm Bay and offers some excellent tarpon fishing with easy access from two local boat ramps.

Further south the Sebastian River offers protected fishing on windy days. It can be accessed from the Indian River and fished upstream for miles before passage is ended at a flood control gate. The river has mangrove shorelines, a railroad bridge, grass and mud flats, and deep holes that harbor waiting predator fish. The river also offers outstanding kayak and canoe fishing.

The Intracoastal Waterway coincides with the Indian River along this stretch of Florida's East Coast with access to the Atlantic Ocean available through Sebastian Inlet. The many islands that characterize the region were created by dredging operations in the 1950s to deepen and widen the Intracoastal Waterway. The material dredged up to deepen and widen the river is referred to as spoil. That dredging material was dumped outside the channel to form many spoil islands, creating yet another fishing structure in the river. Some islands are now submerged as a result of winds, waves, and hurricanes, but all create potentially fishy areas. Many gator trout have been caught around these manmade islands. Anglers should refer to area charts to identify potential boating hazards related to the submerged islands.

The Sebastian offshore area is blessed with a diversity of fish-holding structure, too. On any given day the choice of locations to fish will depend on the species you want to catch. The area includes wrecks and rock piles that provide great bottom fishing for snapper and grouper. The wrecks and rock piles are very productive fishing grounds and only a 10- to 12-mile run before the fishing begins.

If the target of the day is dolphin or wahoo, it's the open water that will provide the action. Big game fish can be caught from along the beach all the way out to the Gulf Stream. In the deeper water, anglers will find plenty of hills and valleys that hold fish. Anglers should study a good chart and locate the structure where distinct and large changes in depth occur.

Sonar equipment should be used to pinpoint the hills or valleys for best fishing success. Captain Billy Poertner operates Imagine That Fishing Charters out of Sebastian. He is an expert in live bait fishing for wahoo and other pelagic species. He says, "Locating a hill on the ocean floor where the depth changes from 1,000 feet to 650 is the kind of area to look for. The hill or valley will create an upwelling, which carries nutrients up to the surface. This is the beginning of the food chain in these productive waters. The nutrients attract small baitfish, the small baitfish attract larger fish, and the larger fish attract the targeted pelagics we all love to catch."

Captain Poertner likes to fish the west edge of the Gulf Stream where eddies form and temperature changes occur. "Sometimes just a small temperature break, say from 79.1 to 80.0, is all that it takes for the different nutrients to occur, resulting in an incredible bite." He advises anglers to always keep tabs on the water temperature and the water depths that are holding fish. "Certain depth ranges hold fish on various days, but so do temperature breaks. Finding these ranges is a key to offshore success."

Shallow water off the beaches can be very productive when baitfish are present. Captain Poertner says, "When the bait is really plentiful on the beach, that's where I fish." He also likes to fish the numerous shoals available out of Sebastian Inlet. He mentions Pelican Flats, a shoal about 18 miles northeast of Sebastian Inlet as an example. He advises anglers to be sure to fish the whole shoal. "I think the biggest mistake anglers make is to just fish the inside edge of a flat. After spending hard-earned money, fuel, and time to run all the way out there, anglers should not be content to fish only 50 percent of it."

Sometimes the structure comes in the form of another fish. Captain Billy tells anglers to be ready when the unexpected appears. "No matter what structure you fish, always have a pitch bait ready when an opportunity arises." That opportunity could be a free-swimming manta ray with a cobia or two beneath it. "While you're running to and from different fishing grounds, you may pass through a large school of rays. If so, take time to stop and check for cobia. The cobia will often be seen swimming beneath the rays."

He says having a livie rigged and ready works great, but artificials will work too. "I love to use a 10-inch Hogey plastic bait on a 2-ounce Hogey jig head or any 2- to 4-ounce jig head with a plastic body about 6 to 8 inches long." Once the cobia is spotted, cast the pitch bait out in front where the fish can see it and hold on. It's almost a certain bite.

With all the emphasis on structure, water depth, upwellings, and temperature, don't forget to keep a watchful eye on the sky. Successful offshore anglers know that a single frigate bird can be one of the best indicators of bait and fish in an area. "Don't forget to look up once in a while; finding a frigate bird is as good as finding a floating board or a weed line when the frigate is working a pod of bait."

The Inshore Bite—Snook-Fishing Residential Docks

Captain Terry Lamielle operates Easy Days Guide Service in the Sebastian area. He says visitors are usually surprised at the variety of fish species that can be caught in the Sebastian area on any given day. He names pompano, flounder, seatrout, and redfish as popular targets. His personal favorite fish to target

To avoid unwanted breakoffs, beef up the tackle when fishing for snook around docks. Photo by Capt. Chris Myers.

is snook around the docks and other structure. Fishing around heavy structure adds an element of suspense to the fishing experience and requires good fish fighting techniques. Snook love the structure as an ambush point for passing baitfish and also for the security it provides. Once hooked, they instinctively head for cover and break off unsuspecting or unprepared anglers in the process.

Fishing tackle needs to be beefed up a bit for fishing around structure. Captain Terry says, "When fishing heavy structure, I use a 4000 size reel spooled with 30- to 40-pound-test braided line." Braided line is superior to mono for long and accurate casts and abrasion resistant enough to stand the wear and tear caused when a snook wraps around a dock piling. He adds a 30- to 40-pound fluorocarbon leader before tying on the lure. "I like to have three different lures rigged on rods and ready to cast. I don't want to waste time rigging when fishing a productive dock." The three lures are selected to cover the water column. One rod holds a topwater plug, a second rod is rigged with a suspending lure, and the third rod is set up with a jig head and plastic tail or a D.O.A. plastic shrimp.

If you see a dock where baitfish are being crashed by snook, work it first. Cast a topwater lure into the melee and get ready to hookup. If there are no obvious signs of bait or feeding fish, just start working the docks in a systematic way. Over time you will learn that some docks are more productive than others, but all will hold fish at one time or another. Make a mental note of the productive docks for the next time you fish the area. "I would not pass up any dock unless someone else was already fishing on or around the dock. Working any dock at first light or working a dock with a night light before the sun comes up is always best."

Captain Terry approaches the dock from a distance and works the ends first with a topwater lure. Next he works the sides by casting to the shore and retrieving the lure alongside

When the sun gets higher in the sky, switch to suspending lures for best results. Photo courtesy of Capt. Terry Lamielle.

or through the dock pilings. "I use topwater lures early and switch to suspended baits as the day goes on. The higher the sun, the more likely I am to switch to jig heads with plastic tails because the snook go deeper."

Every angler enjoys the rush of a snook blowing up on a topwater lure. Captain Terry is no different; he says he will never get tired of the excitement created by a topwater bite. "I don't have an absolute favorite topwater lure, but as long as it will retrieve in a walk-the-dog fashion, it will work. Most snook cannot resist that walk-the-dog action." Lures that fill the bill here are Heddon Zara Spooks, MirrOlure Top Dog or Top Pup series, and the original High Roller Stick Bait.

Terry's story is a little different when it comes to suspending baits. He quickly names the Yo-Zuri 3D Fingerling or the Yo-Zuri Jerk-O as his favorite suspending lures. "I have caught everything on the Yo-Zuri 3D Fingerling, in the river and freshwater too." He adds, "The most important factor in the retrieve is the pause after the twitch. I would say as many as 99.9 percent of the strikes come on the pause." He identifies the only remaining factor as the length of a pause, because fish will strike on different patterns on different days. He searches for the desired pause with what he calls the 1, 2, 3 twitch pattern. "I will cast the lure and twitch one time and pause, two twitches and pause, and then three twitches and pause. Vary the length of the pause in the process and you cover all bases. Create the twitches with a short snap of the rod tip; it seems to trigger a strike."

When selecting plastic baits, Captain Terry has a lot of confidence in the D.O.A. Shrimp. The bait skips easily and can be cast to the back of the dock and worked out slowly. Alternatively it can be cast through the dock from side to side, once again being worked out slowly. "Snook like the shadows and shade created by the dock. As the day heats up, the D.O.A. Shrimp is an excellent bait to skip under the dock to entice fish to eat. If I feel the snook want swimming baits, I change over to a paddle tail on a jig head worked deep in the shadows but on a faster retrieve."

As far as color selection goes, Captain Terry subscribes to the popular notion of darker hues in the low light periods and lighter colors as the natural light increases. "The darker colors create a better silhouette in low light conditions, making it easier for the snook to see the lure. It is the contrast that is important to producing visibility in low light conditions. I switch to a lighter color, such as bone, when the sun gets higher in the sky."

Calendar seasons make a difference in how you fish the docks. Captain Terry explains that the techniques discussed above are for use during the prime time fishing months of May through November. Once winter time rolls around and the water temperature falls, he suggests fishing deeper docks and docks over dark mud bottoms. "In the winter I like to target deeper water and mud bottoms. Both of these conditions translate to warmer water that is closer to the snook's comfort level."

Fishing docks for snook presents a challenge not faced on the open flats. Fighting a snook from under a dock is often going to include a dock piling in the scenario; they love to wrap you up and break you off. Proper fish fighting techniques are a must, and some unconventional strategies might come in helpful. Captain Terry's major advice is to leave the 6-pound tackle at home. Heavy tackle can turn the snook's head and make it swim out from under the dock. If the fish doesn't come clear of the pilings, try opening the bail and give the fish slack. This method will sometimes cause the snook to turn around and swim back out the way it went in. When the pressure is relaxed, the fish forgets that it is hooked. If that doesn't work, try to change the angle of attack by moving the boat to a more favorable position to prevent the line from rubbing or wrapping the pilings. If nothing else works, "The final strategy may be to hold your breath and pray it's a dumb one."

Sebastian Pompano

Pompano roam the Indian River Lagoon all year long. They are members of the jack family, but unlike most of their cousins, pompano are considered a prize delicacy when it comes to table fare. They are a silver-colored fish with a forked tail and a narrow body that produces a mighty fight for their size. Some say the pomps will out-pull a jack crevalle of the same size; both are strong fighters. Florida pompano max out at about 20 inches in length and 5 pounds in weight.

Captain Tom Van Horn operates Mosquito Coast Fishing Charters in east central Florida. He says, "The most significant thing anglers may not realize about pompano fishing on the northern Indian River Lagoon is that pompano are a year-round species. Since pompano travel in schools, anglers can be pretty sure that when they find one, they find more. During the summer, pompano roam the Indian River Lagoon shallows in search of small glass minnows. Anglers should break out small jigs or a fly rod once the school of pomps has been found."

Summertime pompano will be foraging along the deeper edges of the grass flats. "They can often be overlooked in the 2- to 3-foot water, but it is not that uncommon to see them. They are also spotted around the edges of spoil islands that line the ICW from the Max Brewer Causeway to the Sebastian Inlet."

As winter approaches and that first cool front blows through, the pompano bite picks up considerably, and locations further south usually get a decent run of pompano. "As the water begins to cool, the pompano schools leave the estuary, making their way out of the lagoon through the inlets into the open ocean. They can also be found just inside the inlets. At Sebastian the large flat inside the inlet is considered prime territory for the pomps. After moving outside, the pompano schools travel up and down the beaches in the troughs feeding on mole crabs (sand fleas), their favorite forage."

Usually around November, serious pompano anglers dust off their gear and keep their eyes and ears open for the news that the pompano have arrived. Experienced pompano anglers know there are two basic ways to fill the cooler with the tasty fish. One technique involves throwing brightly colored jigs at inshore concentrations; the other targets them in the surf.

Brightly colored jigs have long been a pompano staple in the inshore waters. Pink, yellow, and orange are time-tested colors to use on the pomps. Captain Van Horn advises anglers to rig a couple of rods with colorful jigs and tip them with a small piece of fresh shrimp. The added smell of the shrimp helps attract the pomps. "This inshore tactic has worked especially well for me, particularly in the fall. At Sebastian Inlet it's best to have

Pompano are attracted to brightly colored jigs tipped with shrimp and bounced along the bottom. Photo by Capt. Pat Dineen.

a couple rods rigged, because bottom hangs do occur. If you break off, just pick up the other rod and continue fishing."

Any saltwater light-tackle rod and reel combination will catch fish, but serious anglers should choose quality tackle that will last awhile and hold up under saltwater fishing conditions. Most captains agree that quality equipment is cheaper in the long run. Captain Van Horn chooses a St. Croix Tidemaster series rod. "I like a 7-foot medium action, moderate tip rod combined with a 2500 series reel like the Shimano Sahara or comparable size reel. Spool the reel with 10- to 15-pound Sufix Performance Braid line and add 24 inches of 20-pound-test Invisiline leader for an unbeatable combination." Inlet waters are usually clear, and a fluorocarbon leader nearly disappears in the water, leaving the bait to look more natural. More bites will result.

Moving water will be one of the conditions to look for when targeting pompano. Cast shrimp-tipped jigs up-current and bounce them along the bottom in a lift and pause retrieve. "Anglers should fish the incoming tide if they have the opportunity; that's when I do best. Peel the shrimp and pin a small piece on the jig head for scent and also to make the fish hold on after a strike. Pompano will strike hard and fight harder." A bonus to this fishing technique is that it will also catch an assortment of other species. "Sometimes I add a second jig to the outfit to increase the possibility of bites. Occasionally it results in a double hookup."

The second technique common to pompano fishing targets them in the surf during the winter. When surf temperatures reach the 68-degree mark, pompano leave the lagoon seeking warmer water and sand fleas, their favorite winter forage. Pomps will hit artificial baits in the surf, but most surf anglers bait up with peeled shrimp or sand fleas when they can get them. (See chapter 2 for a discussion of how to obtain and rig sand fleas.) If you find a concentration of sand fleas on the beach, it is probably a good place to fish for the pomps.

Captain Van Horn targets pompano in the surf with a 7-foot medium heavy rod fitted with a 4000 series reel. He spools his reel with 20-pound braided line. He says surf rods are not necessary for pompano in the surf. "I like to fish in the first tough along the beach using a terminal rig I tie myself." He begins the rig by attaching a swivel to a Bimini Twist tied to the terminal end of the braided line. Add about 4 feet of 20-pound fluorocarbon leader. Tie in two dropper loops, equally spaced along the leader, using a surgeon knot. Add a snap swivel to the end of the leader to allow ease in changing the weight according to the existing current. Next, cut one leg of each loop near the knot. The result is two long leaders. Add a Daiichi 1/0 Bleeding Bait circle hook to each drop, and it is ready to fish.

In order to enhance this rig he has a little trick up his sleeve.

"Sometimes I alter this rig by adding sound and a float. I slide a small yellow float on the top drop line and three orange-colored beads on the bottom one. The small float will keep the upper hook higher in the water column, and the beads add color to the rig and click together, making some sound to attract fish."

Captain Van Horn buys live shrimp and puts them on ice to use on the pompano. It is not necessary to use whole shrimp. He peels the shrimp and cuts them into several pieces. Pomps don't require large bait; in fact, their mouths are relatively small and better adapted to eating the small pieces of shrimp. "I find the fresh shrimp hold better on the hook than frozen ones. Fresh clams also work, and sand fleas when you can get them."

Captain Terry Lamielle also likes to target the Sebastian Inlet pompano. He agrees with Captain Tom on finding them on an incoming tide. "The pompano usually show up in the lagoon on the incoming tide. Finding them is pretty easy. As you move onto a flat, they will skip out of your boat wake in an effort to escape. When skippers show up, I know I am in the right place. I shut down the engine and drop the Power Pole Shallow Water Anchoring System to hold my boat in place so I can fish the area well before moving." Captain Terry's favorite lure is Doc's Goofy Jig, and he is not alone. Pompano anglers all over Florida recognize this jig as one of the best. "Pompano's preference for colors seems to change from time to time, but I have had the most success on all pink or yellow." Captain Terry's color selection method involves two rods with two different colored jigs. "If I have two people in the boat, I will tie both colors on so one is throwing one color and the other person casts the other color. As the bite gets good, whichever color gets the most bites is what we change to." He says keeping bottom contact with the jig is important while jigging. Let it settle to the bottom, then jerk it up. When the jig hits the bottom, a puff of sand

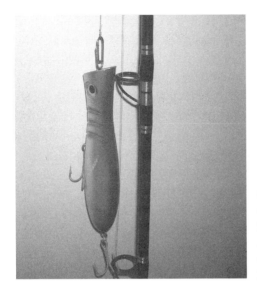

Change plugs, spoons, or bait lines easily by including a Tactical Anglers clip in your rigging. Photo by Capt. Billy Poertner.

comes up like a sand flea on the bottom. The fish see the puff and come to investigate. "Most strikes will occur as the jig falls back toward the bottom."

The Offshore Bite—Trolling Techniques

Offshore, Sebastian offers excellent open water fishing. Several popular pelagic species such as mahi-mahi, wahoo, kingfish, and sailfish are often caught in these productive waters. Captain Billy Poertner reminds anglers to always be on the lookout for temperature changes such as those that naturally occur along the edges of the Gulf Stream.

Open water fishing tackle on Captain Billy's boat consists of 6½-foot rods equipped with Shimano TLD 25 reels. Each reel is spooled with 20-pound high visibility mono. The boat is rigged with Lee's 18-foot outriggers attached to the T-top. Each rigger is capable of deploying two lines plus a teaser line. "I also have two Daiwa bent rods which are rigged with 6/0 Penn Senator reels. I spool them with 100-pound-test braided line and use them for trolling with planers." Years ago anglers used wire lines to pull planers and spoons, but the technological advancement of braided line allows the planer to run deeper without the need of cumbersome wire line.

Captain Billy likes to be prepared for any fishing opportunity that may arise. "I also carry four 7-foot 6-inch rods with Shimano Baitrunner 6500 reels. These outfits are pre-rigged with a Tactical Anglers clip, which allows me to change plugs, spoons, or hooks easily. This is a huge advantage, especially when you get into a school of dolphin."

Fishing from a 23-foot center console has helped Captain Billy develop a few tricks to maximize the trolling spread for smaller vessels. "My shotgun bait is always a medium to large skirted ballyhoo. The skirt is light blue with black markings. Next I like a brightly colored popper, which can be purchased for around $6 to $8 at any local tackle store. These will be rigged with ballyhoo and run from the port and starboard outside riggers. The port-side bait is placed around 70 feet back and the starboard-side bait at around 50 feet."

Since fishing on a small boat makes it difficult to fish six to eight lines the way the larger boats do, Captain Billy uses two teasers in place of fishing lines to attract fish to his spread. "One of my teasers is a squid teaser bar, which I run just far enough back that the teaser bar is out of the water. It is attached to the second eye in my outrigger pole. The next is a dredge system made by Stripteaser. The dredge is run off a cleat on the port side of my vessel. Thanks to an idea I got from George Poveromo, I made a rig to pull the Stripteaser dredge deeper in the water column." The rig Captain Billy uses is a large deep diving plug with no hooks attached. It is fastened to the front of the dredge, and because of its large lip, the hookless lure pulls the teaser deeper than a trolling weight would. "I always fish a naked ballyhoo just behind the dredge and a mullet deep under the dredge."

The sixth fishing line in Captain Billy's spread is a pitch-bait. He keeps it rigged and ready with a naked ballyhoo stored in the Engel cooler. When a fish is raised by a teaser, he can quickly grab the rod and pitch the bait to the sighted fish. "I also have someone reel in the outside rigger to position it behind the teaser when a fish is sighted. Once the bait nears the teaser, just open the bail and let it drop back. Many strikes will occur as the bait drops below and away from the teaser."

His fishing strategy is aimed at maximizing fish catching opportunities from a smaller boat. "I have found that fishing the teasers and dredges in place of additional lines makes it easier to maneuver a boat with a narrow beam." Captain Billy explains that with a center console there is no need to clear all the lines when a fish is hooked. The angler can move to the bow and fight the fish from there. This maneuver allows two things to happen. First, the baits remain in the water and a chance of a double hookup is increased. Second, the captain can instruct another angler to clear the remaining lines as needed without getting in the way of the angler fighting the fish. On larger sportfishing vessels, the wide beam provides plenty of room for all that activity to occur, but on smaller boats it needs to be planned for.

Given the time and effort to go fishing, Captain Billy recommends rigging all baits before hitting the water. It takes much less time to set the spread if you have prepared in advance. He uses an Engel 65-quart cooler, complete with the Engel bait tray system. The cooler holds ice for up to 10 days, and the bait stays cold and fresh. "The advantage of having your baits rigged and ready to redeploy is completely evident when you get on a hot bite. You are not re-rigging baits in a rocking sea and missing what may be valuable fishing time. Given all the maintenance expense, supplies expense, and time spent preparing, it's a shame to miss out on the bite when it turns on."

Advance preparation can also pay off big time if a schoolie

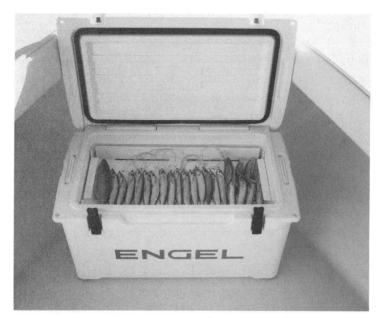

An Engel cooler with a bait tray system can save valuable time when the bite is hot. Photo by Capt. Billy Poertner.

dolphin is caught. This is when anglers want to have some cut bait already prepared in the cooler and pitch-rods ready. "If you get into schoolie dolphin, leave one in the water at all times and the school will stay next to the boat. Use cut bait with a 4/0 hook on 20-pound mono leader and cast to the schooled-up fish. The only other item you will need is a boat brush to scrub down the boat after the excitement settles down."

If you are not experienced with rigging bait, there are several good videos and books available on the market to learn bait rigging techniques. Some captains, including Captain Billy, will accompany you on your boat and instruct you on how to prepare bait, rig rods, set the spread, and execute other related techniques associated with open water fishing. It is a great way to shorten the learning curve and probably catch some fish while you're learning.

Captain Billy is also a proponent of doing something different if the bite is not happening. "When the fishing is slow, don't be afraid to change your tactics. If I am trolling my basic spread without success, I like to change things. I may bring in the squid teaser and use two Stripteaser dredges to cover more water deeper in the column. I may try a split tail mullet with a Sea Witch skirt to add variety to the spread. I may go all naked ballyhoo before it's over, especially if that is the only thing that got whacked on a given day."

Anglers interested in catching only bigger fish can take a lesson from competitive anglers. Tournaments are won by big fish, and tournament anglers are always on the lookout for improved techniques that target larger fish. Take wahoo for example. Tournament anglers say more wahoo are caught trolling at 7 to 10 knots, but bigger ones are caught at 14 to 25 knots. That is exactly why tournament boats troll faster, so if you have the patience to wait for bigger fish, try trolling faster.

Open water anglers should always be on the lookout for birds. "Birds diving on the water indicate that baitfish are being pushed up to the surface from below, and that usually means dolphin or tuna are nearby. Watch the way the birds are moving and try to get in front of them so you can position your baits so the fish are coming to you."

Captain Billy advises anglers to constantly watch for floating debris or weed lines that can hold bait and attract predators. He says, "Remember you don't have to be right on top of the weed lines. I try to stay 30 feet or so away from the debris for the first pass, because I am hoping to catch larger fish that may be hanging around the perimeter of the debris." He circles the debris or weed patch, getting closer with each pass. As he gets within casting distance of the weed line or debris, someone picks up the pitch-rod to be ready in case a fish is seen to cast to.

Targeting Kingfish

Kingfish are a popular and plentiful species all along Florida's East Coast, and they are a relatively easy fish to catch for beginning anglers. Captain Billy uses his 6½-foot rods equipped with Shimano TLD reels to target kingfish. "All of my reels are spooled with 20-pound-test line, and the drags are preset at 3 pounds of drag for strike position and 5 pounds for the additional strike position." If you are using a Star drag system instead of the lever drag, it's better to have the drag set lighter rather than heavier, especially when live bait fishing. "A lighter drag system allows the bait to become fully ingested by allowing the fish to run with the bait before too much resistance is encountered. A tighter drag could pull the bait out of the fish's mouth before the hook is set."

Live bait is preferred by experienced kingfish anglers in pursuit of smoker kings. The term *smoker kings* has different meanings to different people. "That is a question for the ages,"

Kingfish are popular and plentiful targets outside Sebastian Inlet. Photo courtesy of Capt. Billy Poertner.

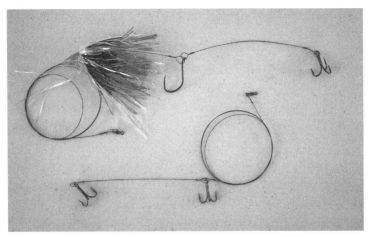

Stinger rigs for kingfish can be either naked (bottom) or skirted (top). Photo by Capt. Billy Poertner.

says Captain Billy. "Depending on whom you ask, you will probably get a different definition. I call a smoker king anything in the 40-pound category or bigger." Ask around, and you will find some anglers who consider a weight of mid-30s and above smoker kingfish. "I prefer live bait for smoker kings because experience has proven it to be the most productive. My bait of choice is blue runners or goggle-eyes. Large pilchards and threadfins are a good second choice. If catching the fish of a lifetime is your goal, live bait fishing is the way to go."

It is a good idea to have several rigs tied and ready to go when heading offshore in search of kingfish. "I use a traditional kingfish stinger rig. It is made by connecting an Owner 4/0 hook with a #4 VMC treble using #6 American Fishing Wire leader. The stinger is attached to my fishing line with a #4 or #6 wire and a SPRO swivel. This rig can be fished from a downrigger or a flatline. It can be fished naked or with a skirt." When rigging live bait, the first hook is placed through the nose, and the stinger rig is placed just behind the dorsal fin and under the spine.

Captain Billy deploys four or five lines while slow trolling for kings. If he is drift-fishing, he uses four or five lines on the windward side and may even fly a kite line or two on the leeward side. (See the kite fishing section in chapter 11). "If I'm slow trolling, I always set my shotgun bait first. Often referred to as the *wayback* line, it is run from the middle of the boat and at least 100 feet back. I then place a starboard rod around 75 feet and a port rod at 50 feet. These baits are staggered to make it easier to fish and make turns without the baits getting tangled." Captain Billy uses downriggers to fish two additional lines about 10 to 15 feet off the bottom. "I change the depth on the downrigger lines throughout the day. If I mark fish consistently at a particular depth, that is where I want the baits located. If the depth machine isn't marking anything, I just change depths to see if I can find a depth that the fish may be holding."

Captain Billy advises anglers to be aware of changing conditions during the day. The currents can cause your lines to tangle and spoil what could be productive fishing time. The wind can also blow your lines together, so be aware of changing conditions and make appropriate adjustments when needed. You may have to change the trolling direction or the distance behind the boat for each line in your spread.

If live bait fishing isn't your thing, there are several other ways to target kingfish. One option used by Captain Billy is to rig a split-tail mullet with a Sea Witch skirt. To fillet the mullet properly, start at the head and fillet the mullet as you would any other fish. When you get to the tail, angle your knife at about 60 degrees and cut through the center of the tail so both fillets will have the tail on them. "I rig the Sea Witch on #8 wire with two stainless steel 7/0 hooks. Use the heavier wire because you're trolling at a faster speed. The heavy wire also allows you to catch several fish on each rig before it is rendered useless."

Run the skirted split-tail mullet rigs on both the port and starboard outrigger and one on a #6 planer board. Captain Billy adds a second planer with a spoon attached when targeting kingfish. "I use about 30 to 35 feet of 100-pound mono leader from the planer to the spoon. Less than 30 feet of leader leaves the spoon too close to the planer, and fish may be spooked. If the leader is much longer than 35 feet, the spoon will rise in the water column and the advantage of the planer board is lost."

Kingfish can be targeted in a variety of locations. A strong outgoing tide or incoming tide at most inlets creates a nice rip and/or color change. Fishing the dirty or green side is a great tactic for targeting kingfish. Captain Billy says that "On an outgoing tide, the bait from the rivers or intercoastals is being pushed out of the inlet, and kings are attracted there to feed. They use the dirty water to ambush smaller baitfish." It's a good idea to fish both sides of the color change if the bite is slow in the dirty water.

Wrecks, reefs, and live bottom (hard bottom) are also great areas to target and locate kingfish. The first main concern for anglers targeting kingfish should be the water temperature in the area of the structure. "I try to fish in the mid to upper 70s for kingfish. There is no reason to fish water temperatures in the high 60s or lower if you want to catch a king." Even when the temperature range is right, a small variation can make a difference in a good day and a great day. Successful kingfish anglers keep a constant eye on the temperature gauge for any variation. "Sometimes a temperature break of 76.8 degrees to 77.4 degrees could be the difference you're looking for. I always note the temperature where strikes are occurring and fish are landed. I then try to keep my baits in close proximity to the structure in that temperature range."

The size of the structure can influence fishing strategy, too. If Captain Billy is fishing a small structure, he will troll across it several times in all directions. He also covers the open water around the structure. "The easiest way to do this is to find your spot on the fathometer and save the waypoint. Next use the navigation screen and cross the spot several times, like cutting a pie." If the current is pushing strong to the north, slow trolling may not work. Under these conditions, it is best to set a drift over the structure or anchor up and use a chum line to attract the fish. "I prefer to use these tactics only when there is a large structure on the bottom, I am marking fish or have already caught fish, and all other conditions are right. I would want to have good bait deployed, and I would want the water temperature to be in the preferred range."

A good kingfish bite can be exciting, and many fish can be caught over a short period of time. With a bag limit of two fish per person, Captain Billy reminds anglers to be conservation minded. "Our fishing resource is fragile, and we need to do all we can to preserve it. If anglers will keep only those fish they plan to eat, it will help ensure our fishery for many years to come."

Trolling for Wahoo

A screaming reel from a hooked-up wahoo is at the top of the excitement list for most offshore anglers. Wahoo are not caught nearly as often as kingfish, but when you hook one, you know you have a fight on your hands. Captain Billy has specific suggestions for targeting wahoo, and they start with planers. "I like using planers trolled at about 6 to 9 knots. I rig up with black and purple or pink and white Sea Witches for targeting wahoo. I get the heaviest I can find, 2 ounces or more. I use bonito strips, split-tail mullet, and also strips of mahi-mahi as my preferred bait." He admits that using strips of mahi-mahi sounds crazy to most anglers but insists that if

Wahoo are normally caught deeper in the water column than kingfish.
Photo by Capt. Chad Starling.

you are targeting wahoo, it increases the probability that you will hook one. "It's interesting," he says; "usually I get nothing but wahoo when using the mahi-mahi strips. When you hear a reel screaming, you will know that you have caught one."

Using planers to deploy the wahoo baits is preferred for several reasons. He says, "The planers are better to get the baits deep in the water column without the drift-back associated with downriggers." Planers can be used inline—meaning they are attached to line with which you are fishing—or tied to cleats. Use a #8 brass snap swivel and a rubber band to attach the fishing line to the tied-off planers. To use the swivel technique, let the baited mainline out around 25 to 40 feet behind the boat. Place a rubber band around the line, back through itself, and attach it to the swivel. Attach the snap swivel to the mono or cable that is attached to the deployed planer and begin to let out more line. The snap swivel will continue down the cable until it reaches the planer. Once a fish hits the bait, the rubber band will break and the angler can fight the fish without the planer.

Captain Billy says, "I rig several snap swivels and rubber bands ahead of time so it's a simple process to bait a new line and send it out. If you rinse the swivels in fresh water after use, they will last you several fishing trips." Captain Billy adds one piece of advice: "While fishing this way, I always run a skirted ballyhoo way back. I like the blue-and-white skirt the best. I always use skirted ballyhoo when trolling fast for wahoo. The skirt prevents the ballyhoo from washing out quickly."

As a final piece of advice he says to always check to see where the eastern and western edges of the Gulf Stream are before heading out. "The eastern edge can be quite a run, but the western edge is usually around the 20- to 26-mile mark. It's along the edge of the stream where you will find nice temperature changes and eddies. The chances of catching wahoo increase considerably in those areas."

Charter Captains

Captain Terry Lamielle

Hometown: Palm Bay, Florida
Business: Easy Days Guide Service
Phone number: 321-537-5346 or 321-725-7255
E-mail address: zaracrazy@aol.com
Web site: www.easydaysfishing.com

Captain Lamielle's advice to visiting anglers: Any angler fishing an area for the first time should take it slow until he or she gets familiar with the waters, or hire a local guide who has spent many hours on the waters to school himself in the best techniques, lures, and locations for specific times of the year. Don't fish all seasons as if they were the same. Approach a new fishing destination by researching it before your trip. Check with local tackle shops, friends, or coworkers or attend a couple seminars presented by local guides. Fishing maps can also be of great help. Maps show underwater structure such as creek channels, wrecks, and contour breaks. Don't forget to mark the places where you catch fish so you can return in the future. When on the water, have courtesy for other anglers and try to make everyone's fishing trip a pleasurable one. In the end, it is time on the water that makes the difference between highly successful anglers and average anglers.

Captain Billy Poertner

> Hometown: Hobe Sound, Florida
> Business: Imagine That Fishing Charters
> Phone number: 772-245-8229
> E-mail address: captbilly@imaginethatfishingcharters.com
> Web site: www.imaginethatfishingcharters.com

Captain Poertner's advice to visiting anglers: New anglers to an area should pick a few fishing locations and get to know them well. With the constant changing of fuel prices and the economy the way it is, you can spend a lot of money chasing fish. My grandfather once told me, "you can't catch fish if you don't have a hook in the water." I recommend concentrating on good locations and fishing them thoroughly. I spend most of my tournament days fishing, not doing the run and gun method. Don't get me wrong; you can catch a lot of fish that way, but I honestly believe that learning the area you wish to fish will pay big dividends and eliminate some of the run and gun fishing that some people do.

Captain Tom Van Horn

Hometown: Orlando Area, Florida
Business: Mosquito Coast Fishing Charters
Phone number: 407-416-1187 cell
E-mail address: mosquitocoast@cfl.rr.com
Web site: www.irl-fishing.com

Captain Van Horn's advice to visiting anglers: Visiting anglers should visit a local bait shop and ask for advice. He suggests Black Dog Bait and Tackle on Melbourne Beach. Tackle shops are in the business of selling bait, and if they can help you catch fish, they will sell more bait. There is nothing that beats local experts for telling you exactly where, how, and when to fish. Once the fishing location is reached, pay careful attention to the local anglers fishing there. In most cases, they will also share their fishing knowledge freely. When fishing in the lagoon and estuaries, watch for pompano skipping in the wake behind your boat. When they are frightened by the approaching boat, pompano will come to the surface and skip on their side like a rock skipped across the water. When you start seeing multiple pompano skip, you are in the right spot. Pompano are often overlooked as a fun fish to catch, and they are very tasty on the dinner plate.

Area Hotspots

Offshore, Sebastian Inlet anglers can easily locate Pelican Flats and The Pines on a Top Spot map. Kingfish, cobia, and dolphin are common targets. The large flat just inside the inlet will produce trout, reds, snook, pompano, and more. Look for the Highway 1 Bridge over the Sebastian River and follow the river inland for some great snook and tarpon fishing along the shorelines and the docks. When the seas are calm, small boats can use the inlet to access super redfish catching outside the inlet. Just take all the necessary precautions, because Sebastian Inlet is known as a treacherous inlet to navigate.

Fishing-Friendly Lodging and Glorious Galleys

Marsh Landings Restaurant

> 44 North Broadway Street
> Fellsmere, FL 32948-6601
> Phone number: 772-571-8622

Go back to pioneer days and dine in a historic setting. Frog legs, catfish, gator tail, fried green tomatoes, and swamp cabbage. Near Sebastian. Recommended by Capt. Terry Lamielle.

Squid Lips OverWater Grill

> 1660 Indian River Drive
> Sebastian, FL 32958
> Phone number: 772-589-3828

The service is always great, and many days they have live music. Plenty of dock space accessible on the Indian River. There is a cleaning table on the dock, and for a small fee they will cook your fish for you. Recommended by Capt. Billy Poertner.

Bait and Tackle

Honest John's Fish Camp

> 750 Old Florida Trail
> Melbourne Beach, FL 32951
> Phone number: 321-727-2923

Go back in time to this quaint little spot on the Indian River. Bait and tackle, light refreshments. Boat ramp, boat storage, canoe and kayak rentals. Recommended by Capt. Terry Lamielle.

Black Dog Bait and Tackle

207 Ocean Avenue
Melbourne, FL 32951
Phone number: 321-725-1200

Black Dog offers a full line of live and frozen baits plus rods, reels, and tackle. Plenty of surf fishing gear. Open seven days a week; if you are running late, just call. They will wait. Recommended by Capt. Tom Van Horn.

Fishing Lessons for Life—Resuscitating Fish

If the decision has been made to release a fish, don't just throw it back into the water. A landed fish is a stressed fish and needs some time to recover. If you stop and think about it, fish really

Take all the time required to resuscitate a fish before releasing it back into the wild.

do have a resilience to the handling they get from anglers, and they often swim away from the encounter to be caught another day. Once the hook has been removed and the photos taken, resuscitation is often necessary to execute a successful live release. It is an investment in the future of fishing to take the time to help a stressed fish recover before being released back into the wild. Larger predators have a sense of knowing when one of their prey is stressed, and they have no qualms about taking an easy meal.

Everyone recognizes the acronym CPR as standing for a method of reviving humans and animals from cardiac arrest. In the angling world, the letters have come to mean Catch-Photo-Release. It is the release part of this process that needs the full attention of every angler. Any fish that show an inability to remain upright in the water because of exhaustion should be resuscitated. Stressed fish need to be positioned so that oxygenated water runs through the gills to get the fish breathing again.

Smaller fish can be placed in a livewell for a short period of time to help them recover. Running the aerator will increase the oxygen level and also produce a flow of water that will promote moving the water through the gills of a tired fish, helping it to recuperate. Once the fish revives, it can be released back into its own environment with a pretty good expectation of complete recovery. The larger the fish, the more effort needed to reach this successful conclusion.

Especially with big fish, they will be exhausted after losing a long, hard fight with an angler. At the end of the fight their blood has lost the life-giving properties of oxygen and needs to be replaced. If released immediately, the fish are likely to roll over, belly-up, and just die without proper attention. They just don't have enough energy left in their bodies to swim and re-oxygenate themselves.

Many anglers still use a method of resuscitation that moves the fish forward and backward to force water through the gills in both directions. Recent scientific studies suggest this procedure is not the most efficient method for reviving a fish. The studies show that a forward-only motion is most beneficial to the fish. The resuscitation process must transfer oxygen from the water to the bloodstream. To do this efficiently, the water must flow from front to back. In other words, the water needs to enter the mouth and exit the gills. Savvy anglers are now promoting a method that grabs the fish by the lower jaw and moves it in an S-shaped or figure-8 pattern. If it is a toothy fish, a lip-gripper tool can be used to complete the revival. Either of these patterns ensures the front to back water flow necessary for efficient entry of oxygen into the blood stream.

There is no rule of thumb for how long it takes to revive a fish; it depends on how long the fight lasted and how much oxygen was lost in the battle. The process must continue until the fish gains enough energy to swim off on its own. The fish will indicate when it is ready to go. Once its strength returns, it will kick strongly to escape your grasp. At this point simply let it swim away.

Keep an eye on the fish until it swims out of sight and keep an eye on the surface even longer. Sometimes resuscitated fish will swim off, only to resurface, belly up, because they were not fully revived. If resurfacing occurs, try to retrieve the fish and start the process over again. Be sure the fish has a good strong kick before you release it a second time.

Large gamefish like tarpon and billfish can be resuscitated by using the boat. Get a good firm grip on the fish and have the captain put the boat in forward gear. Idle along slowly, pulling the fish alongside the boat causing water to rush through the gills to provide the life-saving oxygenation.

As catch-and-release fishing becomes more popular among anglers, the use of proper resuscitation techniques is critical to fish mortality rates. Anglers should develop a code of conduct that encourages the use of best techniques for releasing fish. As anglers take responsibility for their impact on each individual fish, the whole fishery resource will benefit. If kids learn the importance of resuscitating fish before release, it is another conservation technique they can use for the rest of their lives.

PART 3

Florida's Treasure Coast

8

~~~~~~~~~~~~~~~~~

Vero Beach and Fort Pierce

Vero Beach is the beginning of Florida's Treasure Coast. The name relates to the 1715 wreck of the Spanish treasure fleet when a hurricane struck the area. The entire fleet of eleven ships was lost, and only five have since been located. The remaining six linger in the ocean depths as the target of treasure hunters to this day. Citizens have long reported finding coins and jewelry washing up on local beaches, and treasure hunters can be found searching the area with sophisticated equipment. The wrecks occurred along the barrier islands that separate the Indian River from the Atlantic Ocean.

Fort Pierce, one of the oldest cities in Florida, became the hub of industry on the Treasure Coast with the opening of the East Coast Railroad in the 1920s. Commercial fishing and fish processing and canning plants provided jobs for the local residents. Pineapple and citrus production increased once the railroad provided the necessary transportation to move the products to market. Unfortunately, the pineapple industry collapsed after World War II, but the citrus industry continues to this day. Indian River citrus became world famous as the benchmark by which all other citrus products are judged.

Today the area is well connected to the rest of the world by the St. Lucie County International Airport, the Port of Fort Pierce, Interstate 95, Highway 70, and the Florida Turnpike. The region is home to the Smithsonian Marine Station, Harbor Branch Oceanographic Institute, Indian River Community College, and the Manatee Observation and Education Center.

Fort Pierce Inlet offers plenty of inshore and offshore fishing action for visiting anglers. The offshore bite is similar to that at St. Lucie Inlet, and the offshore fishing discussed in the next chapter applies to Fort Pierce also.

Characteristics of the Fishing Area

The Treasure Coast provides anglers a wide choice of fishing areas. Captain Joe Ward operates Captain Joe's River Charters in Fort Pierce. He says area visitors are usually surprised by the variety of fishing opportunities the area offers. Grass flats make up a large portion of the fishing grounds. Area flats are very large and can range in water depth from less than 1 foot to 5 feet. There are a wide variety of grasses providing habitat and food to the region's fish. Turtle grass and manatee grass are the two major habitats anglers will find in the area. Turtle grass can be recognized by its wide flat blades reaching as high as 30 inches from the lagoon's bottom. Manatee grass can be identified by its slim cylindrical blades. It is no larger than a string of spaghetti and reaches a maximum height of only about 12 inches. Locating either of these area grasses can increase fishing success.

Given the area's tidal flow, the tidal cuts found on the flats create great fishing spots. Fishing the cuts should be coordinated with the tides for best results. Captain Charlie Conner operates Captain Charlie's Fish Tales Charters in the Fort Pierce area. He says, "Tidal cuts are natural waterways carved out over time by the moving tides. The cuts provide the perfect ambush point for predator fish." Determine where the cut runs and how the water is moving through it and use that information to your advantage. Cast up-tide so your bait or lure will travel across the shallow flats and drop off the edges of the cuts. Fish are lazy and will sit facing into the tide waiting for a meal to drift to them. "I don't always have a choice in the tides, but love the first part of the outgoing tide to fish. I also like to work along the edges while drifting along with the tides. When fishing the tidal cuts, I prefer moving water. Incoming or outgoing tide is not as important as the fact that the water is moving through the cut."

Dock anglers certainly won't be disappointed in the Vero to Fort Pierce area. Plenty of boat docks line the Indian River shoreline, mixing manmade structure with nature's grass flats. Combinations of the two make perfect ambush points for many species of fish. Popular fish species like redfish, snook, and seatrout are the likely outcome of tossing artificial or natural bait under or around the docks. Don't be surprised, however, if you hook up with flounder or snapper when fishing the docks.

The Fort Pierce Inlet offers rock jetties, more docks, and a turning basin as additional fish holding structures. The jetties can be fished from shore as well as from powerboats and even paddle craft. The inlet is famous for its snook fishing, which is good all the way from the entrance, characterized by rock jetties, west along the docks lining the inlet. Many of the docks are lighted, attracting monster snook to feed under the lights. The Ship Turning and Docking Basin averages 25 feet deep, providing yet another choice for area anglers. The Turning Basin is a particularly good wintertime alternative as fish seek the comfort of the deeper water.

Two Fort Pierce bridges provide easy access to more good fishing. The South Bridge in Fort Pierce has catwalks on both sides of the bridge for anglers without access to a boat. Seaway Drive crosses the Indian River over the South Bridge and takes shorebound anglers to the south end of the inlet. There is easy access and parking on both sides of the bridge and a boat ramp at the northwest corner of the bridge. First-time anglers can enjoy a good fishing experience from the catwalks while learning firsthand about the tides, currents, and species of fish the area has to offer. The North Bridge, known as the North Causeway, provides fishing only from the bank or from

Huge seatrout roam the grass flats around Vero Beach and Fort Pierce. Photo by Capt. Charlie Conner.

the bridge itself. Captain Conner says, "The North Bridge has always been productive for snook around the fenders. On the east side, visitors will find a boat ramp and local park with nice facilities to spend the day fishing with the family."

Channel edges and channel markers throughout the river can hold a number of species during the year. Just like the cuts, the channel markers are more productive when the water is moving. Anglers and scientist agree that Fort Pierce is near the end of the range for catching redfish on Florida's East Coast. As anglers travel south, the redfishing gets tougher, the snook fishing gets better, and the seatrout get huge.

Captain Rob Ward is an expert offshore angler and son of Captain Joe Ward. He describes offshore fishing out of the Fort Pierce Inlet as some of the best all-around offshore fishing on the east coast. "From bottom fishing for snapper and grouper to trolling for kingfish, sailfish, dolphin, and cobia, this part of

Florida's East Coast is second to none." Regardless of the targeted fish, the numerous wrecks and reefs in the area offer the perfect setting to bend a rod with the possibility of a trophy offshore fish.

The Inshore Bite—Gator Trout

Trout fishing in the Fort Pierce area has long been an attraction to big-fish anglers. The locale is well known for large trout that can exceed 30 inches in length. Big trout can be caught all year long, but the most productive times are spring to autumn, when baitfishes abound in the river. Captain Conner says, "Depending on the time of year, you can find big seatrout on the grass flats. Spring, summer, and fall, the trout are feeding in shallow water from 1 to 4 feet deep. As long as the bait schools are prevalent on the river, the big trout will be nearby."

Wintertime brings additional challenges by adding water temperature to the variables affecting fishing success. Cold weather fishing strategy revolves around finding the warmest water. A couple of degrees' change in water temperature can make all the difference when targeting trout on the flats. "In the wintertime when the water temperatures drop, look to deeper flats in the 5- to 7-foot range." Those deeper flats provide a comfort level the fish are seeking in cold weather periods.

The best locations for spotted seatrout on the flats are sand holes where turtle grass or manatee grass grows up around a spot and creates an edge. The sand holes are washed out by the tides and are generally deeper than the surrounding grassy area. The trout will lie in the sand spot and wait for the tides to push baitfish across the holes. "Fish are generally lazy and want the most food for the least amount of effort." Big trout are usually loners, but they can be anywhere on any given grass flat. Captain Conner advises anglers to "Work deeper sand holes and near the edges of the flats to find the big boys. They will feed in shallow water at first light or at sunset, but during the day you can find them sitting where the food source will come to them."

To maximize your opportunity to catch gator trout, Captain Conner says, "Learn to read the water. My eyes are constantly scanning the water around me to see what is happening on the flats." High on his list is taking the time to learn the bottom structure of the area to be fished. "Learning the bottom of the areas that you want to fish is important in finding out what the water will do on the tides and where the fish will likely be waiting for their next meal. Since most flats are very large, taking time to learn the bottom contours will narrow the possibilities you have to cover." The conditions to be looking for include where water flows with the tides, where drop-offs signal the edges of a flat, tidal cuts that will carry the tide and food across the flats, and deep sand holes that will hold big fish on any tide.

Captain Charlie says, "It takes time to learn, but it will be time well spent to know the bottom layout of any flat. Success is a result of patience. The more time you spend looking, the more activity you will see." Sometimes you see fish, sometimes you see diving birds, or sometimes you see bait. He goes on to explain that anglers should always be looking for bait. "Look for the bait, and you will find fish. Many kinds of baitfish inhabit the river, and fishing around schools of bait is one of the best ways to find fish."

One of his favorite fishing seasons is summer, when acres of glass minnows invade area waters. "Every fish likes to eat glass minnows. When you look out over the water and it appears to be raining in certain spots, it will most likely be glass minnows. You are seeing little dimples in the water made by the swimming bait. Fish around the edges of the dimples, and you will catch trout."

Expert trout anglers fish different water depths during the day. "If you always expect fish to be in one area at one depth, you will find that often you are not as successful as when you fish different depths." If the trout are not biting, change lures, try other areas, and work different water depths to locate fish. "I like to drift across a flat when prospect fishing. It allows me to cover a very large area and find where the trout are feeding and what they are feeding on."

Another requirement for catching gator trout is stealth. Anglers must approach the fishing area in an unobtrusive and undetectable manner for best results. The big gator trout are much more in tune with their surroundings than the smaller schoolie trout that will be found closer to the boat and less likely to bolt at an unexpected sound. Captain Conner advises anglers to practice stealth as a habit, not just on occasion. "Approaching flats with stealth is essential. Noise in shallow water carries a long way and can effectively eliminate your chances of catching any fish in any area, let alone a gator. Move across flats slowly and keep the noise down. Banging a hatch or dropping a lure can make the fish scatter quickly. Enough said!"

Dock fishing is no different from flats fishing when it comes to stealth. Docks should be approached quietly. Captain Conner says, "When fishing docks, approach them quietly and keep as far away as possible to reduce the chance of scaring off the fish. Fish will sit under and around the front of docks, so just get close enough to be able to cast to them." He also advises anglers to fish with patience. "Cast your lure or bait under the dock and let it sit. Don't be hasty to start your retrieve. The longer it is under the dock, the more chance you have of catching fish."

Some artificial bait is designed to be fished slowly. Captain Conner recommends D.O.A. Shrimp for gator trout around the docks. "D.O.A. Shrimp are excellent lures to work around docks. To increase your chances of catching a big trout, cast it under the dock and work it out slowly." He says if he had his druthers he would never bring the bait out from under or around the dock until he was hooked up. "Just give it a short, quick pop to move it and let the lure settle down right back

Make up to 15 casts to a fishy-looking dock before moving to the next one.

under the dock without pulling it out." He also likes D.O.A. Terror Eyz for fishing the docks. They imitate small baitfish, and they catch big trout. Regardless of the bait, he suggests making 10 to 15 casts before moving to another dock.

Determining which dock to fish at a particular time depends on water depths, time of day, and tides. Boat docks have many depths depending on their location in the river, and it is important to log which docks are deep and which ones are shallow. Captain Conner prefers to fish the deeper docks during the day once the sun has begun to heat up the shallow water, causing the fish to seek cooler surroundings. Shallow docks are best fished at first light. Docks are a favorite ambush point for many fish, so don't be surprised if your search for gator trout results in hooking a few other species like redfish and snook, too.

Use the tides to your advantage when fishing around docks. "Fishing up-tide around docks allows anglers to cast or drift their bait or lure under the dock and keep it there. Have a couple different rods set up for different lures or baits so you don't have to waste time making changes during the best fishing time. The rule of thumb is *match the hatch*, so try to determine what the trout are eating and choose a lure accordingly." Pinfish and pigfish are also bountiful throughout the summer, so try a D.O.A. Terror Eyz or live pigfish for big trout. "It's one way of using the tried and true method of matching your bait to what the fish are feeding on." Experienced anglers develop a pretty good idea of what bait to use at a particular time of the year. Being able to change colors or bait profiles can make the difference between success and failure in catching gator trout.

Equipment choice for gator trout is the same as general flats fishing; it does not have to be heavy-duty tackle. A medium or a medium-heavy spinning rod will fill the bill for gator trout. Use the medium on the open flats and step up to the medium-heavy around docks where a little more backbone is beneficial for turning heads and starting a big trout in the right direction. Captain Conner's choice of reels on the flats is a Shimano Stradic 2500. "The 2500, spooled with 10- to 15-pound-test braided line, will perform well for most any fish you encounter on the flats. The other advantage is that its light weight will not tire you out during a full day's fishing excursion." He cites the strength and abrasion-resistant properties of braid as a great advantage to anglers. He also likes the sensitivity of the braid in transmitting the actual bite of a fish to the angler. "I love using braided line. Ten to 15-pound-test braided line provides you all the strength you need and also gives you fantastic feel in the line. You will find that you miss fewer fish because you can feel the fish pick up the lure or bait."

A slightly heavier outfit should be used around docks. "I use a medium-heavy rod that is rated for 10- to 20-pound line. A reel similar to a Stradic 4000 with 20-pound braid and a 25-pound fluorocarbon leader will give you a little more advantage when pulling fish out from under a dock." He reminds anglers to always check the drag setting regularly, and don't be afraid to test the backbone of the rod when fishing around docks. "You have seconds to turn a big fish hooked under a dock, so adjust your drag to a level that will increase your chances of wrestling it out from under the dock."

Anglers just beginning their quest for a gator trout should start with a popping cork, according to Captain Conner. "For new anglers in search of trout, I always recommend starting out with a popping cork and live shrimp." He adds a popping cork to his mainline, followed by a fluorocarbon leader. "Fluorocarbon leaders are a must for targeting big trout. They resist abrasion and are relatively invisible in the water." A circle hook or even a jig head can be tied to the leader, which should be slightly shorter than the water depth being fished. The popping cork set-up, baited with live shrimp, is cast along the grass flats and worked with short jerks created by the wrist to cause the cork to pop. The noise sounds like feeding fish, and the trout are attracted to the area. Captain Conner describes the popping cork rig as a prospecting tool to help anglers find fish by slowly working it across the flats. If you spot a sand hole on the flat, cast the popping cork past the sand hole and slowly pop it back across the hole. Gator trout are predator fish and will ambush the live shrimp when it appears in the hole.

Once the popping cork technique has been perfected with live shrimp, Captain Conner suggests changing to artificial bait on the float. "To take the next step in learning to fish a grass flat for gator trout, tie on a D.O.A. plastic Shrimp to your popping cork and work it vigorously across the flat. You will be surprised at what you can catch this way." He says the technique is the same and once mastered eliminates the need for live bait. Paddle tail plastic baits or even plastic jerkbaits will work well under the cork, too.

In addition to the plastic shrimp, Captain Conner likes to use plastic jerkbaits, topwater lures, and suspending lures on the flats for gator trout. "When using jerkbaits, I like a light

Topwater and suspending baits work well in low-light conditions for gator trout. Photo by Capt. Charlie Conner.

jig head, preferably a ¹⁄₁₆ ounce. D.O.A. makes what I consider the perfect jig head for fishing the flats. With short, slow jerks along the bottom, it will jump up and over the grass. Most bites will come on the fall of the lure, so always be ready for that soft pickup of a trout." This is where the braided line gives a distinct advantage to the angler. Light bites will be detected more easily when using braided line.

Topwater and suspending lures are a great choice early in the morning or late evenings. A combination of low light conditions and the noise from these lures entices any fish, including the gator trout, to take a whack at a perceived intruder or potential dinner. The topwater baits create commotion on the water, depending on the action created by the angler, and the explosive strike of a gator trout on a topwater lure is as exciting as it gets. Suspending lures usually make noise, too, with a built-in rattle to help attract the predators. "Work these lures at different speeds to find out which speed produces a strike, and then repeat the action. On windy days, I like suspending baits instead of topwater baits. They swim just under the surface, producing a profile that is more visible to the fish on a windy day than topwater lures."

There are numerous brands of good topwater and suspending lures on the market, so Captain Conner recommends spending some time in local tackle shops to get their input on what lures work best in the area you will be fishing. His personal preference is MirrOlure and Rapala brands. He says, "If I could only have one topwater lure for gator trout, it would be a Rapala Skitterwalk. Nothing can get a big trout angrier than walking the dog with a Skitterwalk. Change the retrieve until you find what they are wanting on a given day. Work it fast and hard or slow and easy and get great topwater results." He claims color isn't as important as presentation. "Work the Skitterwalk with rod tip high or low, but be sure you achieve that side-to-side sway as you pop it across the surface."

Captain Charlie's top choice for suspending lures is a MirrOlure. "My all-time favorite bait for gator trout is the MirrOlure MirrOdine." It comes in two sizes and a variety of effective colors to match the hatch. By sharply popping it, the angler can make the lure dart erratically just under the surface of the water. On windy days when a topwater lure does not work so well, he turns to the MirrOdine to go subsurface. "I call them my windy day topwater lures because of their proven effectiveness on windy days."

The Inshore Bite—Snapper and Grouper

The Fort Pierce Inlet, area bridges, channel edges along the ICW, and docks are favorite fishing locations for anglers seeking grouper and snapper. Captain Joe Ward says, "For the snapper, I would fish along the channel edges and around structure such as bridges, rock piles, and docks. For grouper I like the inlet, the Intracoastal Waterway, around rocky structures, and under local bridges."

Anglers will catch both mangrove snapper and grouper while fishing the area, but targeting a specific one requires different setups, according to Captain Joe. "Snapper rigs can be light outfits, but when grouper are on your mind, you need to beef up the tackle. You could hook a really big one."

Snapper Fishing

The snapper Captain Joe refers to are mangrove snapper. Offshore mangroves can grow larger than 15 pounds. The Florida record is 16 pounds 8 ounces. The inshore variety is regularly caught at 1 to 5 pounds. They usually appear grayish red but can change to a copperish color. Their official name is gray snapper, with some anglers referring to them as mangos. Many anglers like to target mangrove snapper for the dinner table because they have a very white and tasty meat. Mangrove snapper tend to congregate in schools, so once you find one

Inshore snapper weighing 1 to 5 pounds are regularly caught on crustaceans and small baitfish.

there are normally more around. In their natural environment, they feed on crustaceans and small fish.

Mangrove snapper got their name from the mangrove trees that provide cover and food, especially for the juvenile fish. They hide in the roots of shoreline mangroves looking for their next meal and avoiding larger predators in the food chain. The snapper part of their name designates them as part of the larger snapper family, which includes almost 100 species worldwide. The name could just as easily come from the fact that they are very aggressive toward anglers removing a hook. If you ever get bit by one, you remember it, because they snap down with canine-like teeth and don't let go. It's sure to be a bloodletting experience. They should always be handled with caution. The bigger ones venture out from the mangrove roots seeking an ambush point to surprise their next meal, and that's why Captain Joe likes to target structure.

Mangroves are known to be notorious bait stealers, so be sure to bring plenty of bait. Captain Joe likes shrimp or silver jennies. The silver jenny is a cousin to the striped mojarra and can be caught in the Fort Pierce area with a cast net, usually over sand bottom. The shrimp are hooked in the traditional way, crossways under the horn. The jennies are best used live, hooked on their bottom side near the tail. If they are large enough, they can be hooked through the lips. Either way the jennies make a great snapper bait and are available year-round.

When Captain Joe Ward targets snapper he prefers to use a medium-weight rod with a sensitive tip to feel the bite. He chooses a small-sized spinning reel spooled with 10-pound braid. "For snapper fishing, light mainline will work just fine. I like to add about 36 inches of 20-pound fluorocarbon leader before tying on a #2 long shank hook and a ½- to 1-ounce weight." Snapper can be very leader shy, and the fluorocarbon leader is less visible in the water than mono and will normally produce more bites. Captain Joe likes the long shank hook simply because experience has shown it to be most effective on snapper.

The size of the weight will depend on the current in the location you are fishing. The stronger the current, the larger the weight should be. The idea is to pull the bait near the bottom and keep it there without it lifting in the current. Once the bait is found by a snapper, there is often a feeding frenzy, with competitive fish trying to get in on the feed bag. Concentrate your fishing along the channel edges or near any structure with current running over it. Captain Joe says the time of day for fishing snapper doesn't matter if you have other important ingredients. "If you find live structure and a moving tide, the time of day really doesn't matter. Mangos can be caught all day long."

A good fishing location for larger snapper can be found by trying various spots along the ICW channel edge or fish-loving structure like the bridges, rock piles, or docks. Captain Joe advises anglers to keep an eye on the sonar and watch for structure when prospecting in the river. Underwater structure can pay off big with snapper, but it is harder to locate than bridges or docks. Any structure becomes home to barnacles and other marine growth that attracts small baitfish, which in turn attract the snappers.

Once you find a concentration of snapper, be prepared for a hard bite, but don't set the hook hard. Captain Joe advises, "Once the first snapper takes the bait count to 3 then pull—not a hard hook-set, but a lifting motion." If the fish is not hooked on the first pull, the sight of the bait slowly getting away will often elicit a more aggressive second bite and the hookup is successful.

Some anglers use chumming techniques to rile up the mangos and start a feeding frenzy. The chum tends to make the fish more aggressive and less inclined to refuse a baited hook as the fish compete for the offered morsels of cut-up fish chum. A frozen bag of chum can be purchased from a local bait and tackle store and hung over the side, up-current from the targeted structure. Once the feeding starts, a baited hook can be

Mango snappers can also be caught on well-placed artificial baits. This one succumbed to a D.O.A. Shrimp. Photo by Jerry McBride.

drifted into the chum line with a pretty good expectation of a bite.

Mangrove snapper are famous for their bait-stealing ability, but once hooked they are very aggressive fighters. The mango's fight is much harder than you would first expect from a fish its size. Anglers have to be on their toes to get the fish away from the structure when using light tackle. Its brothers, sisters, and cousins have no qualms about taking the bait for themselves, sometimes taking it out of the mouth of the first fish to get it. This behavior causes hooked fish to generally head straight for the structure once they have food locked in their teeth. It is a natural instinct for mangos to protect their meal and eat it in the privacy of a hideaway in the structure. The result for the unsuspecting angler is a hang-up or a cutoff. If the structure is hooked, open the bail and let the line go slack. Sometimes the hook will free itself, or, if there is any bait left on the hook, another fish will strike and dislodge it, allowing the angler to retrieve and rebait.

Artificial lures can also be used to target mangrove snapper. One good choice is the D.O.A. Tiny Terror Eyz. It simulates a small crab, one of the mangrove's favorite meals. Anglers should fish the lure close to the structure; the possibility of snags and hang-ups is high, but the satisfaction of fooling a nice mangrove snapper makes the effort worthwhile. D.O.A. Shrimp will also bring some nice mangroves to the boat. Regardless of the bait selected, natural or artificial, anglers are thrilled with the fight of the scrappy mangrove snapper and delighted with the taste on a dinner plate. According to Captain Joe, "One of the best things about mangrove snapper is their taste when served with homemade tartar sauce."

Mangrove snapper are also a great fish to target with kids. Once found, they are usually schooled up and can provide non-stop action for the kids. Use a small hook and small bait for some continuous action.

Fort Pierce—Grouper in the River

Fishing for grouper in the Indian River is not all that different from bottom fishing in the ocean. The fish will be around heavy structure and want to take the angler right back to it when hooked. Once a big grouper gets in a hole and spreads its fins, it's pretty hard to get it out. Anglers need to turn the fish's head before it gets locked up in its hole. Captain Joe advises anglers to beef up the rod and reel and use heavier line to keep from being cut off or hung up by a big fish. "I would use medium to heavy tackle and up to 60-pound-test line when targeting river grouper." Some grouper are found right alongside the mangrove snapper, but you won't get the big ones out using light snapper tackle. The best spots for grouper are the Intracoastal Waterway along the channel edges, rock piles in the inlet and river, and the area bridges.

Trolling can also be an effective method in the Intracoastal along the channel edges. Use your favorite deep diving lure

Diving lures are controlled by the size of the lip. Use long lips for gags in deeper water and shorter lips for shallower water.

and pull it along the edge of the channel. There are areas of limestone edges that were carved out when the Corps of Engineers dredged the Intracoastal. The grouper will be nearby. Keep an eye on the sonar as you troll and mark rock piles to fish later. The one drawback with trolling is an occasional lost lure because the treble hook will snag some of the structure, and you might not always get the lure back. One trick to avoid hang-ups is to remove the trebles and replace them with circle hooks—they are not as likely to snag.

Captain Joe has his favorite color for trolling. "I like the deep diving plugs with orange/yellow colors for trolling the ICW. Set the drag tight, so you can pull them away from the structure when they strike." The bigger the lip, the deeper these divers go. Use different sizes to fish different depths as you prospect different areas to find where they are holding. Once a strike occurs, try to keep the bait in that level of the water column.

Fishing rock piles in the river or in the inlet will produce plenty of gag grouper, but live bait is the preferred offering here. Captain Joe adds a 5/0 hook to a 60-pound fluorocarbon leader on his heavy rigs to target the grouper around the piles. He will downsize the leader if not getting bites because the fish can be leader shy. Downsize in small increments to find the size you can get by with. The leader should be as strong as possible but not a detriment to getting bites. Captain Joe's selection of weight will depend on the current: as small as possible, but big enough to hold the bait on the bottom. The weight can be as small as 1 ounce or as large as 8 ounces, so be prepared for the current you find and rig enough weight to keep the bait on the bottom. His preferred bait for grouper is live pinfish. Pins can be caught by hook and line, captured in fish traps, or caught with a cast net. Regardless of how you get them, they are candy to the grouper.

The same tackle and same technique can be used around the area bridges to target grouper. Determine the size sinker you need for the current and bait with a pinfish. Captain Joe suggests fishing around the bridge fenders for best results. "A good grouper in the river is from keeper size of 24 inches to about 32 inches. My personal best is 31 inches, weighing in at 9 pounds." He also advises anglers to find and fish structure. When the grouper bite is not on, move to the next location.

The Offshore Bite—On the Bottom

Like many offshore fish species, snapper and grouper have been named as overfished species and a closure is being considered at the time of this writing. This rule does not mean you can't catch them, but you certainly don't want to keep them if regulations prohibit it. As more and more fish become subject to intermittent closures, be sure to check current regulations to determine which fish are legal to catch and which are not. When a closure exists, simply practice catch-photo-release (CPR), enjoy the fight, and send them back to the deep.

Even with closures on popular fish, there are many alternative catches that can replace them on the dinner table.

Much of Captain Rob Ward's offshore fishing relates to reefs. "Reef fishing is an all-year-long activity. Grouper fishing is great in the winter, and snapper fishing is good during the summer months. Just be sure to check the current regulations." He says summer can also be outstanding for kingfish as a great break from the bottom fishing. Reefs are great fishing spots because they are natural habitat for the baitfish that predators seek. The locations of reefs are easily obtained on local area maps and Internet sites.

A typical bottom fishing excursion will include rods specifically rigged for snapper and grouper as well as rods for the kingfish. Captain Rob prefers 7-foot 9-inch Star Rods for the snapper and grouper. He adds a Shimano Speedmaster reel spooled with 30-pound Momoi Blue Diamond monofilament line. A 5/0 live bait hook is used for snapper and an 11/0 circle hook for grouper. Captain Rob's leaders are made from 50- to 60-pound fluorocarbon. "The length of the leader will depend on water clarity. In dirty water I like about 6 to 8 feet. If the water is clear, I lengthen the leader substantially, going to 25 or 30 feet." When the bite is slow, anglers should consider a longer leader. The longer leader gives more of an illusion of free swimming bait and will sometimes make the difference between failure and success.

For those times when he takes a break from bottom fishing, Captain Rob has a couple of 7-foot Crowder kingfish rods on board. He spools his Avet reels with 20-pound Momoi Blue Diamond mono especially for the kings. Unlike braid, mono stretches and prevents early breakoffs from hard-hitting king mackerel. The terminal tackle for kings includes #4 wire leader and 4x treble hooks. He can use some of the same bait he gathers for bottom fishing on the kingfish rigs.

There is no other way to say it. Captain Rob is a live bait

fisherman at heart. "I love to fish with live bait. I use a variety of baits, depending on what is available. The common ones are sardines, cigar minnows, thread fin herring, and greenies." All these baits can be obtained using Sabiki rigs or cast-netting (see chapter 11). "When bait is available on the beach, I will cast-net them using a 14-foot cast-net with 1-inch mesh. My net weighs 26 pounds to get it down over the bait quickly. After that, all you need is a good livewell to keep the bait fresh." Captain Rob will continue gathering bait until he has at least 10 to 12 dozen. "I hate running out of bait when the bite finally turns on."

Prefishing activities include tying several extra leaders. When fishing reefs for snapper and grouper, you will lose some terminal tackle in the process. Snapper and grouper love to come out of hiding to grab a bite and then run back to the safety of their rocky lairs. Tying leaders at the dock adds fishing time on the water. "When going bottom fishing, I generally make 10 to 15 extra leaders before I leave the dock. Then, I head to some favorite buoys to fill the livewell with bait."

Captain Rob always has a reef in mind when he starts out in the morning, but he realizes it may take stops at several reefs before finding a productive one. "I may anchor on several spots before I find where the fish are lying." Every day is different, and just because fish were on a reef one day does not guarantee they will be there the next.

Once a productive location is found, Captain Rob likes to remind anglers how snappers feed. The larger the snapper gets, the larger the prey it includes in its diet. The really big fish will eat shrimp, squid, and octopus. Their main food source, however, is smaller fishes and crustaceans found on the flat bottom areas next to the reefs.

When setting the hook on snapper, keep in mind that they feed slowly. They need to be given a little time after the bite is detected before setting the hook. Set the hook too quickly on a snapper and you will miss it. "When snapper fishing, I will let them eat for a few seconds before setting the hook. Then I set the hook hard."

This is different from grouper fishing, according to Captain Rob. "Grouper are ready to hook as soon as you detect a bite. Once they hit, just start reeling as fast as you can. I usually fish with a very tight drag." He says if very large fish are biting, crank the drag all the way down. "For big fish I don't use any drag. You have to get them off the bottom."

Charter Captains

Captain Charlie Conner

> Hometown: Port St. Lucie, Florida
> Business: Captain Charlie's Fish Tales Charters
> Phone number: 772-284-3852
> E-mail address: captaincharlie@fishtalescharter.com
> Web site: www.fishtalescharter.com

Captain Charlie's advice: Inshore saltwater fishing is both fun and exciting for all ages, and long-term success depends on three words: patience, patience, patience! Take the time to study the area you intend to fish. Make mental notes or record fishing successes and failures in a log. Make note of the tides and when they are productive, watch the water for any unusual movement or activity, and learn the bottom structure to know where to fish. Success does not come overnight. It takes time to learn any fishing area, but with patience you will become successful in your fishing endeavors.

Captain Joe Ward

> Hometown: Fort Pierce, Florida
> Business: Captain Joe's River Charters
> Phone number: 772-201-5770

E-mail address: cward11605@aol.com
Web site: www.captjoeward.com

Captain Joe's advice: Years of fishing experience have taught Captain Joe to keep it simple, and that is his advice to anglers. He says any fishing trip should include a trip to a local tackle shop where anglers can ask about what's biting and where they are biting. Local guides can also be questioned about the best bets for fishing, and they are normally willing and able to help. If it is in your budget, hire a local guide. You will get a great amount of knowledge for your money and improve your catch rate considerably. On the conservation side, practice catch-photo-and-release (CPR) as much as possible to support the fishery. If you are harvesting fish, keep just enough for your next meal. Anglers should respect and protect the environment but still enjoy the outdoors.

Captain Rob Ward

Hometown: Fort Pierce, Florida
Phone number: 772-201-5775
E-mail address: robward2008@hotmail.com

Captain Rob's advice: The best advice I can give newbies to the area is to get to know the area before you fish it. This would apply everywhere, not just in Fort Pierce. Ask local tackle shops for suggestions on what time of year to be here for the species you want to target. New anglers to an area can shorten the learning curve by hiring a guide the first couple times they go out. A guide will teach you where to go, when to go, and how to fish for the time of year you are visiting.

Wintertime has some of the best pompano fishing anywhere, and it is just offshore. Spanish mackerel are also abundant in the winter—so much so, even fly-fishing addicts get in on the game. Try to plan a trip in the summer to experience some smoker kingfish catching in the 40- to 50-pound range.

Light-tackle king fishing can be the most exciting fishing around.

Area Hotspots

Harbor Branch Oceanographic Institute is located north of Fort Pierce. The flats to the north of the institute hold plenty of trout and redfish. Close to downtown is the Fort Pierce Turning Basin. It holds big snook and goliath grouper in addition to many other varieties. Target the Bear Point area, south of the Turning Basin and on the east side of the river, for trout, snook, and reds on the flats.

Shorebound anglers can try the catwalks on the South Bridge, Harbour Pointe Park, and the south jetty. Beach access is available at the south jetty and all along A1A south. That stretch of A1A has beach access on the east side and river access on the west. Herman's Bay Beach and Pepper Park Beach are popular for whiting and pompano.

Anglers wanting to test the offshore waters can try The Cove near Vero Beach for bottom fish, pompano, and kingfish or the Mulliphen Reef for a good variety of species, including bottom fish, amberjack, and kingfish.

Fishing-Friendly Lodging and Glorious Galleys

12-A Buoy Restaurant

> 22 Fisherman's Wharf
> Fort Pierce, FL 34950
> Phone number: 772-672-4524

Great place for seafood, oysters on the half shell, and many specialties that are outstanding. Near the water, and they will cook your catch for you. At the base of the South Bridge. Recommended by Capt. Charlie Conner.

Dockside Inn

1160 Seaway Drive
Fort Pierce, FL 34949
Phone number: 800-286-1745

Dockside downsized in 2010 but still has 31 rooms and the same dockage it had in the past. The complex sits right on the water of Fort Pierce Inlet with snook fishing off the docks. Bait shop on the premises. Recommended by Capt. Joe Ward and the author.

Dave's Diner

1011 Seaway Drive
Fort Pierce, FL 34949-3143
Phone number: 772-460-2810

Simple food at a great price. Breakfast and lunch. Fisherman's box lunches available. Recommended by Capt. Joe Ward and the author.

Bait and Tackle

The Back Country

1800 U.S. Highway 1
Vero Beach, Florida
Phone number: 772-567-6665

Hands down one of the best outfitters on the Treasure Coast. Owner Eric Davis is a guide himself, and he knows what you will need to catch the big one. The store specializes in fly, spin, and light tackle equipment and supplies. Recommended by Capt. Marcia Foosaner.

The Fishing Center of St. Lucie

300 S. U.S. Highway 1
Fort Pierce, FL 34950
Phone number: 772-465-7637

Wide selection of bait and tackle for all needs on the river or in the ocean. Competitive prices and great service. Largest selection of D.O.A. lures in the area. Will special-order for your needs. Recommended by Capt. Charlie Conner.

White's Tackle

106 U.S. Highway 1
Fort Pierce, FL
Phone number: 772-461-6909

A long-time favorite of Fort Pierce anglers. Onshore, offshore, and archery too. Recommended by Capt. Melinda Buckley.

Fishing Lessons for Life—Safety First

Nothing should be more important to the angling public than personal safety. No fishing trip would be worth it if the end result was some kind of injury that prevented future fishing temporarily or even permanently. Some safety issues are common sense while others relate to regulatory requirements. Fishing is not a dangerous sport, but carelessness on the part of the angler can make it so. The major issues include wearing proper clothing, using life-saving equipment, and showing common courtesy while fishing.

The simplest safety issue to conquer is that of wearing proper clothing. From head to toe, there is clothing that is specifically designed to protect anglers from the elements. Wide-brim hats or baseball caps protect the head and face from sunburn. Medical science has proven that protecting eyes from those UVA and UVB rays is absolutely necessary for good eye health. Polarized sunglasses protect the eyes while making it easier to spot fish and other underwater objects. Long-sleeved shirts are better sun protection than short-sleeved ones. If a short-sleeved shirt is worn, it should be complemented with plenty of sunblock. The same is true with pants. Selecting long pants as opposed to shorts is the wiser decision, but shorts and lots of sunblock work well, too. Shoes are also an important decision. Wading anglers need to protect their feet from rocks and other sharp objects that might be encountered. The same is true for anglers walking along the shore. Boaters should choose a pair of shoes with nonslip properties to keep them from falling on a wet deck.

State regulations vary about who must wear a personal flotation device (PFD). In Florida, for example, a child under the age of 6 must wear a USCG-approved Type I, II, or III PFD while onboard a vessel less than 26 feet in length while the vessel is under way. Once a boat reaches a fishing spot and is anchored, the PFD can be legally removed, but it is not a bad idea to just leave it on. Additionally, the boat operator is responsible for having a PFD on board for each individual in the vessel. Vessels longer than 16 feet must also have an approved throwable PFD on board. Anglers and boaters must know the requirements for their specific fishing location.

Using fishing equipment safely is often mistakenly left to chance. Young anglers, especially, should be taught the proper use of rods and reels. The most important issue is casting. It is extremely important to have the presence of mind to know what obstacles are around before a cast is made. Anglers should visually check behind them before a back cast snags another person or a tree or anything else. Nothing spoils a fishing trip faster than one angler hooking another. That type of accident can easily require a trip to the emergency room and an end to the day's fishing. Anglers should also avoid laying equipment down in the boat where others might trip over it. Boats are somewhat confining, and a fall can result in serious injury.

Common sense will go a long way in preventing fishing injures, and preplanning will go a long way in ensuring the success of a fishing trip. The first item on the angler's checklist should be a first aid kit. A small kit with basic supplies can come in handy for the minor mishaps that might occur. Plenty of liquids should be brought and consumed on the trip. Drinking plenty of water or other healthy drinks will prevent dehydration or heat stroke. Sunblock has already been mentioned, but don't forget some type of lip balm for protecting the lips. Insects are also often encountered on fishing trips, so have some insect repellent on hand.

It is hard to anticipate all the mishaps that might occur, but to make every fishing trip as safe as possible, plan ahead and think safety first.

9

Port St. Lucie, Jensen Beach, and Stuart

The stretch of water and land from Port St. Lucie to Stuart makes up the southern end of Florida's Treasure Coast. The area developed mostly as a result of commercial fishing, ranching, and pineapple farming. Port St. Lucie and Stuart have long been known for their good fishing. Their proximity to the inlet, which gives access to excellent sail fishing opportunities, gave rise to a moniker they share with the rest of the Treasure Coast: Sailfish Capital of the World. In the late 1800s, Jensen Beach was dubbed Pineapple Capital of the World, as about 1 million boxes of pineapples were shipped during the summer harvests. That title was soon lost as the East Coast Railroad came and brought with it the importation of pineapples from Cuba. These imports and losses to freezing weather combined to end the pineapple trade.

Modern development in Port St. Lucie did not begin in earnest until the 1950s. Before that it was mostly uninhabited, comprising only a fishing camp, a few businesses, and farms. There were few roads in the area, so development centered along U.S. Highway 1. Further development was encouraged in 1959 when a bridge was built over the St. Lucie River that gave automobile access to the city.

A residential boom began about this time as the General Development Corporation purchased property in the area and promoted it in the northeastern United States. Historians report that full-page newspaper ads drew the interest of retirees eager to move to the tropical climate of Florida. Ten dollars down and $10 a month could buy an 80 by 125-foot lot, and homes could be bought for as little as $9,000. As the population boom got underway, land that had been purchased for $6 an acre by ranchers was selling for $225 per acre. The resulting development from this business venture was the foundation for what is known today as the city of Port St. Lucie.

Early Jensen Beach settlers were the Ais and Seminole Indians. The Ais people were basically hunters and gatherers, living off the land. Their lifestyle revolved around the local rivers and the ocean. Their primary means of transportation was dugout canoes, which they also used for fishing. There is no evidence that they farmed, but they gathered wild berries and edible plants for food and for ornamentation. The Seminoles came later as refugees from Alabama and Georgia, where they had been pushed out by wars and settlers.

By the mid-1800s, local settlers were experiencing what may have been the first of the region's habitat problems. Fresh water was entering the Indian River in amounts large enough to reduce the salinity and cause harm to saltwater fish. The local settlers' answer to this phenomenon was to cut an inlet from the ocean to the Indian River near the mouth of the St. Lucie River. The original cut was 5 feet deep by about 30 feet wide. Improvements over time have brought the inlet to its present state as a modern navigation channel known as the St. Lucie Inlet.

The settlement and growth of Stuart was directly connected to the fishing and wildlife opportunities in the area. Some of the first tourists to the area came from the northern United States only to find slim accommodations. The first hotel was a houseboat brought to the area by John Danforth, a hunting guide. He later built the Danforth Hotel, which catered to visiting sportsmen. Tourism continued and fueled additional growth. A famous early visitor was President Grover Cleveland, who came to the area to hunt and fish. Tourism spurred a boat-building industry and fishing industry to accommodate the increasing presence of anglers and tourists. The Dixie Highway was completed in the 1920s to include a bridge across the St. Lucie River, opening the area to the same development boom experienced in Jensen Beach.

The Stuart area was one of the first to be involved in Florida fishery conservation efforts. An exceptional sailfish run in 1941 resulted in tremendous overkill and waste of the popular sportfish. Records from the Stuart Sailfish Club document that as many as 5,000 sailfish were caught in a 90-day period. Commentary from the day indicated that many sails were caught and released, but many more were slaughtered and dumped into the river. The unwanted waste of this extraordinary event prompted a local sailfish guide to provide an answer to the problem. Captain Curt Whiticar, himself a member of the club, suggested and designed a special button to be awarded to anglers who caught and released a sailfish. Anglers responded positively to the idea and a catch-and-release fishery was created. To this day the Stuart Sailfish Club awards anglers for practicing catch-and-release fishing.

Characteristics of the Fishing Area

This beautiful area of Florida from Jensen Beach to Stuart includes the southernmost waters of the Indian River Lagoon. The Indian River Lagoon system is the most biologically diverse estuary in North America. As reported on IndianRiverLagoon.com, there are more than 4,000 species of plants and animals that make their home in this watershed, including a number of threatened and endangered species.

The lagoon ends at Hobe Sound just north of Jupiter Inlet. As you travel further south, toward West Palm and Fort Lauderdale, the fishery becomes more of an offshore fishery, with fewer inshore waters to investigate. As with most of the

Indian River Lagoon, there are plenty of grass flats, sandbars, deep channels, and cuts for anglers to explore. The St. Lucie River, its tributaries, and many residential canals are lined with docks and seawalls. For offshore anglers, deep water and the Gulf Stream are as close as 9 miles. Successful bluewater fishing can actually be accomplished in a half-day fishing trip.

Captain Marcia Foosaner is a well-known and experienced angler in local waters. She offers fishing charters in the area, mostly on foot with fly rod in hand. "Plenty of docks line the lagoon and the St. Lucie River. They are true fish magnets. There are some oyster bars to fish, but most have been destroyed by the water quality issues inherent in the area." She adds that many of the previously fishy oyster bars are now covered over by sand from shifting currents, storms, or strong tides. The remaining bars are only remnants and not viable as a primary fishing target, although they will hold fish at times.

The terrain under the surface on the flats changed dramatically in a month's time with hurricanes Frances and Jeanne, according to Captain Marcia. Changes in the flats still occur, even without hurricanes, but normally those changes are gradual. Anglers should be aware of the possibility, though, because shifting terrain of flats will change the feeding pattern of fish. Only regular trips to the flats will keep the serious angler on fish. Sometimes fish can be found in the same spot for weeks, other times only for days.

Turtle grass and eel grass are indigenous to area waters. The flat, straplike blades of the turtle grass and the long, bright green, ribbonlike leaves of the eel grass provide nursery grounds for many species of fish. The actual amount of grass on the flats tends to vary with environmental conditions. Captain Marcia says, "The amount of turtle and eel grass on the flats seems to be determined by our water quality. In the summer it is affected by lake water being dumped on us. In the winter there just seems to be a natural die-off, leaving more of the sand exposed." She says more sand on the flats is not a bad

There are numerous places between Fort Pierce and Stuart giving anglers roadside access to excellent wade fishing. Photo by Karen Presley.

thing for winter fishing, but grass habitat is a desirable condition for the summer. "The channels and cuts around the flats become a mainstay for fish if our water temperatures drop during the winter." Fish will stage in the deeper water and move to the flats to feed and warm themselves once the water temperatures have naturally warmed.

"One of the best things about this area is the fact that there are several dozen places one can just walk into the water from the roadside and catch fish," says Captain Marcia. "This includes the beaches."

Captain Melinda Buckley, known locally as Captain Melly B, fishes area waters from Fort Pierce to Jupiter Inlet. She says, "If you like diversity, this is the area for you. We are very fortunate to have a wide variety of habitat all around us. We have mangroves, grass flats, spoil islands, oyster bars, sandbars, jetties, beaches, artificial reefs, docks, bridges, and locks." She also mentions the fact that you do not need a boat to enjoy area fishing. "We have great accessibility to engage in wade fishing, beach fishing, and kayak fishing." Along with this habitat

Juvenile tarpon are great starter fish for kids and inexperienced tarpon anglers in the North Fork of the St. Lucie River. Photo by Capt. Chris Myers.

diversity are a variety of species of fish to catch. They include but are not limited to snook, trout, redfish, ladyfish, snapper, flounder, pompano, jack crevalle, grouper, Spanish mackerel, bluefish, sharks, and tarpon.

The North Fork of the St. Lucie River regularly attracts tarpon during the summer months. A favorite method of catching these summer residents is by sight casting to rolling fish in the tannin-stained waters.

Referred to as juvenile tarpon, these willing combatants are mostly smaller fish ranging up to 50 pounds, with a smattering of larger ones showing up occasionally. Captain Marcia targets these silver kings with flies or on occasion with a D.O.A. Gold Glitter Shrimp and a spinning outfit. "This is a yearly event with some years better than others," she says. "It is a wonderful opportunity for a first-time tarpon outing. I refer to them as starter fish, and I love fishing for them."

There are also several bridges that provide excellent fishing for large tarpon and snook. Among them are a railroad bridge, the Roosevelt Bridge, and the Sewall's Point Bridge (known to locals as the Ten-Cent Bridge), all spanning the St. Lucie River. The D.O.A. Terror Eyz is a favorite lure around the bridges.

Offshore anglers abound in this stretch of the Atlantic Ocean, using the St. Lucie Inlet to access excellent bluewater fishing with sailfish as one of the popular targets (see the next chapter for information on sailfishing the Treasure Coast). Plenty of dolphinfish, kingfish, wahoo, and bottom species are regularly caught on offshore boats. During the summer when ocean conditions are mild, plenty of small boats will join the action.

The Inshore Bite—Wading with a Fly Rod

The abundance of fish and the availability of wading opportunities attract many fly-casting anglers to this region of Florida's East Coast. Some don't have boats, and others simply leave theirs at home because they want to enjoy the experience of finding and catching quality fish on fly. "My absolute favorite way to fish the flats is on foot with a fly rod on the falling tide," says Captain Marcia. Falling tides give fish fewer places to go. They are forced to seek holes, ditches, cuts, or channels adjacent to the flats. In shallow water the visibility is better, and even in the deeper cuts and depressions, fish will often be sighted moving or sitting and waiting for their next meal. "I love the hunt. Most of what I need is either in my pockets, in my wader pouch, or tied to me."

Wade fishing offers an alternative to fishing from a boat, an alternative that some say is more successful. Captain Marcia says the first and most important advantage of wade fishing is the silent approach it provides; the second is the low profile. Both allow the angler to get closer to the fish. "I'm talking about water that ranges from inches to 2 feet. I find and

The combination of wading and fly-fishing gives anglers the advantages of stealth in stalking fish on the flats.

catch fish that have their backs out of the water, they are in so shallow. I have often almost stepped on fish that people dream about catching. It's crazy to try and fish these conditions any other way."

Snook and trout are the most prevalent fish found while wade fishing the flats. "You would think they would always be sitting in holes, but they are not. They sit where they feel like sitting, and, like a bonefish, the snook will match terrain they are sitting on. I have seen 25-pound snook just vanish in front of me on the flats—while I was looking at them. I find most of my snook sitting high up on the grass."

The key to wade fishing is focus, even when there are not a lot of fish being spotted. "Most anglers, including me, when looking for something to cast to, might get complacent for lack of seeing any fish. Complacency is your worst enemy, and it takes crazy amounts of discipline to walk around on a flat for hours in hopes of seeing a few fish." Captain Marcia reminds wade anglers not to start sloshing around, blind casting without a target, or yelling to a companion on the water. "That fish you have been stalking for 30 minutes or more will bolt because of the noise, and you will then know exactly where she was—after the fact. Sometimes I think they even hear the fly and bolt."

Making a bad cast and nearly hitting a fish on the head sometimes results in a strike, but that is not the norm. Captain Marcia says she may have done that about six times in her lifetime. On those occasions the fish may have struck out of anger or fright, but hitting a fish with the fly or lining one will not normally result in a hookup. She simply chalks those occasions up to fisherman's luck when a lined fish does strike.

The ideal situation for Captain Marcia is to have a fish facing her straight on or at a slight angle. "We all know we can't have the perfectly positioned fish every time. I try to move to a more suitable location for a presentation if the fish will give me time; I don't just cast in a hurry."

One successful approach to fish on the flats includes looking things over calmly and making a decision on the best approach to each particular fish. "I often start by short casting and hope the fish wants it so badly that it comes after the fly. Unfortunately that is not the norm for a *sitting* fish. That approach is more successful if the fish is cruising." Sometimes a cast needs to be long and beyond the fish so the fly can be stripped into the strike zone. "If I can get the fly about 8 to 12 inches in front of the fish without it spooking, I can get a strike. I usually retrieve a fly slower rather than faster and sometimes barely move it at all." She describes big snook as lazy, and a slow-moving fly can be the ticket to success.

Trout are more likely to be found in sand holes than snook, but her wading, fly-fishing approach is basically the same for either fish. "I find big trout spookier than snook, but there really isn't a better way to approach them, so I fish for them the same way." One exception to her normal approach is when

Trout are more likely to be found in sand holes than snook, but the fly-fishing approach is basically the same for either fish. Photo by Capt. Chris Myers.

there are large schools of mullet milling around on the flats. "I will fish mullet schools by casting randomly into the school." That said, the strategy has three results: a strike, lining or hitting a fish, or no fish at all. She uses this random cast approach during low light conditions when the fish can't normally be sighted. "I can't see them, but sense they are there by the behavior of the bait. Skittish bait often indicates the existence of predators near the school." Still relying on patience and focus, she always studies the bait school for some indication of the presence of fish before making a cast.

If Captain Marcia travels to her location by boat, she likes to float in the last 50 yards without engine or trolling motor running. "My float-in approach has two goals; the first is stealth, and the second is an opportunity to listen and observe the area I will be fishing." If she has clients, it gives them time to get themselves together and ready for the action before getting close to where they will get out and wade. "I don't want them stomping all over the boat, slamming hatches, or dropping rods on the deck as we get to the desired location. Watch a heron in the water stalking its prey. That's me. I walk like that looking for my next target." She thinks that even a trolling motor in shallow water is a deterrent to successful fishing. Even kayaks, which are generally stealthy vessels, are showing up with trolling motors running. "Whose idea was that? Think hard about that stealthy kayak you bought to get into those shallow areas to fish. I don't think the trolling motor is aiding the quest."

Fly-fishing should not be complicated, and it doesn't have to be, according to Captain Marcia. "I have probably simplified fly-fishing to a fault, but that's the way I think it should be. For example, I started fishing with a straight piece of leader without concern for the traditional tapered one." Tapered leaders required tying different sizes of line together to create the tapered leader. Eliminating the knots actually resulted in a more efficient cast and retrieve. "Those knots up and down the line got in the way of fishing on the flats when there were grass and weeds present. The solid leader has made no difference in my casting, and the fly is presented and tracks without picking up debris. I simply put a loop in the fly line and a loop in the leader. I loop mainline and leader together, tie on my fly with another loop knot, and I am ready to fish." She does not add a shock leader and says the only time she uses anything heavier than 30-pound test is when she fishes for mackerel. "If I am targeting mackerel, I will go to 40-pound leader, but never use any wire."

Summer or winter really doesn't matter when it comes to the process of fly-fishing. A few simple adjustments will prepare anglers for trophy catches in either season. "I'm a Florida girl, born and raised, so in the winter months, when the water goes below 70 degrees, I don my waders and wading shoes for additional protection from the elements and off I go. In the winter I do adjust my tackle by downsizing somewhat." She says she will sometimes fish equipment as light as a 4 weight, but a 6 weight or a 7 weight is her average outfit. "I will use the 6 weight most of the time since it is substantial enough to land most of the fish I catch in the winter."

One decision fly casters have to make is the choice between floating or sinking line. Captain Marcia has simplified that too. "I have nine fly reels and only two have a true floating line, and one of the two is just an extra spool that I never use." She says floating line is rarely in her arsenal unless she is throwing a fly that floats. "I never like floating line much anyway, because it is colored." The intermediate lines are usually colorless-clear to gray hues. Strip an unweighted-fly-using floating line and it will rise every time, and it may rise too high in the water column. She recommends using an intermediate sinking line with a shorter leader so the fly will stay down better, no matter how you strip it. "Some of the channels I fish have a pretty good current in them. The inlet is a perfect example of needing an intermediate sinking line. You will have much better success in fast-moving water if you use a sinking line." Captain Marcia likes to use intermediate line even in shallow water in the winter. "On the flats I really don't want my fly to rise; I like it to kind of 'scoot' along the sand. Intermediate line tends to pull the fly at its level, keeping it down in the strike zone. I personally think keeping the fly down makes a big difference in my success." She says it also provides the option to fish deeper if needed.

She shortens her leaders a bit, using 4-foot-long leaders as a norm in the winter and 8-foot leaders in the summer. "I don't find the winter fish very leader shy, but sometimes that shortened leader is a big help in windy conditions." She recommends leaders of at least 20- to 25-pound test and says that 25-pound leader is probably ideal for winter conditions. "I re-tie less frequently with the 25-pound leader, and, as I stated earlier, these winter fish really are not normally leader shy."

Captain Marcia ties her own flies and has a personal array of "concoctions" that work for her. "I use small Clouser Deep

As the water temperatures rise in the spring, the bigger snook begin to show on the flats. Photo by Jerry McBride.

Minnow flies that look like spin-fishing lead-head jigs. "I refer to this combination fly and jig as a *Fig* after showing one to a fishing friend from the West Palm Beach Fishing Club. His name is Barry Brimacomb. When I showed him the fly he looked at it and said, 'The Foosaner jig, call it a Fig.' I've been calling it that ever since." When choosing colors, she uses plenty of white and gold. She describes one personal favorite as standard red-and-white Clouser Deep Minnows. Another favorite is the "good old standby, chartreuse and white." Naming pompano as one of her favorite winter targets, she ties sand flea imitation flies. Her advice to anglers in pursuit of pompano is to "put plenty of gold in the pattern."

As winter transitions to summer, Marcia likes to move up to a beefier rod, one with some backbone for larger fish. "In between the winter and summer seasons, I tend to come up a few notches to a 7- or 8-weight rod. If the days get warmer and the water warms in the shallows, a few early snook can show up, and I don't like to be caught light handed." During this period, when the water is becoming a little warmer each day, bigger fish start to invade the flats. She starts lengthening her leaders and changing fly patterns in preparation for the early snook. "I'm still carrying my winter fly patterns, but adding a few Deceivers or small baitfish patterns during the transition to warmer weather and the possibility of bigger fish."

When summer temperatures become an everyday occurrence, the only change needed is the size of the gear. The fish will be bigger, a bit more leader shy, and preferring larger baits. "When summer rolls around in earnest, I will go to the 9 weight and even a 10 if I throw really large flies. I make my determination based on the size of the fish I see in previous trips to the flats." The main thing, according to Captain Marcia, is not to be undergunned when the big snook, tarpon, and jack crevalle start to invade the flats. A friend of mine once described the need to beef up the tackle, saying, "Don't take a knife to a gun fight."

Leader size and length should also be increased for summer fly-fishing. "My leader size increases to 25 to 30 pound for the summer fish. I rarely use anything heavier, but I certainly don't want anything lighter in the summer." She prefers a leader of about 8 feet in the summer. Her fly patterns will increase in size to as large as 3 to 4 inches in length. Her favorite summer fly color is red and white. It includes spun deer hair in the pattern to make it float. "It is by far my best big trout and snook fly. I have used it almost exclusively for fishing during the summer months for as long as I have been fly-fishing."

The summer fishery includes the possibility of some giant fish on the beach. Some years are better than others, but every year the surf gives fly-rodders the opportunity to catch quality fish on fly. Captain Marcia says, "The surf fishery can, most years, be one of the things I enjoy most about living here. Steady activity can be gained by walking the beach and sight fishing for snook. Most beaches will hold fish, but the places with structure and the St. Lucie Inlet are prime fishing territory." She spends many days from June through September toting a 9- or 10-weight fly outfit in search of snook and tarpon on Lake Atlantic.

Wade fishing for tarpon on the beach normally results in big fish, not the juveniles. "As a general rule, the fish are larger on the beach, and I get the best part of them if they jump a few times and break me off, or jump and throw the fly. In fact I decrease my leader size to ensure that outcome much of the time." She says she has caught enough of those big tarpon and doesn't really desire the long fight anymore. "I personally do not increase my leader size for tarpon, but if I wanted to think about fighting that fish to the end, I would use 50- to 80-pound leader."

Tarpon will eat a variety of offerings from a fly angler. Captain Marcia likes the standard long-nosed variety. "I like typical tarpon flies, but tarpon eat such a wide variety of stuff, they sometimes surprise me with what they will strike. If I showed you some of the things I have caught them on you would laugh. I have hooked tarpon on anything from a little 2-inch length of orange chenille to typical or maybe not-so-typical tarpon flies."

She thinks black makes the tarpon mad and aggressive, leading her to a fondness for a fly called Black Death. Created by legendary fly tier Stu Apte, the Black Death fly features the long nose for less wind resistance and long casts. Its body and tail are tied from contrasting black and red material for great visibility in the water.

As summer progresses toward fall, nothing but the bigger gear is needed. It is likely that big tarpon will be available within casting range of the beaches. The only drawback could be weather roughing up the ocean and wind, making it difficult to fly cast.

Although most of Captain Marcia's fishing is done while wading with a fly rod, she will from time to time pick up a spinning outfit because it allows her to use topwater lures and experience the explosive strike of a tarpon or snook on the surface. "If I use the spin outfit at all, it is with a topwater lure in the summer, because I love the strike." She doesn't like to use the topwater lures right out of the box. "My topwater lures are all altered for the sake of the fish. I never *ever* use a topwater with three treble hooks. Three treble hooks are totally unnecessary and bad for the fish. I always pinch barbs and remove one of the trebles if it does not affect the balance and performance of the lure."

She says there is an alternative lure that will work equally well if not better when you consider the hookup ratio of topwater baits. The hookup ratio using topwater baits is only about 50 to 60 percent. "You can increase the hookup rate considerably using a D.O.A. Shrimp. The D.O.A. Shrimp is hands down the best *go-to bait* in my tackle box." She describes it as fish friendly because it has only one hook to allow easy removal from the fish. The hook in this bait rides point-up, allowing relatively weedless retrieves in shallow, grassy water. "The D.O.A. Shrimp is effective on almost all fish, but without reservation it is the best lure I have ever thrown at a tarpon."

Her spinning reel is spooled with braided line, usually 15- to 20-pound test, with leader of 20- to 30-pound test, the same as she uses with flies. She prefers a 7- to 7½-foot medium/light rod and a 3000 size Shimano reel to medium/heavy rod with a 4000 sized reel. "These rods will cover 90 percent of the fishing I do in the lagoon."

Savvy anglers understand that many fish are run over with boats instead of being brought to the boat by rod and reel. It may not even be a place you planned to fish on your current outing, but if you want to fish it tomorrow, you should not run over it today. "I try to avoid running over an area that I like to fish. I can think of five or six places in the lagoon that have provided me with some pretty good fishing over the years where I can no longer expect to catch fish. They have been run over so many times the fish have moved on." It is a situation that's hard to understand. A boat on plane can run over some pretty shallow water, and sometimes it seems they do it just because they can. The motive must be to save a few minutes by leaving the channel and taking a shortcut. "The fact is they are destroying good fishing spots and showing bad manners if other anglers are present on the flats. Common sense could go a long way in making better fishing for everyone."

Imagine spending 20 to 30 minutes floating quietly into a fishing location at dawn, getting out of the boat, approaching your fishing hole, and having someone come barreling through the flat at top speed. Or worse yet, have someone pull up on the flat with engine running and throw a cast net over the bait pod you just spent time approaching with intentions of fishing. It is rude of the perpetrator and disheartening for the angler.

Captain Marcia says, "As long as I beat the crowd I can do some pretty good catching, but it gets more difficult all the time. I wish more anglers would learn the advantages of not running over the shallow-water flats. I believe they would catch more fish and not ruin the fishing for other anglers." Some of these anglers who run in shallow water may not even understand how shallow quality fish can be; others just don't seem to have respect for their fellow anglers. "I think it was Flip Pallet that said, 'If you keep running through a fish's house, he will eventually move.' Truer words were never spoken."

Snook Fishing the Inlet

Snook is definitely one of the most popular fish in this area of the Indian River Lagoon. Captain Melly says that during the summer the snook head to the inlets and beaches to spawn. "A medium/heavy Crowder rod paired with a Penn Sargus 5000 reel, spooled with 30- to 50-pound braided line is my rig of choice. I add 4 feet of 40- to 60-pound fluorocarbon leader and a circle hook for a winning combination on a moving tide." She favors free-lining live bait on the outgoing tide, but as long as the water is moving, she says the chances of a hookup are good when fishing around the jetties or near bait pods on the beach.

Schools of greenies and pilchards can be found in the morning around the inlet, along the beach, and near wrecks close to shore. The Bull Shark Barge just south of the St. Lucie Inlet is a popular bait-gathering and fishing location. The structure is a steel barge mistakenly sunk in the location about 20 years ago. The barge sits upside down in about 45 feet of water on the ocean floor. It is usually easy to locate by the overabundance of boats catching bait and fishing in the area. Watch for dimpling bait on the surface of the water and diving pelicans to locate the bait. Use a Sabiki rig on the wrecks or cast net on the beach to capture enough bait for the days fishing. There are also several bait shops that frequently have live bait. Sometimes in the summer there is a live bait boat near Sandsprit Park, first thing in the morning. Anglers can drive their boats right up to the floating bait shop and purchase fresh live bait.

Once the angler is settled in the fishing location, the bite will either be an explosive topwater bite or a more subtle tapping bite. The most exciting bite is when it happens on top. Those bites will make the angler think the snook saw the bait coming. "The bite on free-lined live bait can be an explosion on the surface as the snook nails the bait as soon as it hits. I use circle hooks, so once the snook grabs the bait, I just wind tight and hang on. Let the circle hook do its job." Sometimes the bite can feel like a couple light taps. The snook will suck in the bait, spit it out, only to suck it back in again. "If anglers start retrieving the line too soon, they can yank the bait away from the fish. It is not uncommon for a hungry snook to take more than one swipe at the bait, so anglers want to be patient and see if the snook comes back after the initial hit before reeling in the bait to check on it." If a bite occurs, but the bait is still lively when retrieved, toss it right back out. If the bait is lifeless, put on a fresh one before casting again.

A D.O.A. Shrimp fooled this snook off the St. Lucie Inlet jetties.

There are an attached and detached jetties at the end of the St. Lucie Inlet. Those jetties and the Hole in the Wall are popular fishing locations. The Hole in the Wall is easily spotted along the south side of the inlet. A channel coming out of the mangroves empties into a tidal pool before connecting to the inlet. The popularity of these locations requires some common courtesy among anglers if everyone is going to enjoy the experience. Captain Melly reminds everyone to be mindful of other anglers when fishing these areas.

One requirement when fishing in close proximity of other anglers is not to come between vessels and the structure they are fishing. "Several boats can fish the same area when lined up properly. Sometimes approaching anglers need to hold off and observe conditions. Determine where the current is going and where the existing fishing lines are in relation to the current. Most anglers at the jetties are anchored and fishing stationary positions. Set up your boat so you do not interfere with someone else's fishing."

Anglers fishing the Hole in the Wall are often drifting in the current outside the tidal pool. If someone anchors along this stretch, the opportunity for drifting is limited and not as effective. In this case the best alternative is to keep your distance and anchor too.

When too many people are already fishing a particular spot, it may be necessary to move on and try again later when a spot opens up to give access. The beaches, docks, and bridges in the area offer superb alternative locations to fish without having to travel far. Common courtesy goes a long way when fishing a popular area and should be practiced by all anglers.

Captain Buckley suggests anglers prepare for the summer snook bite by watching the weather and the tides. She says July and August are the prime months for snook in the inlet, and sometimes the weather can be dicey. Pick the most favorable conditions if you can. "A hard east wind coupled with an outgoing tide makes it difficult to reach the beach in search of bait pods to fish. Those same conditions make it difficult to fish the jetty, too, because the water will be churned and rough." She says some protection can be found on those windy days by fishing the inlet shoreline. "The Hole in the Wall area provides more protection from the wind, but due to high boat traffic, anglers will want to be ever ready for wakes of passing vessels in the channel."

Lighter equipment can be used, but it is not recommended by conservation-minded anglers. The lighter equipment prolongs the fight and tires out the fish. Since the summer fish are spawning, they must be handled with care. Captain Buckley advises anglers to "Leave them in the water while removing the hook. If they swallow the hook, don't try to remove it. Cut the line as close to the hook as possible and let Mother Nature take care of the rest."

To take advantage of a photo op, she recommends leaving the fish in the water while the photographer gets the camera ready. Support the fish with one hand under the belly and hold it horizontally. Raise the fish for a picture and quickly return it to the water to be revived before release. She says you should never hang a big snook by the jaw because it can damage internal organs and result in a dead snook. It is not uncommon to have multiple catches of big snook in the summer. Captain Melly says, "We respectfully ask visiting anglers to just catch a few, then move on to another species. Some may think it is cool to brag of high numbers of snook battled in one day, but at what cost to the spawning fish in the inlet?" There are plenty of alternatives to snook in the area. Anglers can enjoy a few summer snook and then run just a couple miles outside the inlet to use the rest of their bait on kingfish, bonito, barracuda, snapper, and summer sailfish.

Fishing Bridges and Residential Docks

Once fall rolls around, the snook start to move back inshore to the docks and bridges. Captain Melly identifies two of the area's famous snook spots as the Ten-Cent Bridge and the Roosevelt Bridge in Stuart. Some of the best fishing around the docks and bridges occurs when the mullet show up for the fall run. Captain Melly says the D.O.A. Big Fish Lure (BFL) works well to imitate swimming mullet. "The D.O.A. Baitbuster is also a great bait to *match the hatch* in lieu of live mullet." Gulp! Jerkbaits in Smelt or New Penny rigged on a jig head are included in her arsenal and make a great presentation when tossed around the bridges. She also likes to fish the D.O.A. Glow Shrimp slowly bounced on the bottom. As always with the shrimp imitations, slowly is the operative word.

Fishing the bridges is most productive for snook when keeping the bait deep. Some anglers prefer to anchor, throw out some live bait, and wait for the snook to find it. Anglers who like to fool the snook with artificials are more likely to use a trolling motor to position the boat for making casts to the bridge pilings. A D.O.A. Terror Eyz bounced off the bottom is

The author is shown here with a big snook caught on a D.O.A. Terror Eyz bounced off the bottom near the Ten-Cent Bridge. Photo by Capt. Chris Myers.

deadly on bridge snook. Cast the lure up-current and bounce it along the bottom until a big snook picks it up. These are big fish, and the equipment needs to match the task. A heavy action rod with at least 20-pound braid will work fine. Add about 2 feet of 40- or 50-pound fluorocarbon leader before attaching the Terror Eyz. The drag needs to be tighter than normal to keep these bruisers away from the structure and potential cutoffs. A savvy fishing partner can help with landing the fish by using the trolling motor to steer away from the structure once the hookup occurs.

There are also plenty of snook to be caught around the area's residential docks. Most shorelines are lined with docks, offering plenty of opportunity to prospect for snook. Moving water is an important element of fishing the docks. Pick fishing times by the tides to ensure a period of moving water to improve your success.

Moving water can be incoming or outgoing, just so long as it's moving. It is important to note the direction the water is moving when fishing docks, because it will affect your bait presentation. Captain Melly prefers to let a bait sweep by or beneath a dock rather than be sucked under it toward a wall. "I guess you would say it's better to have current perpendicular to the side of the dock. The fish will be staging under the dock with their noses in the current waiting for bait to come by so they can ambush it." She recommends presenting live or artificial bait up-current so it flows naturally with the current back to the dock. Retrieving bait against the current will not appear natural and will not get as many strikes.

Captain Melly likes to remind anglers about the importance of leader size when fishing the docks. "Some conditions result in letting your bait pass under the dock between pilings. This situation requires a strong leader. I recommend no less than a 30- to 40-pound leader around the docks, because once you hook a fish, it will try to dance around the pilings and cut you off." If anglers want to be on the safe side of this decision, it would not hurt to beef up to 50- or 60-pound leader. If the fish appear leader shy it may be necessary to reduce the size and try again.

Some docks can be fishier than others because of the rate of water flow, whether the dock attracts bait to interest the predators, and whether there is enough structure to make both the baitfish and predator fish happy. "When looking for docks to fish, the ones that have bait hanging out are more likely to have predator fish nearby." She says that doesn't mean a dock has to have bait to hold fish. "Any dock may have a snook or big trout hunkered down beneath it waiting for a meal to come by. It definitely does not hurt to make a few casts to see if anyone is home." Once you locate these otherwise fishless-looking docks, make a mental note that they were productive. For whatever reason, the fish were there then, and they are likely to be there the next time under similar conditions.

Even the physical structure of docks is an important consideration when choosing which dock to spend some time on. "Some docks create a better *happy place* for the fish than others, based on the way they are designed. Baitfish prefer places where they can hide and take cover easily when threatened. A predator fish likes a place it can hide and wait for his meal to come by and still feel like it can't be seen." The Indian River along the Treasure Coast is populated by many extremely high docks constructed to accommodate large vessels. "These high docks do not provide as much shade in the day or shadow lines at night due to their height. Additionally, the lights at night do not cast the same shadow as a shorter dock. I prefer a lower dock with more shadows. I also like the T-shaped docks because they create more shadows and ambush points."

Fishing the docks at night offers a special opportunity for anglers. Fish will often be sitting out in the shadows beyond the light reflecting on the water's surface. As baitfish and shrimp pass through the light, the fish will see an easy meal and ambush them from their perch in the shadows. Anglers get an easy shot at producing a natural presentation when these conditions exist. Captain Melly instructs anglers to cast up-current near the dark edges and let the bait sweep through the lighted surface and into the shadows again. "This presentation is one of the easiest to make and at the same time one of the most effective for fishing residential docks." She adds this advice when determining which dock to target: "When night-fishing docks, I like a dock that has a strong light source close to the water. These lights create distinct shadow lines. A dim light does not seem to attract as much bait and does not create distinctive shadow lines. The green lights like the Hydro Glow lights create the conditions I like to fish at night."

Lure selection for night fishing is similar to that for any other fishing. It should relate to matching the hatch. "If you see shrimp popping under the dock, then try to use a live shrimp; D.O.A. Shrimp, my favorite color is glow; Berkley

When the mullet run starts in the fall, big jack crevalle and other species invade the area, feeding on the migrating mullet. Photo by Paul MacInnis.

Rattle Shrimp, where I like the rootbeer glitter; or a lure that resembles shrimp, like a small tried and true bucktail jig."

On the other hand, if the bait seen around the dock is finfish, try a baitfish-imitating plug. "When mullet or other baitfishes are present around the docks, I like to throw topwater plugs. MirrOlure's Top Pup is one of my favorites around the docks, under the lights. If I don't get a strike on top, I switch to something subsurface like a MirrOlure MirrOdine, Gulp! Jerkbait, or a Yo-Zuri Crystal Minnow."

Captain Melly's final advice when fishing around the docks is not to overlook other possibilities that might exist close by. "Don't get so focused on fishing the docks that you miss other activity going on in the near vicinity of the docks." In the St. Lucie River, for example, some docks have seawalls between them that often attract fish. "Big jack crevalle and snook will cruise those walls between the docks trapping bait up against the walls." The main thing is to always be on the lookout for any activity on the water that is out of the ordinary and be willing to check it out.

Anglers may catch a bonus fish inside the inlet once the mullet run starts in the fall. Big jack crevalle invade the area, feeding on the migrating mullet. A feeding frenzy won't be hard to spot as the marauding jacks crash the surface in feeding frenzies. It is a sight to behold, and if you hook up you will have a major fight on your hands. Captain Buckley says, "The big jacks are a blast to catch on light tackle. Most of the D.O.A. lures or a big Yo-Zuri popper produces great explosive bites and long blistering runs." She recommends removing the treble hooks from lures and replacing them with J-hooks when targeting big jacks. This simple alteration makes releasing the fish much easier. "Replacing the trebles with J-hooks is safer for both the fish and the angler!"

Trout in the Indian River

Plenty of seatrout are caught in the Indian River between Fort Pierce and Stuart, regardless of your fishing platform. Kayakers, waders, shore-based anglers, and anglers fishing from powerboats all enjoy the trout bite in this area with an opportunity to catch a trophy. Lighter fishing equipment is used when targeting trout. "For trout fishing I use a 7-foot Shimano Terramar medium action rod with a fast taper," says Captain Melly. "I add a Shimano 2500 Symetre spooled with 10- to 15-pound PowerPro braid." She adds a 20-pound fluorocarbon leader before attaching an artificial lure or a hook for live bait fishing.

Captain Buckley advises shore-based anglers to cross over the Jensen Beach Causeway to reach Hutchinson Island. The island has numerous places to wade-fish along the east shoreline. Herman's Bay just north of Nettles Island is the first good spot, but anglers will find plenty more locations all the way north to Fort Pierce. "As you travel north on highway A1A, you will see numerous locations to park your car and start wading or kayaking. Live shrimp on a popping cork will get you trout, along with a variety of other species, providing fun for all ages."

Topwater lures like the Top Pup or Skitterwalk in early morning or late afternoon periods are a favorite of Captain

Buckley's. "I like to walk the dog with topwater lures in low-light conditions. I get the side-to-side action by twitching the rod as I retrieve the bait. This action is excellent to get the trout's attention and bring on an exciting topwater strike." As the sun comes up she prefers soft plastics such as Gulp! Jerkbait or Gulp! Shrimp, D.O.A. Glow Shrimp, or the Berkley Rattle Shrimp.

Wading or drifting anglers should look for potholes on the flat. Potholes are sandy areas in the grass that are normally a little deeper terrain, providing the perfect ambush spot for predator fish. Big trout are often spotted lying in the sandy potholes. Making a cast beyond the fish and bringing it back over the hole will often elicit a strike. Even when you don't see a fish in the pothole, make a cast to check it out. Sometimes big trout lie in the grass waiting to ambush baitfish as they cross the sandy depression. Any time anglers wade or drift the flats, potholes should be prime casting targets.

If the wind is strong from the west, it might be better to fish the west side of the river to gain some protection from high winds. Captain Melly says the west side of the river also contains productive grass flats and numerous docks to fish around. "Fishing close to the docks will produce snook and redfish. Move out away from the docks and trout will be more likely." She says anglers should be patient once a trout is caught. If you catch one trout, there are usually more in the neighborhood, so take time to make several casts in the same area before moving on.

Experienced anglers keep an eye out for baitfish. "If you see nervous water caused by baitfish, you definitely want to cast all around them. The reason they are nervous is probably a predator in the vicinity thinking about eating them." Captain Melly keeps several rods rigged with several choices of bait for times when bait is sighted. She normally tries to imitate the bait she sees, but if that doesn't work, she will cast something different. "If matching the hatch doesn't work, I like to throw something totally different. This strategy often gets a predator's attention and I get a strike. For example, try throwing a shrimp in the middle of the minnows, if throwing the smelt-colored Gulp! did not trigger a bite."

Captain Buckley names Sailfish Flats and Marcia's Flat in Stuart as additional popular fishing destinations for people in search of trout and snook. Anglers should check with a local bait and tackle shop for the exact location of these popular and productive fishing spots.

In Jensen Beach, you can launch your boat at the Jensen Beach Causeway and run north to Herman's Bay, the power plant, and Bear Point. In Fort Pierce, you have the Black Pearl Ramp and the Stan Blum Ramp, which is a short run to the Harbor Branch area, and in Vero Beach you have Round Island, where you can launch your boat and start fishing almost immediately.

The Offshore Bite—Tuna and More

The adventuresome angler will find the pinnacle of Florida offshore angling outside Stuart and the St. Lucie Inlet. Captain Scott Fawcett operates Boneshaker Charters out of his hometown of Jensen Beach. He describes this area as one that offers plenty of inshore species and all the sought-after offshore fish. He has a real passion for traveling the 65 miles to fishing grounds known as "The Corner." He says the 65-mile run sounds far only if you are from South Florida, where the west side of the Gulf Stream is so close. "If anglers are willing to make the 65-mile run to the other side of the Gulf Stream, the rewards are often mind blowing. If I hadn't seen it with my own eyes and been a part of it many times myself over the past years, I would never believe that Florida offered an offshore fishery such as this."

Captain Scotty describes a fishery that many probably imagine only in their dreams. He describes surface water erupting with yellowfin tuna in the 50- to 100-pound class. "It is not unusual in this area for the radar to be freckled with packs of birds marking tuna in every direction. Schools of puffer fish will be balled up on top with 25- to 70-pound dolphin taking their turns at gorging themselves. The sonar will show hard boomerang images marking wahoo stacked up like cordwood under the boat." Throw in an occasional billfish skyrocketing through a bait pod or cutting on some small skipjacks, and it is easy to see why it truly is a mind-blowing experience.

The area is characterized by all the important offshore elements needed in a premier fishing location. "Throw in rips, color changes, and bottom structures that rival any other in the world and you have The Corner, approximately 65 miles northeast of Stuart and the St. Lucie Inlet."

One of Captain Scotty's favorite targets is tuna. He describes the area he likes to fish as extreme. "The geography of the area we are fishing is pretty extreme in comparison to most of the land and water off the Florida coast, or even the eastern seaboard for that matter." He describes the area as an underwater peninsula. Flats and reefs extend off the Bahamas Banks then quickly drop off to 2,500 feet of water in three main stages. The seafloor levels out and then slopes off again at about 300 feet, 800 feet, and 1,300 feet before leveling out at about 2500 feet. "All these edges and drop-offs cause substantial tide rips and temperature breaks and quite often hold bait and sargassum weed. While tuna fishing, we are primarily fishing the birds and the actual fish which are blowing up around us. Experience has taught me, however, that even though we are seeing the action on the surface, it is related to the bottom structure in one way or another."

A typical day of tuna fishing requires more planning and more time allotted for the trip. The preparation begins the day before. Chores include fueling the boat, checking the oil, filling the water tank, acquiring food, drinks, and ice, purchasing and rigging bait, and checking tackle. "Our plan is to leave at about

3:30 in the morning, and there are not many places open for business, so everything is done the day before. After all the preliminary tasks are done, we try to catch a few winks and rest the best we can in anticipation of the thrills to come."

Most charter captains meet up early with their mate to make final preparations before the clients show up at the 3:30 departure time. Those final preparations include pulling out the rods that had been spooled with fresh line the day before and rigging them for the day's fishing.

On a typical tuna trip, Captain Scotty includes four 20-pound Fin-Nor reels, six 50-pound LRS Shimanos, and two 80-pound Lindgren-Pitman electric reels on bent-butt rods. All his rods are custom made by Crowder Rods in Stuart, Florida. "The 20-pound rods are for any sails, white marlin, or dolphinfish that may rise to our teasers." These are referred to as pitch rods and will be used to cast to the rising fish. His choice of rod and reel for pitching is a 6½-foot Crowder with a Fin-Nor Marquesa spooled with 20-pound line.

This is opportunistic fishing, and it's best to be prepared with the baited rods. The 50-pound rods are all rigged with long 100-pound-test fluorocarbon leaders, fresh hand-tied Sea Witches, and 8/0 Mustad 9175 hooks. The hooks will be sharpened before rigging with ballyhoo. The 80-pound rods are spooled with 300-pound-test line to handle the really big fish that can be encountered. "We pull larger baits on the 80s, like Hawaiian Eyes or Mold Crafts with ballyhoo rigged on 220-pound extra hard Momoi leader. The hook is a number 10 J-hook."

On Captain Scotty's boat, the 50-pound rods are baited with medium-sized ballyhoo before deployment. It is the mate's job to have at least 50 rigged ballyhoos ready to go. These rigs do not use snap swivels or short leaders because Captain Scotty thinks bigger fish are inclined to shy away from the extra hardware. One of the 50s will pull a diving plug like a Braid Runner or a Marauder designed by luremaker Dennis Braid. Captain

Scotty particularly likes darker colors but says they all seem to work.

In addition to the medium ballyhoo rigged for trolling, there are 20 or so dink baits readied for the 20-pound pitch rods. Captain Scotty's dink baits are small to medium ballyhoo rigged with a smaller hook and leader in comparison to the day's norm. The smaller ballyhoo are rigged on 6-foot 60-pound leaders and 7/0 Mustad circle hooks for this application. Finally, a half-dozen big baits are rigged for the 80-pound rods with plenty more horse ballyhoo in the cooler if needed for later rigging.

The first few hours of a tuna trip are conducted in the dark. Captain Scotty gives everyone a lightstick or a strobe light for safety. "The radar is fired up and the spotlight turned on as we make our way to the inlet. Once the ocean is reached, I adjust the radar for the cruise, and we all settle in for about a 2½-hour ride to the fishing grounds. The departure time is calculated so we reach our destination at The Corner just as the sun is starting to break over the horizon." Once the fishing destination is reached, the radar is switched to bird mode and the riggers are dropped into position. The birds are usually marked on the radar very quickly, and a course is set to intercept the closed pack of feeding birds. All the rods are baited and ready to deploy.

Starting about a mile out from the birds, the engine is slowed and the approach begins, with everyone watching for the birds. At about three-fourths of a mile, the birds become visible to the naked eye. At this point a check of the water surface will reveal the busting, feeding fish below the birds. The engine is cut further to reach a trolling speed of 6½ to 8½ knots, and all the baits are deployed as quickly as possible, along with a couple of squid chains as teasers. "A normal approach will take us alongside the school. We continue forward until we reach a position where we can make a wide turn that will present the bait in front of the tuna."

When the first rod goes down, Captain Scotty continues to troll away, hoping for another hookup. The anglers are jigging their baits in an effort to entice yet another fish. "It is not unusual to have six or eight bent poles on the first bite of the day on a new school of fish. After the first bite, the rods are rebaited and deployed and we attempt to catch more fish."

Offshore fishing is very dependent on weather conditions and its effect on the radar. "Rain, clouds, and big waves interfere with radar signals and can make it hard to locate fish. Instinct and experience are important during these foul weather times to be successful. One thing is for sure, the fish are there, and when you find them under adverse conditions, they seem to cooperate better than ever."

Birds are definitely a desirable indicator of fish in the area, but seeing no birds does not mean not catching fish. "If the birds are not showing the way we want them to, we deploy a mullet dredge [see chapter 10] to enhance the bite." Some captains add dusters in front of each mullet to add some flash and color. Mullet are preferred by most captains, but ballyhoo can be used for the dredges. The problem is, they wash out too quickly and lose their appeal. Bottom line, however: pulling a dredge can increase your odds of hooking up. "If all goes as planned, by 11:00 we are done with the tuna; we put out a couple wahoo lures and chug along to the bottom grounds."

Once the bottom ground is reached, the crew rigs up for bottom fishing and drops the baits (see chapter 4). The plan is to catch a couple snapper and grouper on the deep drops and head back home by about 2:00 p.m. "We have that 2½-hour ride back to the inlet when we just relax a little and discuss the day. As we near the inlet, we start to hose off the bridge and outriggers and start to clean up the boat. When we get back to the dock, we unload the boat, take some pictures, and start cleaning the fish." The fresh fish fillets are bagged and given to the customers before boat cleaning is completed to end the day. "I usually finish a tuna trip about 7:30 p.m. or so and head home to play with my little boy and tuck him into bed." Captain Scotty describes The Corner as "an amazing place. I feel very fortunate to have been able to fish The Corner. If you are ever lucky enough to experience it on a good day, it will change you for life. If people realized what went on there on a regular day, I would be booked every day of the season." He likes to remind anglers that it is still just fishing and there are bad days, too, but day-in and day-out odds are good that fish will be caught at The Corner.

Charter Captains

Captain Marcia Foosaner

Hometown: Palm City, Florida
Business: "Gotcha" Charters
Phone number: 772-708-7689
E-mail address: fishalot1@mindspring.com
Note: Fly-only charters, limited basis

Captain Marcia's advice for visiting anglers: I would not be comfortable fishing an area I have never fished before without hiring a guide (and I am one). There is no substitute for local knowledge, and a guide can provide that. Checking with the local fishing stores will yield some good information, but that is not quite good enough. There is too much water to learn in a day or even a weekend trip. If you are bringing your own boat to fish from, it would be a sure waste of your time and money if you ran aground and spent your day either waiting for the tide to free you or paying Sea Tow several hundred dollars to tow you. Targeting a specific species can be seasonal, so question your guide about the best time to come. All this should be done in advance of your trip, not once you get here.

Captain Melinda Buckley, AKA Captain Melly B

Hometown: Stuart, Florida
Business: Buck's Tale Charters
Phone number: 772-607-1309
E-mail address: captmellyb@aol.com
Web site: www.captmellyb.com

Captain Melly's advice for visiting anglers: Hiring a local guide is the best way to learn an unfamiliar area. If hiring a guide is not in the budget, visit local tackle shops such as those listed below for some local knowledge. Ask the proprietors what's biting and what lures are working, and pick up a local map of the area. Another great resource is to find online fishing message boards such as the Florida Sportsman Fishing Forum, where people share local knowledge and fishing reports and even trade fishing trips with each other to share the costs.

Local bait and tackle shops are outstanding sources of current information for anglers. Shown here is the Snook Nook in Jensen Beach.

Captain Scott Fawcett

Hometown: Jensen Beach, Florida
Business: Boneshaker Sportfishing Charters
Phone number: 772-263-0904
E-mail address: fishscottyf@bellsouth.net
Web site: www.boneshakercharters.com

Captain Scott's advice for visiting anglers: A tuna trip is different from the normal nearshore trip out of St. Lucie Inlet; it is longer, and it requires more planning. If you want to target tuna, the first thing you should do is take time to find a captain and crew who consistently do that kind of fishing. A little research can prevent a long and unproductive boat ride. It is best to have a buddy boat on a long trip, but at least file a float plan for your day. Be sure your captain has all the proper licenses and Bahamas cruising permits. Whatever you do, don't underestimate the weather; it can change quickly and get rough. Radar is a must for a tuna trip. Remember, you are going to be 65 miles from home port and must do everything possible to make it a safe trip.

Area Hotspots

Surf anglers can try House of Refuge Beach or the St. Lucie Inlet Beach. The Hole in the Wall at St. Lucie Inlet is a favorite snook hangout, and Hells Gate on the St. Lucie River will get you away from the busy inlet traffic. Waders will find easy access on the south end of Hermann's Bay off A1A, and it is a great place to launch a kayak or just go for a walk. Sailfish Flats is another popular inshore spot. If you want to try the beach, check out Santa Lucea Beach with fly or spin equipment. Offshore anglers can start at the Evans Cary Bridge Pile or the Six-Mile Reef. This area is blessed with numerous wrecks and reefs. You can find their locations at martinreefs.com/pages/locations.html.

Fishing-Friendly Lodging and Glorious Galleys

Mary's Gourmet Diner

> 3310 NE Indian River Drive
> Jensen Beach, FL 34957
> Phone number: 772-334-9488

Looking for some local flavor? This is the place. Small but personal with homemade bread baked daily. Breakfast and lunch. Moderately priced. Don't miss it. Recommended by Capt. Marcia Foosaner and Capt. Rufus Wakeman.

River Palm Cottages & Fish Camp

> 2325 NE Indian River Drive
> Jensen Beach, FL 34957
> Phone number: 772-334-0401 or 800-305-0511

Clean rooms, private beach, fishing dock, and beautiful sunrises characterize this little jewel on the Indian River. The kids can enjoy the pool while the adults enjoy a lush tropical setting for maximum relaxation. A convenient public boat dock

River Palm Cottages are ideal lodging for the angler as well as the family. This view looks east over the beach and boat dock. Mullet schools are mulling in the foreground.

is located about a block away, or, if you prefer, just beach your boat near your cottage. Boat slips are also available. The author visits here every chance he gets. Recommended by Capt. Marcia Foosaner, Capt. Rufus Wakeman, and Capt. Scott Fawcett.

Ocean Breeze Deli and Grocery

2688 NE Dixie Highway
Jensen Beach, FL 34957
Phone number: 772-334-9331

Never mind that it's located next door to a Shell gasoline station; this place is great. You can fill up the boat and get a carryout sandwich to take on your fishing trip, or take it home at the end of the day. Great food, reasonable prices, all cooked to order. Author liked the cheesesteak sandwich. Recommended by Capt. Rufus Wakeman.

New England Fish Market

1419 NE Jensen Beach Boulevard
Jensen Beach, FL 34957
Phone number: 772-334-7324

No frills, just great seafood at a reasonable price. Smoked fish dip and saltines instead of bread. Bibs provided if needed. Lunch and dinner. Recommended by Capt. Marcia Foosaner and Capt. Rufus Wakeman.

11 Maple Street

3224 NE Maple Avenue
Jensen Beach, FL 34957
Phone number: 772-334-7714

Wanna eat somewhere really good? Great food, service, and atmosphere. The best restaurant in the world, according to Capt. Rufus Wakeman.

Caribbean Shores Hotel and Cottages

2625 NE Indian River Drive
Jensen Beach, Florida 34957
Phone number: 772-334-4759

A tranquil setting and relaxed atmosphere. Fish off the 300-foot pier, bring your boat, or enjoy their canoes and kayaks. Heated pool and hammocks swaying in the palm trees make this a great place to relax. Recommended by Capt. Marcia Foosaner.

Four Fish Inn and Marina

2225 NE Indian River Drive
Jensen Beach, FL 33957
Phone number: 772-334-0936

Full-service marina and trailer parking. Slips and storage available. Boat ramp ¼ mile to the south. Relaxing hotel, Keys atmosphere. The inn is nonsmoking and no pets. Especially good for bigger boats. Recommended by Capt. Billy Poertner.

Bait and Tackle

John B's Fly and Light Tackle

4326 SE Federal Highway
Stuart, FL 34997
Phone number: 772-287-6535

This shop sells, services, and repairs spin, casting, conventional, and offshore rods and reels. Fly tying materials and lots of different artificial baits. Recommended by Capt. Melinda Buckley and Capt. Marcia Foosaner.

Snook Nook Bait and Tackle

3595 NE Indian River Drive
Jensen Beach, FL 34957
Phone number: 772-334-2145

Complete line of bait and tackle, inshore and off. Rod and reel repair. Guide services, too. Call Henry or Freddie for the latest action reports or book an expert guide. Recommended by Capt. Melinda Buckley, Capt. Marcia Foosaner, and Capt. Rufus Wakeman.

Billy Bones Bait and Tackle

10602 S. Federal Highway
Port St. Lucie, FL 34952
Phone number: 772-335-3715

Live and frozen baits, tackle for inshore and off. Not sure what you need to catch the big one? Just ask Captain Bruce. Recommended by Capt. Melinda Buckley and Capt. Marcia Foosaner.

Finest Kind Offshore Tackle

3585 SE St. Lucie Blvd
Stuart, FL 34997
Phone number: 888-777-9789

Full-service marina in Port Salerno. Bait and tackle, offshore and inshore charter boats. Online store, too. Recommended by Capt. Rufus Wakeman and Capt. Scott Fawcett.

Southern Angler

4695 SE Dixie Highway
Stuart, FL 34997
Phone number: 772-223-1300

Southern Angler is the Treasure Coast's most complete fly shop. A place that remembers your name from the first time you walk in. They carry top-notch tackle, inshore and offshore, and have first-class people to help with your fishing questions. Recommended by Capt. Scott Fawcett.

Fishing Lessons for Life—Fishing Ethics

Good fishing etiquette can result in better fishing for everyone. Kids, especially, need to learn the proper way to conduct themselves when fishing around other anglers. If taught proper fishing ethics, kids will grow up with a sense of caring and responsibility for their own actions and also for the fishing resource. Respecting the rights of others is identified by many professional anglers as the one principle of ethical angling that is violated more than any other.

Proper fishing ethics begins with respect for other anglers. Any time there are anglers fishing in close proximity to each other, there are opportunities to show respect. Casting from boat or shore should be accomplished without crossing other anglers' lines. Likewise, when one angler is fighting a fish, other anglers should remove their lines from the water to prevent tangling of lines and loss of the fish.

Approaching shallow-water flats where fish can be super spooky must be done in a stealthy manner for best results. When other people are already fishing on the flat, an uncaring angler who runs the main motor all the way up on the flat usually blows out the fishing for everyone. Proper behavior requires anglers to give everyone plenty of room. It's no big deal to move a little further down the shoreline or move to another location altogether. Unfortunately for many anglers, seeing one fellow with a fish on is an invitation to run up beside him and fish. Shouting matches result, and the fun of fishing is diminished.

Boating anglers should be respectful at the boat dock. Boat

ramps are another opportunity for anglers to come in close proximity. Respectful behavior at the boat ramp means doing everything you can to reduce congestion. The boat should be prepared for launching in a staging area well away from the ramp. Insert the plug, remove retaining straps, and attach the dock lines before approaching the ramp. The boat should also be preloaded with tackle, bait, coolers, and other equipment to be used on the day's trip. The use of common sense at the ramp will prevent ramp rage and conflict with other boaters. It's not just the anglers trying to get on and off the water; it's also the recreational boaters who use the same facilities.

Kids need to learn environmental ethics, too. Environmental ethics are about conservation and refer to taking care of the resource, which is the environment you are in while fishing. Anglers should avoid leaving prop scars in shallow-water grass beds. There are a few simple things anglers can do to reduce prop scarring. Use maps to study fishing areas and familiarize yourself with water depths, wear polarized sunglasses that allow you to locate shallow areas more easily, and raise the main engine and use the trolling motor while navigating shallow water.

Anglers should also be mindful of trash and debris in the fishing area. This is one of the simplest of all ethical behaviors to teach. Anglers should not be litterbugs, distributing their trash all over the fishing environment. In fact, it is easy to take out more trash than you bring in. When adults demonstrate this behavior on a regular basis, children will pick it up and learn to be good stewards of the resource. It is a sad state of affairs to find a dead bird tangled in discarded monofilament line that prevented it from flying and feeding. The discarded line caused its death, and it would have been so simple for the angler to have properly disposed of the line. Picking up and disposing of trash is a win-win proposition. The result is a clean, litter-free shoreline as opposed to one cluttered with trash and debris.

Anglers can and should be role models to make the future of fishing more enjoyable for all participants. Good fishing ethics are as simple as the thoughtful application of the Golden Rule toward other anglers, the fishery resource, and the environment. Treat your fellow anglers the way you would like to be treated by them.

10

~~~~~~~~~~

Lake Worth, Jupiter, Palm Beach, and Boca Raton

This southernmost portion of the Treasure Coast is rich in history relating economic activity to the Atlantic Ocean. Early explorers documented the existence of the natural inlets as far back as the 1500s. Settlers to the area quickly recognized the economic value of open trade lanes connecting the area to the ocean and were aggressive in upgrading existing natural inlets and creating two additional inlets. Today the county of Palm Beach is home to four navigable inlets connecting the area to the rest of the world by water. Each of the inlets was opened and closed to the sea many times by the forces of nature through the years. The persistence of early settlers and later residents paid off, however, and all four inlets are fully navigable today.

Historians recognize Jupiter Inlet as one of the major natural inlets on the east coast of Florida. Being a natural inlet does not mean the inlet is forever open. Hurricanes and winds would often fill the inlet with sand, making passage impossible. In those early days, a lack of heavy equipment forced settlers to open the inlet with shovels and manpower. Digging a ditch to start the water flowing would allow the incoming tide to reopen the inlet until the next storm closed it. Periodic dredging has prevented closure of the inlet and maintained it in a navigable state in more recent years. A lighthouse was

Jupiter Inlet is well known as a departure point to catch sailfish. Photo by Capt. Bouncer Smith.

built in 1859 that still stands today. Jupiter Inlet is known as a dangerous inlet to navigate, and boaters should beware.

Lake Worth Inlet is a manmade inlet connecting the Atlantic to the ICW. Lake Worth was once a freshwater lake, until an early pioneer cut a trench to the ocean, lowering the water in the lake to sea level and providing a shipping lane for area goods. The inlet was moved several times until about 1917, when it was opened at its current location. By 1965 the inlet had improved rock jetties and been deepened to 33 feet. The deepening by the Corps of Engineers met with some resistance by local residents who feared the deeper inlet would capture more sand, leaving less to drift down on area beaches. Today the inlet is maintained at a depth of 35 feet.

Historical records indicate that Palm Beach County citizens were discussing the possibility of creating another inlet from the southern part of Lake Worth to the ocean as early as 1913. These discussions came to fruition in March of 1927 when a third inlet was created. The South Lake Worth Inlet (also called the Boynton Inlet) was opened as an additional shipping and transportation route, but the main reason was for health and sanitation issues related to the declining water quality in Lake Worth. This inlet, like those before it, was plagued with filling by Mother Nature's forces. Higher, longer jetties and a sand transfer operation help keep the inlet open today.

The fourth and southernmost inlet in the county is Boca Raton Inlet. It was originally a natural inlet, but its location has changed over the years. It was not until 1967 when high winds closed the inlet once again, causing the water in Lake Boca Raton to stagnate. Once the local newspaper reported that the water in the lake was polluted, city officials began activities that would reopen the inlet and keep it open to this day. The city continues to maintain the inlet at its present size of about 150 feet wide and 10 feet deep. The north jetty is 650 feet long, and the south jetty is 800 feet long.

More recent history of the area includes a true habitat reconstruction success story in the Lake Worth Lagoon. During the 1920s, dredging and filling operations along the edge of the Lake Worth Lagoon resulted in deep holes that accumulated sediments and became devoid of oxygen. The result was an area unsuitable for marine life. This *dead zone* was an area north of the Lake Worth Bridge and adjacent to the Lake Worth Municipal Golf Course.

A project to revive the zone was undertaken in a city, county, state, and federal government partnership. The result of the partnership was a revitalized and useful wetland habitat in the lagoon. The Palm Beach County Web site reports the following successes for the Snook Islands Natural Area, which was completed in 2005:

- Restored 100 acres of wetland habitat in the Lake Worth Lagoon.
- Filled deep holes with 1.2 million cubic yards of sand from Peanut Island that had been previously dredged to maintain the Intracoastal Waterway and inlets.

- Graded fill to wetland elevations, creating four islands and submerged land suitable for seagrass.
- Eliminated erosion and created a natural shoreline along 1.2 linear miles of the lagoon.
- Removed exotic plant species like Australian pine, Brazilian pepper tree, and seaside mahoe from 5 acres of shoreline and restored 1.7 acres of existing mangrove fringe.
- Planted 11 acres of mangroves and 3.8 acres of spartina (commonly known as cordgrass) along the shoreline and on the islands.
- Stabilized mangrove planting areas with 28,000 tons of limestone boulders.
- Created 2.2 acres of oyster reefs.
- Restored 40 acres of shallow subtidal habitats to promote seagrass colonization.

Captain Danny Barrow operates Silver Lining Fish Charters on the Lake Worth Lagoon and the nearshore waters of central and southern Palm Beach County. He describes the cleanup and revitalization as the rebirth of a lagoon. "This project in the Lake Worth Lagoon in central Palm Beach County was once a dead zone. A 10-foot-thick layer of muck was all the 2-mile stretch of water had to offer. With grant money, the Palm Bay County Environmental Resource Management Department built the Snook Islands, and today the area thrives as an aquatic nursery and hosts some great snook fishing at times."

Characteristics of the Fishing Area

The four ocean inlets and all the connecting waters inside the barrier islands provide an unending array of fishing opportunities for local and visiting anglers. Jupiter Inlet is a natural inlet with a rock jetty that can be a great location for snook fishing. The Loxahatchee River empties into the Atlantic Ocean through Jupiter Inlet, creating what some have called a haven for sharks and shark fishermen. Lake Worth Inlet floods the inland area, providing excellent fishing on the backcountry flats and shorelines.

Hobe Sound has plenty of grass flats and oyster bars for the shallow-water angler. Captain Chad McGann operates Fly and Light Tackle Fishing in the area. He identifies a variety of fish that can be caught on the flats of the Sound. "You can find a host of desirable species such as snook, trout, tarpon, pompano, snapper, grouper, ladyfish, bluefish, jacks, and occasionally redfish. I've even caught a few bonefish, but we are a little too far north to expect them regularly. There are also some less desirable fish like catfish, lizardfish, poisonous rock fish, and puffers that will pull drag as well."

There are numerous elongated rock outcroppings throughout the revitalized island chain called Snook Islands. Many of the outcroppings are totally submerged at high tide and exposed at low tide. The west side of the area is populated by spartina grass with mangrove trees growing along the shoreline. Captain Danny says, "The larger islands are surrounded by granite boulders on three sides, leaving the westward sides exposed, allowing the incoming tide to flood the mangrove area that was planted on the interior of each island. The eastern side of the island chain parallels the ICW and is much deeper than the interior side of the project."

The inlets provide rock jetties, and the connecting waterways have bridges and lighted docks that are particularly good for night fishing. During the hot Florida summers, a night fishing trip can be a comfortable and productive activity. For the nearshore anglers, the waters off the beach have scattered rock outcroppings that tend to hold fish. The beach fishing can be accessed either by boat or by shore.

Plenty of boat ramps give anglers easy access to the water, and several bait shops and marinas provide all essential supplies and services. The area is well marked and easily navigable by expert and novice alike. Water-accessible restaurants are a welcome respite for lunch or a way to end a day of fishing.

The Inshore Bite—Fishing the Revitalized Snook Islands

The Snook Islands were designed for shallow-water fishing, but understanding the cautions associated with skinny water are a must for venturing out in the Snook Island area. Proper entry and exit will result in more fish caught and less time stranded on a shallow sandbar at low tide. The area is practically impossible to enter from the north on a low tide. Captain Danny advises anglers, "It's shallow, so enter on the high tide at the southern end if the draft of your boat allows. Fish your way out heading north and the tide will be your friend." He says an alternative method for fishing the island chain is to enter from the north and use an electric trolling motor. Always be mindful of the shallow areas in relation to the tide. The trolling motor method allows you to fish your way south through the islands before turning around and exiting back to the north. "If I get into the fish, I use the trolling motor to hold the boat in position while I work the entire zone." The quiet trolling motor is much more effective than a noisy outboard in these conditions. He says the entire area is a bird sanctuary, so walking on the islands is prohibited.

Fishing the island chain in the early morning is prime time for topwater fishing lures. Captain Danny recommends topwater baits like the Heddon Super Spook Jr. and Rapala Skitterwalk to produce some fantastic topwater action. "I like to fish the points of the rock outcroppings early in the morning. I use a walk-the-dog presentation with a topwater lure fished parallel to the outcroppings. I have found this approach to be very productive, especially on an outgoing tide." He prefers spin cast or conventional reels spooled with 10- to 15-pound braid for his island hopping adventures. Add 30- or 40-pound fluorocarbon leader to protect against cutoffs by burly snook. Snook gill plates are very sharp and will cut a line that wraps the fish during the fight. Snook also have a very rough mouth that can cause light leaders to fail from rubbing on the abrasive

Early morning is prime time for huge snook on the Treasure Coast. Photo by John Wilkas.

mouth. "I personally like an 8-foot medium-fast-action rod with enough backbone to pull fish away from any structure. Braided line and heavy leader are also a must when fishing around the rocks."

Later in the day the spartina-covered flats are the best place to continue the action. Captain Danny uses the same outfits but switches to soft plastic baits. "When I fish the spartina grass and flats, I like a 4- or 5-inch plastic bait. The D.O.A. C.A.L. Jerkbaits are my favorite." He rigs the lure weedless, using a 5/0 worm hook when in the grass. The weedless presentation with the hook buried in the plastic body can be thrown into the thickest of cover and retrieved without entangling. Bouncing on the bottom, this bait mimics a shrimp or crab. It will fall into and come out of the grass without fouling. A steady retrieve with varied wrist flicks will keep it swimming and simulating a small baitfish. Either presentation is deadly on the flats.

There is an old saying that silence is golden. Nowhere is this more applicable than when fishing the flats. Stealth plays a big role in the strategy of successful anglers. Stealth is not as critical when fishing 10 feet of water as it in when fishing 1 foot, but why take a chance on spooking fish at any depth? Anglers should always approach fishing areas quietly for best results. Captain Chad McGann gains a level of stealth by drift-fishing when conditions allow it. He says, "I drift-fish all the way from the channel, which is about 10 feet deep, to the mangrove shoreline when the tide is high. At low tide I still drift in as close to the mangroves as I can." He says he prefers the higher phases of the tide because there are a lot of shallows and docks with lights that hold fish on the higher phases of tide. "The fish tend to move out with the tide, making it harder to find them."

The position and speed of the boat are critical elements in successful fishing of the grassy flats. "I almost always use a drift anchor tied to the bow to position the boat into the wind. The drift anchor also slows the drift and allows me to cover the water thoroughly. A 5-gallon bucket will also do the trick." Captain Chad suggests anglers watch ahead of the drift for fishy-looking points that come into casting range. "I will sometimes anchor off the points and fan-cast the area. Points are natural ambush areas for predator fish and should not be overlooked." He suggests using a variety of lures to find out what they are eating on a particular day. It may be a jig one day and topwater lure the next. It's up to the angler to figure out which lure to use on a given day.

Captain Chad's outfit of choice is a medium-action spinning rod with a 3000 or 4000 size reel. Reels are spooled with 10-pound-test Berkley Fireline for maximum casting distance. He adds a 2-foot fluorocarbon trace of 20-pound test to hide the mainline from the fish. To the trace leader he adds a

30-pound bite tippet to guard against the abrasive mouths of snook. All line sections are connected with double uni knots.

Choosing which lure to start the day's fishing usually boils down to past experience. Certain lures produce well and become the angler's go-to lure. Captain Chad's go-to lure is the Cotee Jig's Chubby Grub. It is a shrimp-scented plastic bait that he rigs on a ¼- to ⅜-ounce jig head. "I cast in the direction of the drift so I'm mostly fishing undisturbed water. I cast straight downwind to keep the arc out of the line and gain a better feel for strikes." He lets the lure sink to the bottom before snapping his wrist one to three times to make the lure bounce up and down before settling back to the bottom. "Most of your hits will come as the jig falls, so monitor the slack as you drop your rod, and feel for that bite. Repeat this retrieve all the way back to the boat. You will be surprised how many fish will follow the jig all the way to the boat before striking."

Use the same jig head and a live shrimp for an alternative presentation. Pinch off the tail of a live shrimp and insert the hook in the exposed flesh. Removing the tail releases more scent, which attracts the fish. Fish the rig the same as the jig head and plastic with short, quick wrist flicks to bounce

Pinch the tail off a shrimp and pin it on a jig head through the exposed flesh. Bounce off the bottom or trail behind a drifting boat for good results. Photo by Karen Presley.

it along the bottom. Captain Chad says, "Even when flipping jigs and plastic, I will sometimes drag a jig head with a shrimp behind the boat and pick up a few fish that way."

Captain Chad emphasizes the importance of stealth in improving the hookup ratio; that's why he likes to drift. "If you have a trolling motor, working the shoreline with a jig or lures can be productive, but I like to save my trolling motor for fishing dock lights and bridges at night."

Fishing Bridges and Dock Lights at Night

Snook love dock lights, and anglers do, too. "I like to fish the dock lights and bridges at night, mostly targeting snook," says Captain McGann. Snook are naturally attracted to structure, and the lights add the ingredient of abundant food to the equation. Some anglers even think snook are more eager to feed at night and not as spooky as in the day. The fish don't see an approaching angler in the dark as easily as they do in the sunlight. The combination of structure, lights, and baitfish normally results in a successful fishing trip.

The same equipment used on the flats can be used around the docks and bridges most of the time, but sometimes heavier gear is needed. "I'll often use the same spin equipment as on the flats, but sometimes have to beef up the gear depending on the fish I expect to catch." He prefers 7-foot rods for steering fish around the boat and its many snags. If a fish goes under the boat, the angler needs to stick the rod straight down to clear props, trim tabs, and trolling motors. He says the 7-foot rods are not too long and not too short. During late summer months and into the fall, bigger baits and bigger snook are the norm. "I want medium heavy or heavy spinning rods for the bigger fish. The trace will be 25- to 30-pound fluorocarbon, and the bite tippet will be 30- to 40-pound fluorocarbon." He says it's a no-brainer if you see popping snook in a light; you most certainly stop and fish, but just because you don't see any doesn't mean they aren't there. "Some lights almost always hold fish; some do not. Knowing which docks to spend some time on comes with experience."

A trolling motor can be a great tool for working the lighted docks and bridges. Use the motor to quietly position the boat for the best presentation. If you don't have a trolling motor, set up a drift and cut the engine to silently float by the targeted area. Alternatively you can anchor, again being as quiet as possible so as not to spook the fish. Lighted bridges are characterized by a distinct shadow line created by the lights and structure. Captain Chad recommends anchoring up-current about a boat-length or two from the shadow line. Snook bite better in moving water, so the current is an important element of this strategy. "You can often feed live bait straight behind the boat and get the fish to strike. Or, you can work the shadow line by casting up-current of the shadow line, in the light, and let your bait drift or swim into the shadow at different distances from the boat. Likewise, if you see or hear a fish pop, cast to where the bait will drift toward the feeding action." Proper positioning of the boat allows the angler to drift the bait into the shadows without repeated casting.

The strategy for fishing the bridges with a lure is basically the same as with the live bait. Work the shadow line by casting up-current into the light. Retrieve the lure just inside the shadow line for best results. "The speed of the current will determine how fast your retrieve should be. The fish will be lined up in the shadow line facing the current, looking for food coming at them from the light. It's no secret: snook bite better in moving water, so if there is no current, you'll just have to cast under the bridge and work the shadow line as close as you can."

Captain Chad says one of his secrets for successful dock and bridge fishing in this area relates to the size of the lures. "I like to fish smaller jigs and lures around the lights. The fish in my area have seen everything and have had everything thrown at them. Believe it or not, larger lures tend to scare them off. I generally try to use what the snook are eating." He says around Jupiter the bait is usually pretty small, so he recommends little bucktail or synthetic jigs in white, white/olive, or chartreuse. "Small reasonably lifelike plastic jigs that resemble shrimp or fish work well too." Since he also enjoys fly-fishing, he suggests using small synthetic fiber or polar fleece flies in the same colors as the jigs. Sometimes he ties a fly behind a jig when the bite is slow. "Sometimes I will trail a fly behind a jig on a 20-inch leader to spark a strike when the bite is tough."

Live-bait anglers have great success around the docks. When bait can be cast netted, there is no better way to match the hatch. "When fishing live baits, I use a fairly small hook relative to the size of the bait so it can swim and look natural. If I have finger mullet, 3/0 or 4/0 live-bait hooks work just fine. For small white bait, 4 to 5 inches long, I'll use a 1/0 or 2/0 hook." He says he doesn't normally use circle hooks when fishing under the lights. "Since snook suck the bait in so quickly and you are generally fishing around structure, you have to hit them right away and get them out before they know what's going on. Circle hooks don't always hook the fish under these conditions." It is Captain Chad's experience that the live-bait hooks will generally hook the fish in the mouth, too, because of the quick hook-set. Additionally, they rarely miss the hookup on an aggressive bite.

Live shrimp are a good choice under the lights as well. They can be bought at local bait and tackle shops, which is easier and less time consuming than finding and netting mullet. Even with the shrimp, Captain Chad sticks with the smaller sizes. "I use shrimp around 3 or 4 inches long, maybe smaller. The smaller shrimp is what the snook are used to seeing and eating. You would think any self-respecting snook would gobble down a big live shrimp, but I've seen big shrimp scare them away." He recommends pinning the shrimp on light wire hooks. He says a #1 or #2 hook is just right.

Fly rodders can also have fun catching snook under the

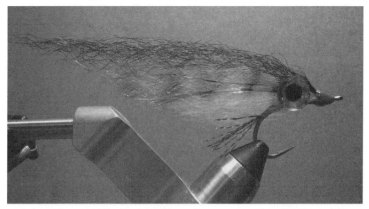

Night snook around docks or bridges will sometimes hit a fly when nothing else will work. This one is called Stu's Flash Mullet, tied by Stuart Patterson. Photo by Stuart Patterson.

lights. Captain Chad is an avid fly fisher with lots of experience. "Snook love a fly," says Captain Chad. "I will often get them to take a fly when they won't take anything else." He uses an 8- or 9-weight rod except for when the bigger fish are present; then he steps up to a 10 weight. He prefers a floating line under the lights with a 20-30-40 tapered fluorocarbon leader. "I tie my own leaders using equal lengths of fluorocarbon to match the length of the fly rod. I usually don't add a bite tippet because the presentation is better without it."

Matching the hatch is the fly fisher's passion. Captain Chad is no different. "I mostly use smaller flies that match the baits common to the area. My hooks will be small, #2 down to as small as #10. In my experience these small hooks will, more often than not, hook the fish in the corner of the mouth, eliminating the need for a bite tippet." He says his best results have come on the higher phases of the tide, when the water is moving more bait through the area. "Try not casting directly on the fish whenever possible, or fish might spook. Cast past them into the shadows and work your fly through the light." He says anglers will often get to watch the fish come out and take the offering when fishing under the lights.

When the current is running fast, the best cast is up-current, allowing the fly to be swept into the light. "Allowing the current to carry the fly to the strike zone is a more natural presentation and not as likely to spook the fish." Notice that this strategy is different from shadow lines on bridges. With lighted dock fishing, the fish are in the shadows and the light, but won't see the bait until it comes through the light. The longer your bait moves through the light on the water, the more likely they will see it and strike. They may take it after it moves into the shadow again, but that is not usually the case.

The Offshore Bite—Sailfish

Anglers unfamiliar with sailfishing along the Treasure Coast are likely unfamiliar with how labor intensive it can be. The hard work has a big payoff, however, when it comes to putting fish in the boat. Captain Rufus Wakeman is a native Florida guide with more than 20 years' fishing experience, much of it chasing sailfish. He says, "Sailfish are available all year long, and the fish can be caught very close to shore. On any given day sails can be caught on a variety of readily available baits." He identifies the best months for sailfish as November through March. "The colder winter months are good, but don't let the time of year dictate your sailfish trip. The Martin County area is not known as the Sailfish Capital of the World by accident."

If you think a huge boat with lots of fancy equipment is needed to catch sailfish, the Treasure Coast fishing experience puts that theory to rest quickly. "You don't need a 60-foot multimillion-dollar sportfishing boat to catch sailfish," according to Captain Rufus. "Any 17- to 30-foot outboard boat will do just fine." A visiting angler who trailers a 17-foot Boston Whaler to Florida for a family vacation can easily head offshore and have a great chance at catching a sail. Captain Rufus says it's not unusual to catch 5 to 10 sailfish in a day. "If live bait can be found, the task gets even easier. The fish are only about 2 to

Trolling live or dead bait could result in an aerial display by an angry sailfish. Photo by Capt. Billy Poertner.

4 miles offshore, and if the weather is good it's the making of a great day of offshore fishing."

The underwater topography of the area is quite unremarkable. "There are no major drop-offs, no huge seamounts rising from the ocean floor, and no really outstanding shoreline variations. The ocean bottom is actually quite boring, with a gradual depth change off the continental slope." Captain Rufus says the slope is a bit more pronounced as you travel south of Jupiter around Palm Beach, but by no means drastic. As one travels north out of Jupiter Inlet, the slope is even more gradual around the Stuart area. Given the gradient in the Stuart area, anglers have to travel about 6 miles offshore to find what Captain Rufus calls *fishable water* for sails.

There is a current edge created by the constantly northward moving Gulf Stream current that makes this area a sailfish haven. "This current is the life force of the fishing up and down the east coast of the United States. The bonus for us, here along the Treasure Coast, is that we have the Stream right here in our own backyard."

There are a few small topographic events that stand out in the area, but they are not all that significant. Two of them are the Loran Tower Ledge, off Hobe Sound, and Pushbutton Hill, located 9 miles off Stuart. The Loran Tower Ledge is a commonly fished area for bottom fish, but if bait is holding there, sailfish and king mackerel are likely too. Pushbutton Hill is a little bit farther offshore than you normally have to go for sailfish, but they do get caught there. All in all, the bottom is quite flat, and the major fish-holding things are the available forage fish and the current edges created by the Gulf Stream.

Trolling dead or live bait around these areas will produce some nice sailfish for lucky anglers. "It is pretty simple fishing. Small boat or large, you only need to put out two or three lines and get ready for the aerial assault of ole spindlebeak himself."

Three Types of Sailfishing

For the uninitiated there are three basic types of sailfishing: tournament sailfishing, trolling, and live baiting. They differ mostly in terms of preparation and intensity. The reward from each is great.

Tournament Sailfishing

Tournament sailfishing is an activity of time-consuming and endless preparation that includes rigging dead bait teasers. "The payoff for all the effort is a good pat on the back, since there are normally no prize moneys involved in the many just-for-fun tournaments. Anglers fish in tough conditions and endure brutal seas all in the name of catching a great fish on light tackle."

Basic trolling for sailfish is a more relaxed endeavor. Preparation time is much less with this type of trolling. Teasers are used, but they are generally artificial instead of dead bait. This is a significant difference in the amount of time needed to prepare for an outing. Live baiting for sailfish is the most relaxed of the three types. Live bait works really well for sailfish and may result in double-digit days. "Anglers are normally going slow and down-sea, bumping the engine in and out of gear to keep the troll speed slow. Using spinning rods on Baitrunner mode makes it an exercise in fun and sport, and usually [brings] lots of success."

To get a real appreciation for sailfishing, anglers can study what tournament anglers go through in preparing and fishing in competition with other anglers. As with any sporting competition, the anglers involved in sailfish tournaments do everything they can to come out on top. Understanding their attention to detail will make anyone seeking sails a better angler.

The teasers used in tournament sailfishing are called dredges. The dredges are used to attract the sails to the trolling spread. They can be quite time consuming and labor intensive to make, but they are the backbone of the fishing system used by competitive anglers. A single dredge can consist of 12 to 48 teaser baits, depending on an individual captain's preference.

Dredges are a star-shaped metal apparatus with six arms and a center pull to connect the tow line. Captain Rufus says, "Large split-tail mullet are placed at two points of each arm of the star. This can result in 12 teasers on each dredge. Some captains like to stack the dredges, resulting in as many as 48 individual split-tail mullet on a dredge system." This may sound like a lot of work, but the resulting illusion of a school of bait swimming below the surface is too much for predator fish to resist.

The dredges are usually pulled on a dedicated electric reel that has about 80 pounds of pulling capacity. These systems are not for everyone, since the reels alone can cost from $2,000 to $4,000. When the dredges are stacked and pulled in tandem, the drag created by this system is tremendous. When you get a bite, you have to get the dredges out of the way. Some anglers use a small block-and-tackle–style pulley to assist in retrieving the dredge for servicing when an encounter with a toothy barracuda or kingfish wreaks havoc with a dredge. According to Captain Rufus, "Those toothy critters also require competitive anglers to have plenty of mullet and ballyhoo prepared for the day's fishing."

Each mullet used on the dredge may take five to ten minutes to prepare by a good deckhand and must be properly brined and iced for maximum potential. "You also need several extra split-tails in case of toothy encounters." A typical day of tournament fishing could require 100 or more prepared mullet. "That's just for the teasers," says Captain Rufus. "You also need rigged ballyhoo to use as trolled bait. I wouldn't start a sailfish trip with fewer than 50 rigged ballyhoos in the cooler." Add it up. That is 150 time-consuming preparations to execute before leaving the dock.

Sometimes when not in a tournament situation, some captains will pull dredges that have real split-tail mullet on the outside of the dredge and artificial Vibra-tail–style fish on the inside. "This system saves on cost and prep time, but diehard skippers will always pull all real mullet in competition." There are also Mylar strips available with decals of baitfish. These are considered the least attractive, but a well-prepared boat would have a few just in case of emergency when they run out of the real thing.

Rods and reels have advanced dramatically in recent years. Captain Rufus prefers a 20-pound-class conventional rod with matching reel. "The rod should have a good set of either roller or silicon carbide style Fuji guides. The standards in the reel industry are Penn and Shimano, with Shimano being the more popular reel, and specifically the TLD 20 in my opinion." He says several new companies have come on the market in recent years. "Reels from Alutecnos, Avet, Accurate, and Daiwa are all very good reels, and you can't go wrong with any of them." He says some of the new companies even offer color coordination. Captain Rufus recalls an old saying: "It's better to look good than feel good." If that instills confidence in your fishing operation, then he says, "Go for it."

Most fishing lines when tested will overtest the stated breaking strength. This is not a problem for recreational anglers, but tournament anglers may be required to use a pretested line. "Most tournaments require anglers to use a tournament-rated line. Ande Tournament Line in 20-pound green is the industry standard. This line is factory tested and certified. Its green color is unmistakable, so any tournament committee member can visually see that the correct line is being used."

Once the rod, reel, and line have been selected, a leader system is included in the rigging. Captain Rufus starts with a Bimini Twist to double about 4 feet of the mainline. He adds up to 15 feet of 60- to 80-pound mono with an Albright special knot, creating a wind-on leader. The Albright will easily pass through the guides on the rod. A small snap swivel completes the rig. When ready to set the spread, the bait leader is connected to the snap swivel and the fishing begins.

Competitive anglers have to abide by IGFA rules when constructing the wind-on leader. The total length allowed is 15 feet for the leader and 20 feet for the double line leader setup. The wind-on leader allows anglers to wind the fish up close since the bait leader, tied to the swivel, is only about 4 feet long.

Recently the National Marine Fisheries Service called on all recreational anglers to use non-offset circle hooks *exclusively* when fishing in a sailfish tournament. Captain Rufus favors the use of the circle hooks. "Circle hooks are a great tool, and they result in an easy hook-set. They are very forgiving to the fish in terms of injury. The hook literally hooks itself in the corner of the jaw and almost never does any damage to the fish by hooking it in the gut."

Using circle hooks can also simplify bait rigging and deployment. Instead of rigging ballyhoo with the hook embedded, they are rigged with a small swivel or wire loop protruding from the front. Storing bait is simpler, too, because there are no hooks to tangle in the cooler. The circle hook remains attached to the leader. Initial baiting or rebaiting is accomplished by simply passing the circle hook through the swivel eye or wire loop attached to the bait.

Setting the spread can be a matter of personal preference. Tournament spreads will include more lines, but the normal spread for chasing sails consists of four deployed baits. Two flatlines are fished about 50 feet behind the boat, and two outrigger baits somewhere between 150 and 200 feet. The baits are pulled at between 4 and 6 miles per hour, which is pretty slow. "The slow speed allows the baits to swim and skip, looking natural in the presentation. Sometimes the flatlines will have a small lead weight incorporated into the chin area." The chin weight is designed to keep the bait underwater. On windy days a colored and weighted skirt of a synthetic material can be added to the outrigger baits to keep them from blowing around in the wind and make them easier to see.

The importance of fresh ballyhoo to tournament anglers cannot be overstated. "Skippers and mates want quality bait only. The ballyhoo should have firm bellies and good color." Captain Rufus recommends the use of kosher salt to firm up the bellies and dry the bait once the baits are rigged and placed in the cooler. He says most good tackle stores will get shipments of fresh ballyhoo the day before the tournament begins and fresh shipments every day of the tournament. "Smaller baits are preferred over larger ones because they are eaten much more easily by the sailfish, and the hookup ratio is better."

Recreational anglers can take a page from the tournament anglers when it comes to setting the spread. Instead of just letting out some line and attaching it to the retaining clip at some random footage, competitive anglers use a special connection. "Tournament crews like to use what is called a floss loop. The floss loop is added to the line at 50 and 150- to 200-foot intervals. The 50-foot loop is for the flatlines, and the other is for the riggers." This system not only provides a connection for the baited line to the clip, it also ensures that the bait is always deployed to the same place it was before. With two loops on all rigs, any rod can be used for either flatline or rigger.

The material used in making the loop is flat waxed dental floss. The loop is created by making a series of half-hitches around the mainline, leaving a loop about ½ inch in diameter to slip in the clip. Captain Rufus favors the loop method for connecting the line to the clips. "This is a really good way to deploy lines, and there is no chance of chafing. The loops also act as a marker on the line, so you know how far away the fish is as you reel in the line." Some anglers even color-coordinate the loops for rigger or flatline, making the baiting and rebaiting even easier. The rods are now ready for action, with maximum ease of use in mind.

As you can see up to this point, the tournament fishing enthusiasts have a lot of work to do before they catch the first fish. Other preparation duties include prepping the boat, checking all the equipment, and packing the food and drinks. Add the expense associated with tournament sailfishing, and you can see why some fun-seeking anglers stick with straight trolling.

Trolling for Sailfish

Trolling is considered the gentleman's way of catching sailfish by some, because it requires more skill than live baiting, but it is not as intense as tournament fishing. It is kind of like chili purists who won't add beans to their favorite chili recipe, but still take steps to ensure it is tasty. "There are those anglers who still enjoy the thrill of the dropback and the hookup of a troll-caught sailfish. These gentleman anglers think live baiting is cheating, because it's just too easy."

Several major things differentiate the tournament anglers from the trollers. "Circle hooks are not mandatory when trolling for sailfish, but some skippers use them out of habit. The mullet dredge is not that important, and an artificial dredge might be used exclusively. Finally, Daisy Chains may be used in place of the dredges." Daisy Chains are rigs that pull mullet, ballyhoo, or even artificial squid. The Daisy Chains skip along the surface or slightly beneath the surface. The dredges might be 4 to 8 feet under the surface and are much more labor intensive. "Sailfish will pay attention to any of these, but most [anglers] agree the dredge is best."

The trolling crowd also likes to prepare the day before. "It is still good to be prepared and have your baits prerigged the night before or on the way out if sea conditions warrant. Either fresh or frozen ballyhoo will work just fine." Captain Rufus reminds anglers that demand is low during the nontournament time of year for fresh ballyhoo, so frozen bait is the norm. His advice is to thaw the bait very slowly overnight. "One method I like to use is a half bag of ice in a 5-gallon bucket, half filled with seawater. This quick brine mixture allows the frozen baits to thaw more slowly than if they were just put in the bucket to thaw." The salty brine also firms up the bait and gives them a more natural appearance. Additional salt can be added after rigging and placement in the cooler. Not only do they look better, they also stay on the hook better.

Live Baiting for Sailfish

Live baiting for sailfish has long been considered *cheating* by some anglers because of its overall effectiveness and ease of application. "Trolling is considered the purist method of fishing for sails. In the few tourneys that recognize live baiting, the troll-caught fish count 300 points while the live bait–caught fish count for only 100 points. This observation alone high-

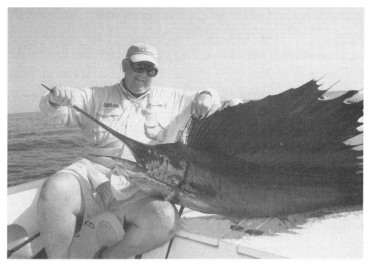

Treasure Coast sailfish can be caught within 2 miles of the beach. Photo by Capt. Freddie Caimotto.

lights the difference in attitude among anglers toward using live bait to catch ole spindlebeak."

Live baiting is very effective and can be done from small boats as well as from large boats. Captain Rufus's initiation into sailfish catching came many years ago. "We didn't even start the day until 2:30 p.m. in a 17-foot Whaler. Only two lines were deployed. The day ended with five sails, caught on light spinning gear, before dark. The key was the live threadfin herring we used for bait." Since that day he has upped his best-day count to 10, but that took him all day. "Records show that some crews have caught as many as 80 sails in a day, on live bait, off the Florida coast. Now that's some snapping sailfish accomplishment."

Live baiting for sails may be very casual for some anglers, but it is very serious for others. "Some crews have the attitude of let's just go out and toss four or five liveys over and wish for the best, and some crews take it to much higher levels. The higher levels involve kite fishing."

The casual approach to live baiting requires suitable rods and reels, a strong mainline, and some prerigged bait. Almost any rod and reel will do, but they have to be strong enough to land a big fish. Twenty-pound-test line should be a minimum, and medium-heavy action rods are a good all-round choice. Sixty to 80-pound leader material should be added before attaching the hook. A snap swivel at the end of the leader makes it easy to change terminal tackle when needed. Head offshore a couple miles and start trolling. Two lines should be pulled 50 to 75 yards back, another at 100 to 125 yards, and the final one will be the wayback, or shotgun line.

That really is all there is to the casual approach. Troll live bait around the area until a hookup is realized, land the fish, and take some photos. Take sufficient time to revive the fish and start the process all over again. If no fish are caught in the area you are fishing, move on to prospect some new territory. For some more enthusiastic anglers, casual live baiting is not enough. They turn to kite fishing.

Kite fishing was invented by the Polynesians a long time ago to aid in getting baits out over the reef while fishing from land. On Florida's East Coast, kite fishing has been taken to extreme levels while fishing from boats. Most knowledgeable captains would identify Jupiter and south to Miami and the Keys as the capital of this high-flying exercise (see chapter 11 for more on kite fishing). "Some crews use one kite and deploy two to three liveys from the kite string and have a fair amount of success, while other crews deploy two kites with three baits off each and they can just crush the fish." The object of the kite is to keep the bait on the surface of the water. The bait, struggling against the pull of the line, drives the fish wild and results in multiple strikes.

The best rods for live bait kite fishing are 20- to 30-pound spinning rods that can handle big spinning reels. Captain Rufus recommends reels like the Shimano 6500 Baitrunner or the Penn 850. "These reels have a large line capacity necessary for the amount of line let out while kite fishing. The far-back baits will have as much as 200 yards of line deployed just to set the presentation. This means anglers will need at least 400 yards of mono on the reel."

The most commonly used baits for sailfish are the goggle-eye (big-eyed scad), threadfin herring (greenie), Spanish sardine, pilchard (scaled sardine), tinker mackerel, speedo (round scad), blue runner, and ballyhoo. Goggle-eyes are the most sought-after bait for sailfish and will command up to $200 a dozen at certain times of the year. To keep these expensive baits lively, bait wells pump up to 1,500 gallons per hour to reoxygenate the water and keep the bait vigorous. "Frisky baits simply catch more sailfish," according to Captain Rufus.

Those frisky baits are usually fitted with a bridle of waxed twine. "I use a needle to sew a crisscrossed bridle just in front of the dorsal fin. Once bridled, the bait is put in the livewell to await its fate. It sounds kind of cruel, but the results are great." When it comes time to rebait, prebridle bait is dipped from the livewell and placed on the hook. When moving to a new location, *used bait* can be put back in the livewell. "I like to call it putting them in the hospital to recover. It is a very efficient system."

Other types of bridles are used in different applications. Baits that will be pulled on flatlines or outriggers are bridled through the eyes. "The bridal is put through the eye socket (not the eyes), and that pulls the bait at a different angle than pulling it off the nose. The bait lasts longer, and when bait is scarce, that is an important difference." The eye bridle can be used on all the baits except the ballyhoo.

Captain Rufus says, "Ballyhoo has its own type of trolling apparatus, and it's a good one. Since the ballyhoo has a bill, it allows for a different bridle." He places a small length of soda straw on the leader before adding the hook. Pin the ballyhoo through the lower jaw in the area before the beak starts. The hook is riding down. Line up the shank of the hook with the bill and slide the drinking straw over the hook and bill. "It works like magic. The rig pulls the bait nice and straight, and it is invisible to the sailfish. This rigging in no way impedes the hookup process." Ballyhoos remain lively for a very long time using this method on flatlines and outriggers. It is not used on kite fishing.

The hooks used for live baiting sailfish depend on the size of the bait being used. "If using goggle-eyes, skippers tend to use a bigger hook, say a 6/0 or even a 7/0 live bait–style hook." These hooks are short shanked and made from thin wire. "Most people use a J-style hook while live baiting because of the possibility of catching other species that are good on the dinner table. Wahoo or mahi-mahi are good examples of bonus fish, caught while searching for sails."

If you are using greenies or sardines, then a smaller hook like a 5/0 would be preferred. Maybe even a 4/0, depending on the size of the bait. "Always match the hook to the size of the bait."

Captain Rufus recalls the old days when the hook selected would have been a Mustad bronze-style *quick-rusting* hook. These hooks were made with a very thin plastic coating that, once sharpened and used, started rusting almost immediately. The result was a hook that disappeared quickly if a fish was lost. "With the invention of the chemically sharpened hooks, such as Owner and Gamakatsu, most anglers are using them. They are extremely sharp and need no sharpening out of the box."

The intent of the quick-rust hooks is not lost on today's conservation-minded anglers. The issue of gut hooking fish is a principal concern to the crews. "Folks do not drop back as far as they used to, and the effort to not gut-hook fish has become paramount. Some anglers have switched to circle hooks with good results; however, the battle over which is better rages on."

In the most extreme case of kite fishing, the captain on the flybridge of a large sportfishing vessel handles the kites. "The mate or mates are in the cockpit attaching the baits to the kite line using small Black's Outrigger Release Clips. The clip is drilled out to allow a certain size swivel to pass through the clip until it encounters a larger swivel that will set it in its proper place on the kite line." The kite line is let out, and it will drag a bait rig out until the next clip comes tight. At that point the next bait is attached and let out. This process continues until all baits are deployed. "The crew that can run six live baits off kites will outfish just about any other crew, just because of the amount of bait in the water."

As the fish is hooked, the captain will usually hit the throttle to quickly remove the slack in the line. This maneuver also trips the release and puts the angler in contact with the fish. "The hookup is a team effort, and communication is the key to success. The angler must play his part by reeling as fast as he can while giving full attention to the movements of the fish. The goal is to release the fish quickly with a minimum amount of stress or damage." Pictures should be taken while the fish is still in the water to increase the chance of survival on release.

One of the key aspects of kite fishing is keeping the boat headed into the wind. This maneuver keeps the baits off the stern and simplifies the process. Holding this heading is much easier to do in a larger boat. "Anglers fishing smaller boats should deploy a sea anchor off the bow to keep the stern downwind and minimize the chances of swamping the boat in heavy seas. The sea anchor must be rigged with a trip-style retrieval line to aid in getting it out of the water quickly once a bite has occurred. If that positioning is not possible, the kites are flown off the bow." Captain Rufus describes kite fishing for sails as "very laborious with lots of different components, but the results are worth the effort."

Tournament anglers, trollers, and live baiters all have to find the fish. According to Captain Rufus, that may be the easy part. "Sailfish are easy to find. Just keep an eye out for the multitude of boats on the horizon. Chances are, that's where the fish are." He says sailfish tend to concentrate in an area and once found can be an easy target. "We used to call that the 'Palm Beach depth finder' when we simply looked for other boats. It has made many a skipper's job much, much easier." He advises sailfish seekers to also listen to the radio for hints of where the fish are. Anglers can also watch the skies for kites deployed in an area. If you see a puff of smoke when the skipper guns the engines to assist in the hookup, that's an indication of fish in the area.

Charter Captains

Captain Danny Barrow

> Hometown: Hypoluxo, Florida
> Business: Silver Lining Fish Charters
> Phone number: 561-253-4100
> E-mail address: captdannybarrow@aol.com
> Web site: www.gosnookfishing.com

Captain Danny's advice to visiting anglers: Captain Danny's advice is as simple and effective as his fishing methods. He says to be patient, be methodical, be quiet, and release your catch unharmed! Patience separates the really successful anglers from the average, methodical anglers leave no cast unthrown, stealthy anglers catch more fish, and catch-and-release anglers are planning for the future.

Captain Chad McGann

> Hometown: Jupiter, Florida
> Business: Fly and Light Tackle Fishing
> Phone number: 561-254-7058
> E-mail address: chadmcgann@bellsouth.net

Captain Chad's advice to visiting anglers: The only advice I'd give to anyone fishing anywhere for the first time would be to use common sense on the water, including being prepared with the proper equipment for the day, and keeping a comfortable distance from other anglers. There is plenty of water out there for everyone; there is no need to intrude on other's fishing. Read and obey markers and signs, they are there for your safety and the safety of others. Don't try teaching cigarette butts or any other trash to swim; place your trash in proper receptacles. Watch out for the shallow spots and have fun.

Captain Rufus Wakeman

Hometown: Palm Beach, Florida
Business: Hot Tuna Charters LLC
Business: River Palm Cottages
Phone number: 772-486-1018
E-mail address: httna@aol.com

Captain Rufus's advice to visiting anglers: Sailfishing is a highly enjoyable sport. Prepare as well as you can the day or evening before. Early preparation will make your day more pleasurable once you get out on the edge, because you don't have a bunch of chores to do. Don't forget to bring your safety gear and a first aid kit on board for those unplanned accidents that can occur. Keep a close eye on the weather for fast developing storms and always be the prudent skipper. Remember that it is only a fish. It's better to practice safe seamanship so you can head out the inlet another day in search of ole spindlebeak.

Area Hotspots

Inshore anglers will find some great fishing in Hobe Sound. Fish the grass flats around and north of Marker 42. Snook Islands and Lake Avenue Bridge in Lake Worth are known snook hotspots. Shorebound anglers can fish the ICW and the beaches around Coral Cove Park on State Road 707 and Phipps Park in Palm Beach, a summer hotspot for tarpon and snook.

Don't overlook the night fishing around the bridges and dock lights in the ICW and the Loxahatchee River.

Offshore anglers will find plenty of fishing close to the beach where the continental shelf drops off to deeper water. The drop can produce cobia, amberjack, snapper, grouper, sailfish, and king mackerel.

Fishing-Friendly Lodging and Glorious Galleys

The Crab House—Jupiter

> 1065 N. Highway A1A
> Jupiter, FL 33477
> Phone number: 561-744-1300

Good food, great view. Waterfront, dockage, casual, live music, outdoor seating. Directly across from the Jupiter Lighthouse. Great for an angler who's been out on the water all day. Recommended by Capt. Chad McGann.

The Square Grouper

> 1111 Love Street
> Jupiter, FL 33477
> Phone number: 561-575-0252

A local landmark, located at Castaway Marina. Outside bar, some dockage, great atmosphere, occasional live music. View of the Jupiter Lighthouse and inlet area. Beer and cocktails. Bar-type food like hot dogs and chicken wings. Recommended by Capt. Chad McGann.

Sailfish Marina

> 98 Lake Drive
> Palm Beach Shores, FL 33404-6218
> Phone number: 561-842-8449

Located at the northern end of the Lake Worth Lagoon. Marina, hotel, and fine dining all in one place. A short boat ride from the Palm Beach Inlet. Recommended by Capt. Danny Barrow.

Bait and Tackle

Fishing Headquarters

> 633 Alternate A1A
> Jupiter, FL 33477
> Phone number: 561-743-7335

Feel free to call the shop any time and talk to Pete or Tom about local conditions, what's in season, local guides, tactics, rigs, baits available, and recent action. Open 7 days a week. Recommended by Capt. Chad McGann.

Juno Bait

> 12214 U.S. Highway 1
> North Palm Beach, FL 33408
> Phone number: 561-694-2797

Owner Todd Mitchell invites everyone to come by and check them out. Live bait and tackle. Open 7 days a week. Recommended by Capt. Chad McGann.

Lott's Brothers Inc.

> 631 Northlake Boulevard
> North Palm Beach, FL 33408-5308
> Phone number: 561-844-0244

Everything from light tackle, fresh and saltwater, to big game fishing tackle. Rod and reel repair. All types of rigged and unrigged bait. Open daily. Recommended by Capt. Danny Barrow.

Boynton Fisherman Supply

618 North Federal Highway
Boynton Beach, FL 33435-4125
Phone number: 561-736-0568

Excellent selection of tackle, fresh and salt. Frozen and live bait. Rod and reel repair. Compete marine supplies. Recommended by Capt. Danny Barrow.

Fishing Lessons for Life—Obeying Fishing Laws

Fishing regulations are made for a reason, and compliance is necessary for healthy growth of the fish population. The sooner all anglers understand the importance of the impact of lawful fishing, the better the resource will be. Responsible angling starts with the individual and needs to be passed on to others, especially children, by setting a good example for them to follow. Fishing should be considered a privilege, and obeying the fishing laws should be recognized as the responsibility that goes along with that great opportunity. Every angler should know the rules and regulations related to the type of fishing they do.

Given the abundance of water in Florida, fisheries management is not a simple matter. It is a scientific process of balancing the impacts of habitat changes, fishing pressure, anglers' desires, and the biological potential of a body of water to grow and support the kinds, sizes, and numbers of fish that anglers want to catch. Fishery managers depend on scientific information to determine the regulations that will maximize a given stock of each fish species. The most important fishing regulations to come from scientific management are size limits, bag limits, and seasons.

Size limits are used to protect spawning-size fish and keep them available for reproduction. Florida fish are measured by one of three methods. Some fish, like spotted seatrout, red drum, and snook, are measured by the total length method. This method takes measurements from the most forward point of the head, with the mouth closed, to the farthest tip of the tail, with the tail pinched together. The fish should be lying on its side during the process. Fish like Spanish mackerel, cobia, and pompano are measured using the fork length method. Fork length measurements are taken from the tip of the jaw or tip of the snout, with mouth closed, to the center of the fork in the tail. The remaining fish species have a bill that extends beyond the lower jaw. These fish are regulated by the lower jaw-fork length measurement method. This procedure measures fish in a straight line from the forward-most part of the lower jaw (tip of the lower jaw) to the fork in the tail. Examples include sailfish and marlin.

Bag limits are used to keep anglers from taking too many fish and depleting the available stock of fish. Bag limits are set for a 24-hour period beginning at midnight and ending the following midnight. This regulation requires that once a bag limit is reached for any particular species, no more of that species can be harvested until after midnight, when a new period begins. It is not legal to catch one limit, return them to shore, and go catch another limit. Stated limits are also possession limits, with one exception for a few Florida reef fish. Details for double bag limits can be found on Myfwc.com.

Fishing seasons are aimed at protecting fish during spawning periods, and concerned anglers should not target those spawning fish, maximizing the reproductive process. Since seasons are set for individual species, they vary greatly from one fish to another. Anglers are responsible for determining when it is legal to harvest their targeted species. If an out-of-season fish is caught, it must be immediately released back into the water using appropriate handling techniques.

Children can learn the rules of legal fishing by taking part in the process of measuring to abide by size limits and counting to abide by bag limits. Explain the importance of seasons and how all the regulations result in more fish to be shared by everyone. Fishing laws and regulations are one part of the conservation puzzle that should be understood and followed by all anglers. Just remember, fishing laws are meant to protect the fishery and make sure there are plenty of fish to be shared by all.

PART 4

Florida's Gold Coast

11

Fort Lauderdale and Miami

Like so much of Florida's East Coast, the Gold Coast, which includes Fort Lauderdale and Miami, did not show significant development until the arrival of the Florida East Coast Railroad. As the population grew and Miami developed an image of a tropical paradise, real estate investors became interested in promoting the area. The outcome was the Florida land boom of the 1920s. The resulting boom created a real estate bubble with characteristics similar to that which occurred in recent years. Real estate prices grew rapidly on the basis of speculation, but when the market was not supported with buyers, the bubble burst.

Additional setbacks like the 1926 Great Miami Hurricane and the Wall Street Crash of 1929 further eroded the economic fabric of the area. The next devastating blow came with the Great Depression, and the first Florida land boom was officially over. The picture of the Gold Coast as a tropical paradise was transformed to a picture of a hot, humid, and remote area with little to offer in the way of economic incentives. It was not until World War II that the economy began to show signs of recovery.

The turnaround for the region came with the war and the creation of a major military base in Fort Lauderdale. Rather than building the infrastructure to house and train the troops, the government used hotels for barracks, movie theaters for classrooms, and golf courses and beaches for field training. Before the war was over, 500,000 enlisted men and 50,000 officers were trained in the area. With the end of the war, many of the military men and women returned to the area, causing a population explosion, renewed economic development, and a return to the image of a tropical paradise.

The area's economy is highly dependent on tourism, with cruise ships, beaches, and charter fishing making up a large part of the tourism appeal. According to the Fort Lauderdale Historical Society, Fort Lauderdale is known as the "Venice of America" because of its extensive system of waterways, including the New River, Intracoastal Waterway, and numerous canals in and around the city. Anglers come from all over the world to enjoy the abundant fishing offered in the area. Because of this demand, the area supports a huge sportfishing fleet and numerous charter fishing operations.

Characteristics of the Fishing Area

Miami is an outstanding place to visit when big game fishing is on your mind. Captain Bouncer Smith, operator of Bouncer's Dusky 33 charters out of Miami, says, "This is one of the greatest places on earth to head for some fishing, because we have so many potential target species available so much of the year. Sailfish are found only 3 miles from the dock, and some days we catch more than a dozen that close. Tarpon are even closer." He reports an average tarpon catch of nearly a fish per hour weighing from 60 to 160 pounds every evening from November through June. This phenomenal fishing occurs only 1 mile from the dock. The area is also blessed with an outstanding swordfish fishery in addition to several other popular species. "We have world-class swordfish only 18 miles from the dock. Then you throw in a few mahi, African pompano, wahoo, kings, amberjacks, and the list goes on. Visitors are in for some great fishing." He adds that all the fishing fun is in addition to everything else the area has to offer on shore.

Captain Poertner agrees with Bouncer on the variety available in this part of the state. "Fishing in 60 to 180 feet of water on any given day provides anglers with the chance to catch kings, sailfish, dolphin, tuna, cobia, and even some wahoo in some months of the year."

Numerous artificial reefs have been created over the years all along the Gold Coast. Water depths of 60 to 180 feet can be very productive fishing grounds. Captain Billy Poertner of Imagine That Charters says, "My best fishing is usually between 90 and 130 feet of water. If you head offshore, the fishing is pretty much the same as in other places in the state. Look for rips, color changes, floating debris, sargassum, and diving birds to locate the fish."

Florida's Gold Coast is big game country when it comes to fishing, and it begins right in the inlets. From late September through October, mullet schools are migrating south, making the tarpon fishing great. Targeting the silver king in the inlets is all about matching the hatch. Captain Bouncer says, "I usually fish live mullet on the surface. Rig up a 20-pound conventional rig complete with circle hook and slow troll for good results." During the mullet run along the beach in the fall, some breeding kingfish return to southern waters in their fall migration. The presence of the mullet and the kings make for another hot Miami bite.

When November rolls around, all the way through April, millions of shrimp migrate out through the inlets in an endless food chain. The shrimp have lived and grown in Biscayne Bay during the winter. Captain Bouncer says, "The tarpon ambush these shrimp as they head out to sea in low-light conditions. Drifting live shrimp on 5/0 circle hooks with those same 20-pound conventional outfits used for mullet will usually produce loads of action from the tarpon." He names Government Cut—the main ship channel from the open ocean to the port of Miami—as a fishing hotspot and says the same tarpon action

Tarpon on fly will make any angler's adrenaline pump. Cast to busting tarpon, strip at a moderate speed, and hang on for the fight of your life. Photo courtesy of Capt. Carl Ball.

can be expected for a mile on either side of the cut. He adds that Haulover Inlet, in the north end of the county, offers the same unbelievable action from November through February.

Shrimp begin to thin out as spring turns to summer, but the tarpon are still there, and they are still hungry. Continue the strategy of matching the hatch and turn to crabs as your go-to bait. This time of year, a tan crab populates the area and tarpon love them. They look exactly like a blue crab except they are tan colored. They range anywhere from ½ inch to 2 inches in width; Captain Bouncer prefers the larger ones. He says, "Just change to a 7/0 circle hook and swap your shrimp for a crab about 2 inches across the back of the shell. Hook the crab through either point about ¼ inch from the edge of the shell." He drifts through the area with the crabs 50 to 100 feet upwind of the boat. If the winds are light, he will add a float about 10 feet above the crabs to keep them near the surface.

Captain Bouncer adds a special note for fly casters interested in a nighttime adventure of a lifetime. "Many nights from January through April, fly-casting to shrimp-busting tarpon can ruin any angler's nerves." Rods should be a 10 to 12 weight of 8½ to 9 feet in length. He recommends white or red Seaducers or Deceivers; sometimes black is good. "The best trips are when you can cast to busting tarpon. Strip the fly at a moderate speed and hang on."

The Inshore Bite—Biscayne Bay

Biscayne Bay lies in the southernmost reaches of the Gold Coast. The bay is about 35 miles long and as wide as 8 miles in places. It offers anglers a variety of fish species to catch. In fact, about every species of fish available anywhere in Florida can be found in Biscayne Bay. Captain Carl Ball operates AWOL Fishing Charters Inc., with a specialty in tarpon, permit, and bonefish. He says, "Redfish are limited in Biscayne Bay, but I catch almost every other species of Florida fish regularly in the bay." The most popular species are snapper, grouper, snook, tarpon, bonefish, permit, barracuda, jack crevalle, shark, ladyfish, bluefish, Spanish mackerel, and pompano. The Biscayne Bay area offers a distinct advantage to anglers with a short window of opportunity in their fishing calendar because of the protection it offers from bad weather. "Biscayne Bay is unique in that you can literally fish for any of the named species 365 days a year in any wind direction and no matter the temperature. This is due to the proximity of the bay to the ocean and the deep ship channel, Government Cut. There is an alternative fishing opportunity for any set of weather conditions." Captain Ball notes the only exception he has ever witnessed to the year-round availability of fishing was the coldest winter in decades that occurred in 2010. The abnormal weather conditions during that time dropped water temperatures well below average, and everything that swam headed for deep water just offshore.

Biscayne Bay averages 10- to 12-foot depths and includes bridges, grass flats, various channels, and multiple islands to fish. To the west of Biscayne Bay lies the mainland of South Florida, and to the east are the barrier islands of Miami Beach/South Beach, Fisher Island, Virginia Key, Key Biscayne, Soldier Key, the Ragged Keys, Sands Key, and Elliot Key. Just south of Key Biscayne is an area called Stiltsville. Dating back to the 1930s, this area is known for homes built on pilings on the edges of grass flats. The homes are weekend getaways, as opposed to full-time residences. The area is now part of Biscayne National Park and offers some outstanding fishing.

Permit in Biscayne Bay

Biscayne Bay permit fishing for Captain Carl Ball means searching from Government Cut south, throughout the entire bay. He identifies the best time of the year as March through November. The key, according to Captain Ball, is warmer weather. Once the water starts cooling, the permit are harder to find. "Permit love hot water. I generally sight-fish them from Key Biscayne south through Stiltsville and on down to Key Largo." Permit like current, and they are found in almost every environment of the bay. "I see them on flats, in channels, and over structure when the water is moving. The hardest part of the hunt is recognizing them before noise spooks them or they see you and flee."

When permit are found on the flats, they are normally in 2 to 4 feet of water and likely feeding on the bottom. Sometimes, in very shallow water, permit tails will be seen protruding above the surface as the fish roam and dig up crabs for their meal. This behavior is known to anglers as tailing. When tailing fish are found, there is no doubt that they are feeding and easier to approach than at other times. Anglers should practice looking through the water to see their dark coloration contrasting with a lighter-colored bottom. They are not easy fish to spot for novice anglers, but it is a skill that definitely can be learned. "When permit feed on the bottom, they appear

Permit love hot weather, so plan your visit accordingly.

slightly darker than the bottom, and they are generally moving. Also watch for mudding, patches of muddy water caused by the digging, to locate them."

Permit can also be found along channel edges or sometimes in the middle of a channel. They are often picking their way through the weeds looking for their next meal. The channel fish are especially difficult fish to spot. "When the permit are in the channels, they may not be sighted unless they are on the surface. In that case, especially on slick calm days, they can be seen pushing a head wake across the surface. Permit have black fins and a brownish tint to their body when seen on the surface. Look for the black highlights to distinguish them from their surroundings. They blend in well with their environment, but experience will teach you how to spot them."

Captain Ball prefers bright sunny days for sight-fishing permit. "They are hard to see if cloudy skies reflect unwanted shadows on the surface." In shallow water you may see what some permit anglers describe as a black fillet knife sticking up out of the water. That knife-looking object is the dorsal fin of a permit. Sometimes anglers see two black objects sticking out. These are the dorsal fin and the tail as the permit cruise the shallow flats looking for their next victim.

Permit holding over structure should be approached carefully. "Our structure is mostly just rubble, and there isn't much of it around." By structure Captain Ball means an old wreck, downed channel markers, or cement pilings from old stilt houses. "I approach permit holding on structure from up-current. They won't be as spooky as permit on the flats. Because of the deeper water, they are not as likely to see you. Cast up-current of the fish and let the current swing your crab in front of them. I use the same tackle on all permit, regardless of where they are found."

The fishing equipment used for permit needs to be capable of handling long blistering runs from large fish. "I like to use a 7½-foot 10- to 20-pound medium-heavy rod. I want it a little heavier than a bonefish rod. The heavier rod is needed to handle the extra strength of the permit. The longer rod also gives longer casts needed on spooky fish." He wants his reels to hold at least 250 yards of mainline. "I use 12- to 15-pound mono and 12- to 15-pound braid." Captain Ball spools his reels with a *top shot* of 150 yards of braid over 100 yards of mono. Different size reels may require more or less mono, but he keeps the braid at about 150 yards. Use enough of the mono/braid combination to fill the reel within ⅛ inch of the top of the spool for best casting performance. "Some guides think the braid spooks the fish; I don't. It casts better and doesn't get all twisted up." Captain Ball doubles the mainline with a Bimini Twist and uses an Albright knot to add a 3- to 4-foot 20-pound test mono leader. "I always use a shock leader with braided line. For a hook I use an Owner Aki 2/0. The hook is very sharp and features a straight eye that gives me a good inline hook-set."

There is no better bait for permit than crabs, so every day

should start with crabs in the livewell if possible. "I start my day with some small blue claw crabs. I like them about the size of a silver dollar." Captain Ball says bigger crabs will work, and a big permit can eat a pretty big crab. He chooses the smaller ones because, presented the choice between the bigger ones and the smaller ones, a permit is more likely to choose the small crab. The small ones are probably just easier to eat and digest. Use the point of the hook to drill a hole in the shell just inside one of the points. Perform the operation slowly to end up with the smallest hole possible. If the hole is too big, the crab can come off too easily. Some permit anglers like to break off the other point to release more scent as an additional attraction to the fish.

When you find permit in schools, they tend to be about the same size. The big ones weighing more than 20 pounds are more likely to be loners, traveling by themselves. Captain Ball warns that if the permit are small, they have a hard time getting the crabs in their mouth. "For small permit, less than 10 pounds, I just use a shrimp for best results." Captain Ball always has two rods baited and ready. One rig is baited with crab and another with shrimp. The crab can be cast to the bigger permit, and the shrimp can be cast either to smaller permit or to bones. "I always have two rods ready. In some spots you could see either bones or permit, so I am ready for both."

Permit will eat crabs either off the surface or from the bottom; they are not that particular. The first rule in presenting the crab is to be sure the permit can see it. "If the presentation is done properly, you can get every permit you see to eat the crab. Hitting them on the head with your crab may spook some fish, but sometimes they will turn around and eat it." Captain Ball says the one thing to avoid is pulling the crab toward the sighted permit. "Pulling a crab toward a permit spooks them every time. Pulling the crab away from the permit and across the surface will get their attention and most likely a bite." Just remember, the crab presentation has to be natural for best

Silver dollar–sized crabs are excellent bait for permit. Here's some proof.
Photo by Capt. Carl Ball.

results, and no self-respecting crab will move directly toward a permit. If the angler can cast the crab in front of the permit, in its field of vision, letting the bait dive to the bottom will also elicit a strike.

Once a bite is sighted or detected by feel, start reeling to take up the slack. When the line comes tight, the drag will be screaming on an initial run of 100 yards or more, depending on the size of the fish. "They will usually run off 100 yards of line and then fight you hard all the way back to the boat."

The fish are extremely tired and stressed by the time they come to the boat. "It's best to scoop them in a net and hold them in the water, giving them time to rest and recover before weighing, measuring, and taking pictures." Captain Ball adds what has become a common warning from conservation-minded guides: "Never weigh them by hanging them by their lower jaw; it can cause internal damage. I loop a small rope around their tail and hang them from that." Another way to successfully and safely weight a fish is to leave it in the net, weigh the whole thing, then deduct the weight of the net.

Patience is recognized as a valuable virtue for any fishing endeavor, but for permit fishing it is needed even more. "Be patient when searching for permit, because there are not a lot of fish, and they are hard to find." Sometimes you may have to stalk a single permit the length of a flat to get the cast. Even then, permit have the uncanny ability to disappear in plain sight; now you see them—now you don't. It's a good day to get five to ten shots at permit, so make every cast count.

Bonefish in Biscayne Bay

Bonefish have been caught up and down the coast of Florida, but most bone fishing takes place from Key Biscayne south to Key West. Captain Ball identifies some of Biscayne Bay's hotspots for bones as the flats around Stiltsville, south to Elliot Key and Caesars Creek. The west shoreline of Biscayne Bay is also known for bonefish as well as for the elusive permit.

Bonefish, according to Captain Ball, prefer beaches, flats, and channels, and, like the permit, the bones like moving water to feed in, but will show up on the beach. "While the beaches generally don't provide much current, bonefish will frequently be seen feeding along the beach or gathered in large schools." Bonefish will also be found in the channels but are extremely difficult to see because of water depth. "Bonefish in the channels are only seen on the calmest days in the clearest channels."

Efficient use of an angler's time and the increased probability of spotting a bone require anglers to concentrate on shallow-water flats. "The most likely place to find bonefish is on the flats in anywhere from 6 inches to 4 feet of water. Moving water is best, and they can be found on both incoming and outgoing tides." When asked what his prime fishing conditions for bonefish would be, Captain Ball replied, "An early morning rising tide has been my best conditions for finding tailing bonefish in the skinny water."

The Biscayne Bay area is home to numerous grass-covered flats. Poling a skiff over these flats will provide the stealthy angler with some shots at bones. "While poling quietly over one of the many turtle grass–covered flats, anglers should look for an indication that bonefish are present. The shallower the water, the more signs of movement you will see." Bonefish will push a head wake that can be seen for quite a distance when moving in the shallow water. "Look for schools in the distance by searching for a patch of disturbed water. Position yourself in front of the nervous water so that it appears to be coming right at you. There is no better position than having the fish coming to you."

Another indication that bonefish are present is spotting the aggressive feeders. When bonefish root in the bottom to find food, their tails rise out of the water, making them easy to spot, especially on calm days. "Tailers are trying to bury their mouth in the sand to extricate critters to eat. The process includes sucking water and sand through their gills to filter out their food. A well-placed shrimp will hook an angler up with a package of greased lightning under these conditions."

As the water depth increases and the sun rises higher in the sky, Captain Ball advises anglers to look for mudding bonefish. Mudding is caused by the same aggressive feeding described before, but in deeper water it creates a cloudy, muddy plume in the water to alert anglers that the bones are near and feeding. "These patches of dirty water create a great opportunity for anglers to hook a bonefish. Deepwater bones are not as spooky as shallow-water fish and easier to approach." Captain Ball likes windy conditions to go along with the mudding, because the bonefish are not as spooky when the wind is blowing.

Like permit, bonefish can be extremely difficult to spot. The easiest ones to see are the ones coming directly at you or the

Bonefish are easier to approach if they can be found tailing or mudding.
Photo by Capt. Carl Ball.

ones moving away from you. When they are swimming parallel to the angler, they are the most difficult to see. "Their shiny sides reflect the bottom when turned sideways to you. They are nearly invisible." Instead of seeing the fish, anglers are more likely to see the fish's shadow. "Look for shadows that are slightly darker than the bottom or shadows that are moving." This ability of bonefish to hide from anglers has led to their common nickname of gray ghost.

The most-often recommended bait for bonefish is live shrimp. "Fly and jigs are also used for bonefish, but shrimp are preferred because they are easy to get and are one of the bonefish's favorite foods."

Captain Ball uses jigs as a backup when shrimp are not available or when he just likes the challenge of fooling a bonefish with an artificial lure. "Bonefish are difficult to catch on jigs because of the noise they make when hitting the water. Stealth is a highly desirable trait when stalking bones. The jigs are best used in deep or dirty water situations or when blind-casting for bones." He suggests tipping jigs with a small piece of shrimp to improve success. "With the jig you want to hop it along the bottom. Expect the bite as the jig falls toward the bottom."

Fly-fishing is an excellent way to fish for bones when the angler is proficient at casting. "Flies can go deep and be fished in the shallowest of water with the least amount of noise. When presenting a fly, anglers need to get the fly in front of the fish and with a few short strips make it look as though the fly is trying to escape." The biggest problem with fly-fishing for bonefish is the lack of casting ability. Bones will be caught only if the fly is placed in front of their line of sight. Most beginners are shocked at how difficult it is to perform that task. It is a game of inches, and poor fly casters do not win. Except for the experienced fly fishers, Captain Ball recommends sticking with live shrimp for bonefish.

Equipment for bonefish can be on the lighter side compared with that for permit. Captain Ball prefers a 7½-foot spinning rod with medium-light action. "An 8- to 17-pound rated rod will handle the bones. I attach a reel with a line capacity of 250 yards to handle the long bonefish runs. I use a topshot strategy, just as with permit." His topshot spooling requires at least 150 yards of 8- to 15-pound braid over a filler of 20-pound mono. Double the mainline with a Bimini Twist and add a 15- to 20-pound mono leader. "The hook can be just about anything that a shrimp will fit on. The most popular bonefish hook is a short shank live bait hook similar to the Owner Aki 2/0."

Depending on how they are hooked, shrimp have a tendency to spin when retrieved. It they spin, they don't look natural. Captain Ball pins them on a live bait hook in a manner that makes them more aerodynamic on the cast and weedless on the retrieve. "I take the tail off to help keep the shrimp from spinning when it is reeled backward. Place the hook through the exposed flesh and back out the belly. Slide the shrimp up the hook, and put the point back up through the belly and out the back. Pin it so the hook point is just barely through the shell. I call it a Texas Rig. You know, like the plastic worms when you want to make them weedless." Removing the tail also releases more scent than a tail-on shrimp and helps to trigger a bite.

Presenting live shrimp to a bonefish is similar to presenting bait to a permit. "To use live shrimp, you want to cast ahead of the school of bonefish and let them approach and find the bait on their own. Reel slowly, and keep your shrimp just above the bottom to position it in front of approaching fish." The cast is made easier if the boat can be positioned up-current from the fish. The current can actually be used to make the presentation more natural. Allow the current to sweep the bait toward the fish. "When the bones are up-current from the angler and moving away, the cast will have to be made beyond them. Let it sit and hope that they find it." The angle of the cast is important, too. A cast that lines even one departing fish is likely to spook the whole school.

Bonefish are known for their lightning speed and long runs. Couple these characteristics with the sheer challenge of catching them and it is easy to see why anglers become obsessed with fishing for the gray ghost. "When you hook a bonefish, it will usually run off 75 to 100 yards of line in about 10 to 15 seconds. It feels much longer, because while it is happening you are not sure it will ever stop." The adrenaline pumps and the excitement runs high, but after that first magnificent run, bonefish are pretty much done. Unlike permit that will fight you all the way to the boat, bonefish come in easily after the long run and a short battle.

Use great caution in handling bonefish. Keep them in the water as much as possible during hook removal and photo taking. "Bonefish have a very low tolerance for being out of the water for a long time, and they are very slow to recuperate. Take a quick picture and return them to the water for resuscitation before release. We can't do too much to ensure our continued access to this valuable fish."

Bonefish are also very susceptible to getting eaten by sharks after being released. "If sharks are seen in the area, and you have a working livewell, place the bonefish in the livewell to revive." Release the fish on your way to the next fishing spot in an area where no sharks are visible.

The wind is your friend when fishing for bones, because you are less visible to the fish when the water surface is wavy. Fish don't notice the splash of a crab or shrimp as much either. The wind also causes the water to be churned up and slightly dirtier, obscuring their vision. "I think fish eat better when the water isn't so clear. When the water is slick, glassy calm, and clear, the bones are very spooky. The permit are too."

The Offshore Bite

More than 100 wrecks of all shapes and sizes dot the seascape offshore Miami. Add the numerous rock piles, rubble, and manmade reefs, and it is a bottom fisher's dream. Some bruising fish are caught off the area structure, and anglers have to beef up the tackle to handle them. Current can be a factor as it can be quite strong. Offshore, bottom fishers measure the weight of their sinkers in pounds instead of ounces.

Locations of fishy wrecks and reefs are readily available on private and government Web sites as well as on commercially available paper maps and electronic charts. One popular wreck, for example, known as the *Deep Freeze*, is described on a Web site as a 210-foot freighter. The wreck is resting on its keel in 135 feet of water. Its uppermost deck is about 110 feet deep. The wreck is home to many large fish like grouper, jacks, and barracuda. Anglers should be aware that the wrecks are also popular with divers, so be on the lookout and fish accordingly.

Outside the inlet, as close as 3 miles, is the often heralded Gulf Stream. Captain Bouncer says when one is fishing along the edge of the Gulf Stream, the kite is king (see kite fishing below). "Live herring, pilchards, sardines, blue runners, or goggle-eyes suspended under a couple of fishing kites is the game in this town. Every bite is a visible event, and hooking the fish is almost foolproof when kite fishing." He says all the popular offshore gamefish are swimming against the current looking for food. The fishing boat is drifting with the current, the same way the baitfish travel. It's not unusual to see two kites suspending baits that are skipping across the surface. The natural presentation of bait dangling from the kites is as close to a guaranteed hookup as it gets. "Gulf Stream kite flying is a super fishing technique with at least 10 possible species likely to bite at any moment."

Given all the possible action available offshore from Miami, Captain Bouncer has developed a great passion for catching swordfish. Swordfishing is not for the faint of heart. It can be physically exhausting, mentally demanding, tiring, stressful, exciting, and exhilarating. So how do we start?

Swordfish—Day or Night

Chasing this monster of the sea means deep water. Swordfish have been reported to swim at depths greater than 2,000 feet, but the escapade starts on land. According to Captain Bouncer Smith, the adventure begins with a tackle check. Here's what we need, or at least what Bouncer needs as he loads his boat for swordfishing exploration: He starts with three 50- to 80-pound class standup rods with 50 or 70 series Penn International reels attached. Each reel is filled three-quarters of the way with 80-pound braid and then a 500-foot top-shot of 80-pound mono. Add a 300-pound test wind-on leader 20 feet long. Attach a 250-pound ball-bearing snap swivel to the leader, and your night fishing rods are ready.

Bouncer adds two 80-pound standup rods with 70 or 80 series Penn International reels. Alternatively he will take only one of the Penn reels and rig another 80-pound standup rod with a Daiwa MP3000 electric/hand-crank power-assisted reel. The power-assisted reels make deep fishing much easier.

These two outfits are spooled with 80-pound braid, leaving room for a top-shot of 100 feet of 300-pound test mono. All the roller guides must be the large type so that wind-on leaders and markers move freely through the guides.

Some of the day's baits are rigged before leaving the dock while others are caught by hook and line on the way out to the fishing grounds. For rigged baits, Bouncer says, "We use bonito strips, kingfish bellies, whole small bonito, tuna, and mackerel most of the time. For the night fishing we need to add several rigged squid about 12 to 14 inches long. All of these baits are about 15 to 18 inches long." All baits are rigged with double Mustad offset 10/0 hooks or hooks of similar quality and size. The bait leaders are about 6 to 8 feet of 300 monofilament line.

Fishing for swordfish during the day is all about getting the bait down deep. Bouncer uses paver bricks to do the job. "We have to make sure we have enough paver bricks for both day and night fishing. We use 6-pound paver bricks and secure them together with a tie wrap and then a band of tape around each end. The fishing line is tied to the tie wrap." Daytime weights need to be about 15 to 20 pounds, so three or four pavers are required. To be fully prepared, Bouncer always ties up about six daytime weights. Nighttime weights are smaller because the fish are not as deep. He makes up 1-pound weights for the evening fishing.

Lights are another necessity of fishing for swords. "We need one or two lights for every rod. Some blue strobes, blue steady lights, green lights, multicolored lights, chemical lights, bright lights, dim lights. Hey! Lights are to swordfishing what assorted lures are to dolphin or marlin fishing." He says the Hydro Glow light or underwater lights fastened to the bottom of the boat are like lights of the city drawing guests to town. Submerged lights hanging 30 feet from the bait are like restaurant signs showing where to get dinner. Small strobe lights or chemical lights close to the bait are like lights on the tables making it easier to see the food.

Paving bricks are used to take swordfish bait to the bottom during daytime fishing. Here is the result. Photo by Capt. Bouncer Smith.

Other supplies needed for the trip include gloves for handling the fish, wax thread for additional rigging, tag sticks and tags for data gathering, gaffs for landing fish, plenty of sodas and water to keep the angler hydrated, and safety lines to keep tackle and anglers in or at least near the boat.

Captain Bouncer normally heads out about 2:00 or 3:00 in the afternoon. His plan includes a stop or two where a few live baits are caught on hook and line. The live bait will be used in the event some fish are spotted on the way to the swordfish grounds. "We have numerous places to stop for bait around markers inside Government Cut and in the ocean. Most of the bait is caught on light spinning tackle using Sabiki rigs. It's not unusual to spot dolphin, sailfish, or marlin on our travels to the swordfish grounds, and most anglers don't want to pass them up."

Running east out of Government Cut for about 18 miles brings anglers to water 1,800 feet deep. Bouncer suggests starting the fishing in 1,600 to 2,000 feet, depending on recent reports from other captains, surface conditions, or just plain gut feelings. He stops the boat dead in the water and drifts for a couple of minutes. During the drift the mate prepares tackle and baits for the fishing. This stop is the first important detail for successful swordfishing adventures. Captain Bouncer says, "The real reason for this stop is to determine the set of the current and the drift of the wind."

Once the current and drift have been determined, the boat is aimed into the current with a plan to drift some "good bottom variations." The boat speed is increased to about 2 knots, and the daytime fishing begins. "We run a single bait out behind the boat on one of the daytime drop rods. This rig contains a strobe light about 6 feet from the bait and a steady light about 30 feet from the bait. Then 100 feet from the bait, we secure a 15- to 20-pound weight to the wind-on leader using 30 feet of 25-pound test mono." The weight is dropped over the side, and the rig runs out behind the boat until there is as much line behind the boat as the depth of the water. Now the boat is stopped, and the rig sinks all the way down to the bottom. As the boat drifts, Captain Bouncer watches the line angle behind the boat until it reaches about 10 to 20 degrees off a vertical plane. At this point more line is released until bottom is found again. "We then put the boat in forward motion, driving into the current as we wind the weight about 30 feet off the bottom. The boat is driven into the current at a rate that keeps the line between 10 and 20 degrees from vertical behind the boat. We now wait for a bite and the fun to begin."

If the rod slams down hard toward the water, an angler may be in for the fish fight of a lifetime. Photo courtesy of Capt. Bouncer Smith.

Day-dropping for swordfish requires keeping the bait near the bottom in deep water. Captain Bouncer outlines five things that can happen in the process of chasing these deepwater critters. First he says you may get a tapping feeling telegraphed through the rod tip. That is a swordfish or other critter hitting your bait with his bill or eating the bait. It is the first indication of interest from a fish. Sometimes the rod will begin to slowly bend down and pull to the south; that is the worst thing that can happen, because the rig has probably snagged the bottom. The rod could slam down hard toward the water. That action is what anglers are looking for; that is a great bite, and you may be in for the fight of a lifetime. Alternatively, the line could go slack, and that is good news requiring a quick response. The captain should speed the boat up into the current. When the line goes slack, the swordfish is headed to the surface while fighting against the weight. When this happens it's good for the angler because it is less work to land the fish. Finally, after an hour with bait on the bottom and nothing has happened, it's time to wind up the rig and check the bait and start the process all over again.

As nighttime comes, the day-dropping procedure for swordfish is retired and replaced with nighttime tactics. All rigs are removed from the water, and the boat is moved to a new location to begin fishing for swords at night. Captain Bouncer says he normally locates water between 1,000 and 2,000 feet deep and is always looking for good bottom. He defines good bottom as an ocean floor with peaks and valleys or drop-offs that attract bait and predators.

The nighttime fishing begins the same way as the day-drop procedure. Stop the boat for a couple minutes and check the drift. With the area to be covered predetermined between 1,000 and 2,000 feet, the drift dictates the starting point. "If the drift is carrying you offshore, start shallow; if the drift is carrying inshore, start deep." Once the drift is determined, four rods are baited and set out at varying depths ranging from 50 to as deep as 600 feet. "We usually fish two rods with 2-liter bottles as floats. The other two rods are fished straight down."

Bait selection for nighttime fishing is varied too. "Usually three rods are baited with squid and one with a small whole fish or large strip of fish. If tinker mackerel are present, then it is two or three mackerel and one or two squid." Tinker mackerel or Boston mackerel are a common baitfish found from Canada to Miami. They follow the cooler water temperatures, so they are not always available. When the tinkers are seen swimming around the boat or have been in the area on recent trips, anglers should plan on catching some on large Sabiki rigs. These migrating fish will range from 1 to 3 pounds and make excellent swordfish bait. Captain Bouncer advises anglers to freeze their surplus and save it for another trip.

All the baits have a light attached 30 feet from the bait, and sometimes a strobe light is added closer to the bait. A portable Hydro Glow fish light is hung off the side of the boat; underwater lights are turned on if available. If the boat is not equipped with the Hydro Glow or built-in underwater lights, the spreader lights can be turned on to attract the swordfish to the boat and baits. Bouncer says you can improve your success by moving the bait. "Your catch results usually go up if you frequently move your straight-down baits up and down the water column by winding up some line and letting down some line as often as the urge strikes you."

Techniques aimed at controlling the drift can also improve fishing success. If the wind is blowing, Captain Bouncer deploys a sea anchor to keep the drift at an absolute minimum. He says the typical drift is about an hour, after which the drift is repeated or a new drift is started. "If we are getting action, we usually run back and make the same drift again; if there was no action on the original drift, we set up another drift at another depth."

Detecting the bite at night has similarities as well as differences compared with the daytime bite. There are several different events that identify the strike and alert the angler to the coming action. The reel may start to click as line is pulled from the reel, the rods fished straight down may go slack as the fish rises with the bait and weight, the float may begin moving off in some direction, you may see a light below the surface moving somewhere around the boat, or you may see a swordfish swim into the lighted area around the boat with your bait light tagging along behind it. "We quit jerking on rods 25 years ago. Anglers should wind to get the line tight and fight the fish with the rod under the arm until the fish runs away from the boat."

When a swordfish is hooked at night, the engines are started, all lines are cleared from the water, and focus is given to landing the hooked fish. "All effort is given to bringing the hookup to a successful conclusion." Captain Bouncer adds this advice for fighting a swordfish: "It is best to fight your swordfish by working the fish up as you keep heading the boat into the current to keep the fish downstream of the boat." Swordfish are strong tough fighters. They frequently come near the boat and then sound back down to the depth where they were hooked. Jumps are not common, but spectacular when they occur. The fish fight will occur as the swordfish dictates. "When the fish charges the boat, wind fast; when the fish runs around the boat, follow him. When he makes a 500-yard run, hold on and the captain will give chase if the run is not straight down. And, finally, when the fight settles down, the angler must pump and wind the fish out of the depths." Bouncer says anglers should expect an hour of fight for every 100 pounds of weight. You do the math; it is not a sport for weaklings.

Swordfish, according to Captain Bouncer, are the very best of what big game fishing has to offer. The challenge begins with finding them; the challenge continues with the fight once you hook one, and the challenge ends only after you land one, as they are very good at escaping. The reward for catching one is a memory that will be with you for the rest of your life.

Kite Fishing for Wahoo

Offshore fishing often starts with gathering live bait for the day's fishing. Captain Poertner says there are two options for obtaining live bait: catch it or buy it. "You can buy goggle-eyes if you are willing and able to pay $80 to $120 per dozen; pilchards can be found for about $25 per dozen." Anglers can catch their own goggle-eyes if they are willing to get up early and be on the water before the sun comes up. "The goggle-eyes bite in the inlet just before sunrise, especially on an incoming tide close to the full moon."

Captain Billy notes the need to put the gogs in the boat fast, because some mornings they will not school up for long. "I actually bought two Daiwa surf rods, the cheapest models I could find, and put roller tips on the ends. The roller tip allows me to use the longer Sabikis with 10 or 12 hooks and not worry about them getting caught up in the eye of the rod. I prefer the R and R tackle HCT 16 for goggle-eyes."

More important, Captain Billy uses both rods at the same time to catch his gogs. He goes to the inlet and puts one rod on the starboard side and one rod on port side as if he were trolling. One rig is a 10-ounce weight and the other is heavier. "As I mark the gogs on the bottom machine, I come dead in the water and the Sabikis drop straight down." The heavier weight prevents the Sabikis from tangling. While Captain Billy unhooks the goggle-eyes from one rod, he's hoping the other rod is getting more goggle-eyes hooked up. "This method allows you to get plenty of bait quickly, since on some mornings those gogs will only school up for 15 to 20 minutes. You have to be quick, especially if you need three or four dozen for a tournament or a run to the islands."

Captain Billy advises anglers to leave the dock with the baitwell full of pilchards or threadfins to maximize the fishing action. During the summer months, these energetic baitfish can be found breaking water and flipping along the beaches and just outside the inlets. To make the cast netting easier, start with a little chum to bring the bait up to the surface and close to the boat. Often, one throw of the net, and you have plenty of bait for the day. This is a great way to obtain a large amount of bait in a short amount of time. Watch for diving birds to help locate the bait.

In the Fort Lauderdale area, Captain Poertner likes the mooring buoys just south of Port Everglades for pilchards and threadfins. "I like to use the glow-in-the-dark with a size 8 hook. I choose the smallest weight possible to deliver the rig to the bait." Cast the rig out and retrieve it back through the baitfish. He says the pilchards and threadfins are normally very cooperative and jump on the tiny lures that make up the Sabiki rig. "In 15 minutes or so you can have several dozen premium baits in the livewell and be on your way to the fishing grounds." He recommends using a normal Sabiki rig to catch the pilchards, but says to be prepared if the ballyhoo are there, which they often are. For the ballyhoo, use a #6 or smaller, long-shank bronze hook. Tip the hook with a small piece of shrimp and free-line it to the ballyhoo.

Baitfish will live longer if removed from the hook with a dehooking device. Dehookers are readily available through tackle shops and can add time to the life expectancy of the bait in the well. Touching the baitfish and removing any of its protective slime will shorten its life, and dead bait is not the bait of choice for wahoo. Captain Billy says, "I recommend using hook removers made especially for removing bait from Sabiki rigs. This saves the baitfish from mishandling and results in livelier bait. The dehookers can be tricky to use at first, but rest assured, once you get the hang of it, you can clear six baits off your line faster than someone grabbing the baits by hand can clear three."

Threadfin and pilchards can be caught with a cast net, but Captain Billy recommends using a net only when catching bait for one day of fishing. The cast net tends to knock a lot of scales off the fish and weaken their immune system. The netted bait does not tend to live as long as those caught by hook and removed with a dehooking tool. "If you are planning to pen up the bait for use over the next few days, I recommend the Sabiki rig to guarantee fresher bait."

When searching for larger baits like blue runners, find some kind of structure that is holding baitfish. Captain Poertner pulls out the Sabiki rigs again to fill the livewell with blue runners, but this time he chooses a larger rig. The same ones used on the threadfin are too small for the blue runners. "I recommend using a larger Sabiki, and always carry a block of chum or two and a bag of shrimp. Many times the blue runners will hit the Sabiki plain, but if they are getting a lot of pressure from other anglers, tipping the hooks with shrimp and putting a block of chum over the side of the boat does the trick."

Captain Poertner says anglers can increase their odds significantly if they take time to bridle baits before deployment. Bridling is a technique that allows bait to swim naturally and live longer. The bridling process involves attaching the bait to the hook without penetrating the bait with the hook. Bridling can be accomplished using a bait needle and a rubber band or dental floss. There are plenty of videos on YouTube that describe the process.

Captain Poertner trailers his boat up and down the southeast coast of Florida from his home base in Hobe Sound. Always in search of the hottest bite, he has a special affection for the Fort Lauderdale area, where he has fished since childhood. The Gulf Stream is located close by and the fishing opportunities are abundant. He also has a special affection for catching wahoo.

Fishing for wahoo can be outstanding in South Florida, especially in the summer and fall months. Most South Florida captains have their favorite locations, and Captain Poertner is no different. "I have my best luck fishing for wahoo in the area from Boca Raton to the Steeple in Sunrise." The Steeple is part of a large church in Sunrise, Florida. It can easily be seen from the water and is a convenient benchmark for the southern end of Captain Billy's wahoo range. "I have fished many days with my grandfather along this stretch of Florida and it is still very productive today."

A growing phenomenon in the offshore fishing world is the introduction of kite fishing. The technique has been around for quite a while, but its popularity is increasing as more anglers try it and enjoy its success. Having grown up in Florida, Captain Billy Poertner has been fishing with kites for more than 20 years. "At first, kite fishing can be intimidating," he says, "but with a little practice, it's not as hard as you may first think. Once you see the action it produces, you will be hooked!"

To get started kite fishing, obtain a small stout rod about 3 feet long. Some anglers take a rod that has been collecting dust in the garage, cut it down to about 3 feet, and place a large eye on the tip. "The guide at the end of the rod is a normal rod tip guide; just make sure you use a heavy-duty one, especially when using electric reels." This rod is used only to control the kite, so simplicity is king. A short rod is better because it will not be an obstruction to the traditional fishing rods and reels. If you want to go all out, you can find a commercially available kite rod for around $140. Reel choice is also up to the individual. You can go the expensive route and buy an electric reel, or the less expensive route by obtaining something like a Penn 113H, which is manual instead of electric. Either reel will do the job.

Captain Poertner has used and recommends the Krystal 601. "I like the Krystal 601 for several reasons. First, its cost is around $650, so it's reasonably inexpensive for an electric reel. It doesn't have the pulling power that some of the larger reels have, so you don't have as much concern with breaking the spars on the kites while you are retrieving them." This reel features sufficient line capacity by holding about 3,000 feet of 130-pound braided line; it will retrieve line at 100 feet per minute and has fish-pulling power of 300 pounds.

Set up your kite fishing system by first spooling the reel with a dependable braided line. Captain Billy uses at least 325 feet of 80-pound braided line on top of 60-pound Dacron backing before adding three clips that will hold the fishing line until a strike occurs. "I usually have 75 feet of braid from the kite to the first clip, 75 feet to the second clip, and then 75 feet to the third clip. I want at least another 100 feet between the third clip and the Dacron filler." He adds, "I use three clips on the kite, but that is really for the advanced kite fishermen. I recommend using only two clips and two fishing outfits for beginning kite fishermen." Place the clips about 75 feet apart to keep the baits from tangling during fishing. Anglers can purchase the kite clips and swivels separately or all in one kit at many local tackle stores or bigger suppliers like West Marine.

Several different manufacturers produce fishing kites. The top two, according to Captain Poertner, are SFE and Tigress kites. "These kites can be used in winds up to 25 knots.

Different wind speeds are handled with a simple adjustment to the bridle that attaches the mainline to the kite. The ability to make the adjustment at the bridle eliminates the need of different kites for different wind speeds."

If the wind gets too strong for the adjustable kites, a special version designed to handle the high winds is necessary. Of course such a need would indicate that fishing conditions have deteriorated considerably, and only the die-hard and experienced anglers will be kite fishing anyway.

Balloons are used to fly the kites when the wind is calm. "I use a helium-filled 40-inch balloon attached to the back of the kite to help it fly in calm winds." Capt. Harry's sells what is called a kite thong. This device is used to secure the balloon to the kite. The thong works better than the alternative, which requires tying the balloon to the center spar with mono and then running a second piece of mono from one top corner to the opposite side of the kite. The mono is secured to the balloon with tape.

When helium is needed to lift the kites, it may be hard to fly three baits. "Under balloon-flying conditions I like to use my large bait on one rod and a small to medium bait on the second rig." For one-stop shopping for kites and accessories Captain Billy recommends buying online at Capt. Harry's. He says they have a tremendous selection, and a simple phone call will put you in touch with a knowledgeable sales person.

If there is no drift available by wind or current, Captain Poertner turns to slow trolling. "If I am slow trolling, I place the wind at my stern, fly the kite off the bow, and fish two flatlines off the stern. Either slow trolling or drifting, I will be fishing both sides of the boat."

Rigging the fishing line begins by running the mainline through the guides and then through a ceramic ring made for kite fishing. "I use the ceramic ring because it allows the line to run across a smooth surface and ensures no sharp edges will cut or fray the fishing line. These rings are found at most

Kite fishing for wahoo is not the traditional way to do it, but it can be highly successful. Photo by Capt. Billy Poertner.

tackle stores." Next, run the mainline through a brightly colored float designed to add visibility to the rig when your bait is deployed. "The weighted float is a great benefit in helping keep the line tight and to make adjustments with smaller baits to keep them in the water." Add a rigging bead before using a double uni knot to add 5 feet of 50-pound fluorocarbon leader. Use an Albright knot to connect a 36-inch piece of #6 to #8 American Fishing Wire leader and finish with a circle hook. "I use Owner Inline circle hooks, 4/0 for smaller baits and 6/0 for larger baits. I hook the baits between the dorsal fin and eyes, right on the spine. The result is bait that keeps its head down while dangling from the kite and makes a lot of commotion on the surface of the water."

The name of Captain Billy's boat is *Imagine That*. The name seems rather appropriate when one imagines fish bait dangling from a kite high overhead in pursuit of the wily wahoo. Many of Captain Billy's techniques used to catch wahoo are traditional and standard for many offshore fish species, but some of them he describes as experimental yet successful for wahoo. He says, "On *Imagine That*, our main kite setup for drift fishing is two kites deployed off the port side of the vessel, which will always be the downwind side." He places a few small split-shot sinkers on opposite corners of each kite. The strategically placed weight makes the kites fly away from each other and allows the crew to deploy one kite off the bow and another from the stern. On the windward side of the boat, up to five lines are fished, depending on the current, wind, and drift.

The drift speed and position of the boat can be controlled by using a drift sock. The sock will slow the boat and also make it drift sideways. "When using a drift sock, I deploy it off the spring line cleat to cause the boat to drift beam to the wind, creating more fishing room." A sea anchor can be used to drift with your bow into the sea if you want to fish off the stern of the boat.

The first line deployed on the windward side is a flatline, with the bait swimming about 75 to 100 feet from the boat. The flatline is rigged with a normal kingfish stinger rig. The next bait is deployed on a second flatline about 60 feet behind the boat. Captain Billy warns, "Make sure the two baits are spread apart as far as possible to prevent tangling. Placing one rod in the bow and the other in the stern will normally do the trick." A mid-depth line can be created by placing 2 or 3-ounce rubber core sinkers on the mainline about 10 to 12 feet in front of the bait. Position the mid-depth line about 50 feet back, and keep it close to the first flatline. The final rod is rigged for deeper fishing by connecting a 16- to 20-ounce breakaway sinker. "This bait should be deployed deep in the water column and continually moved until you find the productive depth. Fish it around 75 feet or so, and if you're not getting hits, try bringing it up or letting it down until that magic depth has been found." Captain Billy recommends goggle-eyes as bait of choice or blue runners if the goggle-eyes are not available.

Pilchards and threadfins work well on the kites, but he advises anglers to use weighted floats. The pilchards and threadfins are lighter and may pop out of the water without the floats.

The traditional method of kite fishing described above will catch plenty of fish, but Captain Poertner has taken targeting wahoo to a new level. "I have been experimenting with kite fishing for wahoo, not the traditional way, but one that's been quite productive." His experimental method does not deploy the kites until favorable conditions have been found for wahoo, and he uses less tackle in the water as part of his strategy. "While I am offshore trolling for wahoo, I always have some live bait and my kite rods rigged and ready to go. If I troll over an area and get a cutoff or two or find floating structure such as large sargassum patches or floating debris, I circle them a time or two to see if there are fish present."

If everything looks right he moves the vessel upwind of the structure and readies the kites on the leeward side of the drift. Two flatlines and one deep line are deployed on the windward side. The deep line is weighted with an 8-ounce sinker attached with copper wire just above the leader. "This weight system allows me to make any line a deep line for quick deployment. Then, when we're back on the troll it's easy to remove the sinker and return to the more traditional trolling spread for offshore pelagics."

As he nears the structure, he starts live-chumming to sweeten the pot. "I deploy the kites and run the kite baits right on top of the water, where they splash and make a lot of commotion." Another part of the strategy is to chum with smaller baits than those you are fishing with. Captain Poertner believes this tactic increases the chances that a wahoo will take your bait, given the choice between a small dinner and a large one. Coupled with the fact that there is very little tackle in the water, Captain Poertner says the live chum and the commotion caused by the kite baits create the illusion of a natural feeding frenzy that even the most stubborn wahoo can't resist. "This is not a traditional way to fish for wahoo, but I have had quite a bit of success with it."

For convenience a three-way rod-holding cluster will slip into an existing gunnel rod holder and simplify making tackle adjustments when needed. Place the kite rod in the middle and a fishing rod on each side for the perfect setup. "The proximity of the rods allows you to make adjustments to the lines more easily when the baits need to be raised or lowered."

Before making a trip to an unfamiliar area, make a few calls or show up the day before to visit a few local tackle shops. Captain Poertner says, "Most local tackle stores will be helpful and tell you where the bite is or isn't. The best advice I can give you would be to just get out on the water and fish." Captain Poertner is a firm believer that the best way to catch quality fish is to spend plenty of time on the water with an eye toward learning something new each trip. "If you can fish with your family or kids, it's even better. My father is a huge part of my tournament team and tries to fish a few tournaments with me each year. It's nice to throw a smoker king on the deck, but when Dad's on the boat, it's even more special." If you want to maximize your fishing fun, include your family and friends in your fishing adventures.

Charter Captains

Captain Carl Ball

> Hometown: Fort Lauderdale, Florida
> Business: AWOL Fishing Charters, Inc.
> Phone number: 954-383-0145
> E-mail address: captball@awolfishingguide.com
> Web site: www.awolfishingguide.com

Captain Ball's advice to visiting anglers: First-time anglers should invest in a Standard Mapping Services chart with satellite view of the Biscayne Bay area. Safe navigation is very important, as unintended vessel groundings south of Key Biscayne are common. Not only can this lead to being high and dry for several hours, the damage done to the grass flats can also last a long time. There are stiff fines associated with any damage caused to the environment by your boat. The maps provide a way to visualize the areas you want to fish before you actually get there. Look for shallow grass flats for the bonefish and permit and locate the various channels that run between the flats. The channels will also hold snapper, grouper, ladyfish, bluefish, pompano, Spanish mackerel, and sharks.

Captain Billy Poertner

Hometown: Hobe Sound, Florida
Business: Imagine That Fishing Charters
Phone number: 772-245-8229
E-mail address: captbilly@imaginethatfishingcharters.com
Web site: www.imaginethatfishingcharters.com

Captain Poertner's advice to visiting anglers: Fishing the Fort Lauderdale area can be very rewarding, and the numbers of species you can target are endless. Trolling for dolphin, live-bait fishing for sailfish, or chasing wahoo might just result in a catch of a lifetime. Since kite fishing in South Florida is very popular, anglers approaching other vessels that may be slow trolling or drifting should keep an eye to the sky to be sure they are not fishing under someone's kites. Do your homework to find a fishing location, start the day with plenty of bait, and just have fun fishing; the catching will take care of itself.

Captain Bouncer Smith

Hometown: Miami, Florida
Business: Bouncer's Dusky 33

Phone number: 305-573-8224
E-mail address: captbouncer@bellsouth.net
Web site: www.captbouncer.com

Captain Smith's advice to visiting anglers: Wherever you fish in the world, spend your first day in the area with a guide, one whose name comes up from more than one source when you are checking into the area. Ask around at tackle shops, marinas, and various media sources. A good guide will reduce the time it takes to understand the local fishing by years. A good Web site designer is not always a good angler, so check around for good references.

If you want to try your hand at swordfish, you should be aware that this is the best of the best of big game fish. They get that reputation because they are not easy to find, they are not easy to fight, and they are good at escaping. Don't expect them to be caught every trip, and don't expect a bite every hour or so. That being said, when you finally catch one, it will be a moment enjoyed and relived for the rest of your life.

Area Hotspots

First-time anglers should try the Stiltsville area for bonefish and permit. Drifting the ocean side of the swim buoys will produce some nice tarpon from just north of Government Cut to 5th Street along the beach. Swordfish anglers should consider the triple lumps, also known as the cones, to start the drift. Kite-fishing anglers can catch sailfish and more in the area from the Government Cut Sea Buoy to 25.48 N. If that stretch doesn't produce, try from Fowey Rocks Lighthouse to the Monument Buoy. Anglers should target 90 to 200 feet of water with the kites for some outstanding fishing opportunities on a variety of species. This is a narrow band of real estate in South Florida waters, but very productive.

Fishing-Friendly Lodging and Glorious Galleys

Monty's South Beach

> 300 Alton Road
> Miami Beach, FL 33139
> Phone number: 305-672-1148

Only 100 feet from Bouncer's boat. Great burgers and nachos. They do a super job with your fish or theirs. Recommended by Capt. Bouncer Smith.

Grandpa's Bakery

> 17 SW 1st Street
> Dania Beach, FL 33004
> Phone number: 954-923-2163

A local favorite since 1957. Breakfast, lunch, and dinner. Fresh baked breads and pastries. Don't miss this one if you are in the area. Recommended by the author.

Silver Sands Beach Resort

> 301 Ocean Drive
> Key Biscayne, FL 33149
> Phone number: 305-361-5441

Great location and price. Overnight boat parking. Choose from rooms or cottages. Recommended by Capt. Carl Ball.

Oasis Sandwich Shop

> 19 Harbor Drive
> Key Biscayne, FL 33149
> Phone number: 305-361-5709

Authentic Cuban cuisine. Cafeteria style. Pick up some great food and take it back to your room or the beach and enjoy. Limited seating, popular with locals. Recommended by Capt. Carl Ball.

The Rusty Pelican

3201 Rickenbacker Causeway
Key Biscayne, FL 33149
Phone number: 305-361-3818

Located on the island of Key Biscayne. Great view of the city of Miami. Fresh seafood that changes with the season. Lunch and dinner, open daily. Recommended by Capt. Carl Ball.

Bait and Tackle

Fort Lauderdale Marina

1900 SE 15th Street
Fort Lauderdale, FL 33316
Phone number: 954-524-8507

North of the inlet and under the bridge. Fuel up and get bait. They carry frozen and live bait. All marine services. Recommended by Capt. Billy Poertner.

Gordon's Bait and Tackle

2627 SW 27th Avenue
Miami, FL 33133
Phone number: 305-856-4665

A little shop with great bait. Fresh live shrimp and crabs. Owned by the same family since the late '70s. Recommended by Capt. Carl Ball.

LMR Custom Rods and Tackle

1495 E Southeast 17th Street
Fort Lauderdale, FL 33316
Phone number: 877-567-7637

Staff are experienced anglers and have everything you need. If they don't have it, they can get it. Recommended by Capt. Carl Ball.

Fishing Lessons for Life—Respect the Resource

Henry David Thoreau is credited with saying, "Many men go fishing all of their lives without knowing it is not fish they are after." If you believe this is true, there is no better statement to underline the need to respect our precious fishing resource. It's not just the fish, it is also the environment in which we fish and the experience we enjoy. Current thinking among many experts relates respect for the resource to the answer to habitat destruction.

Overdevelopment, pollution, and careless anglers all contribute to a declining resource. Rick Roberts, executive director of the Snook Foundation, says, "The problem with habitat is elementary. Without nursery and juvenile fish habitat there are no little fish." Nursery habitat is the beginning of the life cycle for the fish anglers want to catch. Specifically, nursery habitats are marine environments with a greater level of productivity per unit area than other juvenile habitats, and maximum fish reproduction requires abundant healthy habitats. Without the beginning, there can be no end. Mangroves, salt marshes, and seagrass are typical nursery habitats that need to be protected from misguided human actions.

When mangrove stands are removed to build condos and other structures along our shorelines, a necessary habitat is destroyed. When residential and commercial runoffs pollute our salt marshes, habitat is destroyed. When careless anglers run outboard engines in shallow water and create prop scars in seagrass beds, habitat is destroyed. Mr. Roberts says some single species of a few gamefish can be raised in tanks. Redfish are a good example. "Those hatcheries, however, cannot replace mangrove fringe, nursery habitat, and seagrass meadows in producing fish." He reports that when the natural nursery habitat is working full throttle in the late summer, each acre of water produces metric tons of sea life—hatcheries can't match that. "Countless mollusks, all sorts of worms and other beasties, blue crabs, pink shrimp, and so on and so forth share the habitat with our namesake the snook and 280 species of game and forage fishes." It is a no-brainer that our habitat must be protected.

Almost anyone who is on the water regularly will tell you there are fewer fish and fewer habitats than only 20 years ago. Two issues anglers can support are habitat protection and renewal. A great example of a successful renewal project was described in chapter 10: a city, county, state, and federal government partnership that restored 100 acres of wetland habitat in the Lake Worth Lagoon. More projects like the Snook Islands Natural Area need to be undertaken to restore important habitat to the fishery.

Mindful anglers, politicians, and just plain citizens need to be aware of the consequences of their actions for the fragile marine environment. This education needs to be started early in life by teaching our kids the importance of protecting the resource.

Teaching kids simple stuff like picking up trash and proper disposal of monofilament line can help produce a mindset that will translate into habitat protection as they grow older. Teach them that a clean shoreline is more desirable than a dirty one. Teach them that fish need clean water to survive and grow. Teach them to use caution when anchoring in fragile seagrass beds. Teach them to report environmental damage and pollution when observed. The future of fishing could very well depend on early recognition of their role in protecting the fishery resource. Most anglers want that resource to be around for their kids and their grandkids, too, so they should be willing to help protect it.

All anglers should unite behind the goals of protecting and renewing our marine environment and educating others about its importance. The result will be more fish for everyone to enjoy.

ACKNOWLEDGMENTS

This book is intended for fishermen and fisherwomen of all skill levels. It shares numerous tips and suggestions for becoming a better angler. It would not have come to pass without the help of many willing participants.

I gratefully acknowledge the fishing guides and other experts who enthusiastically contributed to the pages of this book. The fishing skills and knowledge they share have been developed by years of experience on the water and by personal observations of a resource that has changed greatly over the years. Their knowledge of the sport is extensive. Their love of the sport and concern for the resource speaks volumes about their character.

I also extend my sincere thanks to the unnamed reviewers of the manuscript for their thoughtful criticisms and suggested revisions. It is a better product because of their critical review and insightful comments.

INDEX

Page numbers in italics refer to illustrations.

Ron Presley is retired professor of economics and a professional fishing guide. He is a licensed U.S. Coast Guard charter boat captain and the secretary/treasurer of the Florida Guides Association.

The University Press of Florida is the scholarly publishing agency for the State University System of Florida, comprising Florida A&M University, Florida Atlantic University, Florida Gulf Coast University, Florida International University, Florida State University, New College of Florida, University of Central Florida, University of Florida, University of North Florida, University of South Florida, and University of West Florida.

WILD FLORIDA
Edited by M. Timothy O'Keefe

Books in this series are written for the many people who visit and/ or move to Florida to participate in our remarkable outdoors, an environment rich in birds, animals and activities, many exclusive to this state. Books in the series will offer readers a variety of formats: Natural history guides, historical outdoor guides, guides to some of Florida's most popular pastimes and activities, and memoirs of outdoors folk and their unique lifestyles.

30 Eco-Trips in Florida: The Best Nature Excursions (and How to Leave Only Your Footprints), by Holly Ambrose (2005)

Hiker's Guide to the Sunshine State, by Sandra Friend (2005)

Fishing Florida's Flats: A Guide to Bonefish, Tarpon, Permit, and Much More, by Jan S. Maizler (2007)

50 Great Walks in Florida, by Lucy Beebe Tobias (2008)

Hiking the Florida Trail: 1,100 Miles, 78 Days, Two Pairs of Boots, and One Heck of an Adventure, by Johnny Molloy (2008)

The Complete Florida Beach Guide, by Mary and Bill Burnham (2008)

The Saltwater Angler's Guide to Florida's Big Bend and Emerald Coast, by Tommy L. Thompson (2009)

Secrets from Florida's Master Anglers, by Ron Presley (2009)

Exploring Florida's Botanical Wonders: A Guide to Ancient Trees, Unique Flora, and Wildflower Walks, by Sandra Friend (2010)

Florida's Fishing Legends and Pioneers, by Doug Kelly (2011)

Fishing Secrets from Florida's East Coast, by Ron Presley (2012)